How To Succeed In Hollywood Without Really Trying

P.S. - You Can't!

How To Succeed In Hollywood Without Really Trying

P.S. - You Can't!

by Melville Shavelson

BearManor Media
2007

How To Succeed In Hollywood Without Really Trying
P.S. – You Can't

© 2007 Melville Shavelson

For information, address:

BearManor Media
P. O. Box 71426
Albany, GA 31708

bearmanormedia.com

Cover design by John Teehan

Typesetting and layout by John Teehan

Published in the USA by BearManor Media

ISBN—1-59393-437-8
978-1-59393-437-8

For Lucy and Rich and Lynne and Patti
and Scott and Karin and Amy
and now Ruth

This is the land of lost content
I see it shining plain,
The happy highways where I went
And cannot come again.

–A.E. Housman

Living in the past has one thing in its favor—it's cheaper.

– Anonymous

Table of Contents

Prologue

I want to do it all over again. Maybe next time I'll get it right.

Yesterday is what I look forward to. There is no rewind for life. Writing about it is the only way I can go back, because writing is my main excuse for living.

I am a writer by choice, a producer through necessity, and a director in self-defense. Three times I have been elected President of the Writers Guild of America, and led that prideful Union through two major strikes, which I believe the writers won. At least, we should have.

I have written movies, plays, novels, television series, and bad checks. My produced screenplays number 35, two of which won Academy Award nominations. I have also directed a dozen the films I've written.

I worked with many of the famous names we all remember, and a few I'd rather forget. For the first time in print you will find here:

The story of the romance between Sophia Loren and Cary Grant, before throwing him over and marrying Carlo Ponti by proxy, the day we were shooting her wedding to Cary in *Houseboat*.

John Wayne's affair that closed down *Trouble Along the Way*, with some real trouble along the way, when he managed to slip the detectives his wife had put on his trail and left town with his South American mistress in the middle of shooting.

The rumored affair between Danny Kaye and Sir Laurence Olivier, which led Jack Rose to inquire, "Who got top billing?" Not to forget Danny and Princess Margaret.

Frank Sinatra, when the Israeli army lined up the most beautiful girls in Tel Aviv for him, and he ran out in the middle of the dedication ceremonies of the Frank Sinatra Arab-Israeli Youth Foundation in Nazareth.

And so forth and so forth ... but for the rest, you'll have to read the book.

With a great deal of help, I've tried to recall how it all was, how I stumbled through an existence after I discovered I would never be Shakespeare, in a town where they'd ask Shakespeare, "What have you done lately?"

And stop asking after he passed thirty-five.

This is the story of Hollywood's Golden Age, and how I enjoyed every moment until it all turned to brass.

In the words of my favorite Sinatra song:

> "I've lived a life that's full,
> I've traveled each and ev'ry highway;
> And more, much more than this,
> I did it my way…"

Chapter 1
Beginnings
April 1, 1917. All Fools Day. Naturally

Nobody was born in a hospital in those days, unless he was sick. I was born, healthy, in the bedroom of the apartment above the toy store my father owned at 1010 Flatbush Avenue, Brooklyn, New York, an address I left as soon as I found out where I was. This took me about five years, to 1922, which made me a lot smarter than the Brooklyn Dodgers, who didn't get up the courage to leave until 1956.

"1010 Flatbush Avenue" were the first words I was taught as soon as I learned to talk. This was, I suppose, in case I was kidnaped and the kidnappers didn't know where to send the ransom note. A lot of good it would have done them, none of our family had enough money, even if they had felt I was worth it. I've never been sure. Besides, unless the note was written in Yiddish, my father wouldn't have bothered reading it. Bills were written in English, anything important was always written in Yiddish, and preferably on the front page of the *Jewish Daily Forward*, my father's Bible. We children—my sister Elsie was five years older than I—were never taught the Yiddish language, so our parents could converse in our presence freely. Of course, I was forced later to learn Hebrew at Hebrew school. I managed to sneak out of a window at almost every class, but since nobody we knew spoke the language, my lack of knowledge was never discovered. Hebrew had value only at Passover, when you had to learn the blessing for wine or you didn't get any. That I learned quickly.

As for Yiddish, what our parents didn't know was that Elsie and I soon learned all the most important words, like schmuck and putz and nudnick, so we could understand what our parents were saying about the relatives.

My mother used Yiddish sparingly. After all, she had come to New York from London, where her family lived in different circumstances than the shlimazls in New York. In England, they were in the Arts, where one of my British cousins—Lydia Sherwood was her stage name—became a noted Shakespearian actress. My uncle Rex was an oboist at the Covent Garden Opera House, and my cousin, Harry Shalson, was a recording star; I have a few of his 78 records, which I played once, which was enough. Only later did I discover that another British uncle was in the fish-and-chips business, and still another was a bookie at a dog-racing track, which renewed my faith in my genes.

Another relative is reputed to be Lauren Bacall, but no one has gotten her to admit it.

As far back as I can remember, my mother often told me she had turned down an offer of matrimony from a gentleman who later became Lord Mayor of London. In spite of her proclaimed disappointment in the life she now led, consisting mainly of arguing with my father and putting in long hours working in the store, I can remember she was always singing songs like, "Peggy O'Neil Was a Girl Who Could Steal," whose lyrics I can still recite from memory, so don't provoke me. Obviously, a woman of her family background couldn't be bothered with the details of bringing up an infant troublemaker like her son, since it wouldn't allow her enough time for her career, which consisted mainly of telling my father how to run the business. So she turned over my care as soon as possible to two young cousins, Hilda and Sarah, who thereupon became known as Little Hilda and Little Sarah, because my mother was Big Hilda and an aunt was Big Sarah. Little Hilda and Little Sarah obviously spoiled me rotten, because they considered me their Barbie Doll. I have seen photographs of myself at the ripe old age of five, riding a new tricycle and still feeding myself from a bottle, obviously as a means of keeping my mouth shut.

But I'm wandering, which I intend to do as often as possible. To get back to beginnings, Dad had come to America from a suburb of Minsk in Russia, escaping one jump ahead of the Cossacks who wanted to impress him into the Czar's army, in which no Jewish boy had survived long enough to rise to the rank of Private. According to his citizenship application, Dad was born in Minsk on June 4, 1883, and crossed the Atlantic from Rotterdam, Holland, on the liner *Rotterdam*, arriving at Ellis Island, on June 10, 1902, without a passport or much of anything else. His immigration papers state it was his intention "to renounce forever all allegiance to any foreign prince, potentate, state, or sovereignty, and particularly to Nicholas II, Emperor of all the Russias," which undoubtedly had Nicholas spending endless hours wondering where he had failed. Whether "Shavelson" was actually a family name or merely the name of a ghetto area in the vicinity of Minsk, I do not know, although my daughter Lynne has said she met some relatives on one of her trips to shoot a documentary in Russia (more on that later), who claimed it truly was the name of a region in the Ukraine.

Joseph Shavelson was a small man, with brown hair and deep blue eyes, from which Paul Newman got the idea. He was always mild and gentle, at least to me, and it is only now, thinking about the stories I heard of the pogroms the family had endured in Minsk, and the fact that he escaped in a perilous (in those days) journey by steerage to New York, with not a penny in his pocket and speaking not a word of English, and managed in the succeeding years to bring over his nine brothers and sisters, and his father and his mother, that I have begun to understand that there was much more to him than met my eye. He was the eldest son and felt it was his duty to save the family. At 19, he had the foresight to realize that a World War was coming, which none of the family in Russia might survive. He knew he didn't have much time.

A letter written by my Uncle Oscar, the first of my father's brothers to be imported gives some indication of what life in Minsk must have been like in The Old Country. (There are some playful photos of Oscar and my dad at a photographer's studio in New York which indicate they had their happy moments; just being young and in a free country was enough.) Oscar, in the U.S., became a pharmacist and his letter, written by hand in 1965, is almost illegible, like a prescription. From what I can make of it, with my notes in brackets, Oscar wrote as follows: "I must have been 4-5 years old. We lived on the outskirts of town named Heine. At that time the house you would call, modern. [This might mean indoor plumbing, but I doubt it.] To enter the house we built a 'succah' for holidays and it was a room to use in summer. Over it we had an attic where we would store some apples in the summer and they tasted so good! Kitchen, three bedrooms, and dining room. [For 11 people.] Garden with fruit trees. A yard with three barns, one cow, two horses, father was busy going to see how many days of Taxes he could earn shoeing horses or anything he could do to make a living. Mother was busy with her children and the store she had in the village...We were very hungry and we knew mother would get us something to eat. Where mother had the store a widow had three daughters and they had a bakery, and the bread was enough to make your mouth water. After awhile, things were getting bad for mother, so we decided to build a store next to our home. The children were getting bigger and there was no one to look out for them. My father had a brother living in Minsk, so my older brother [my father] got a job with him as a clerk. My other brothers were helping him. My mother had it in her mind to come to the U.S., where she had family, three of her brothers were in the drug business [pharmacies, not crack houses]. So she thought she would get me started and she got me a job in Minsk with a man named Rifkind at his 'Apothecary Magazine,' as it is called in Europe…The job was not the best and staying with my uncle was not pleasant. But hope is the greatest remedy…"

The letter trails off here. "Hope" is the proper word to end it. Oscar was even gentler in nature than my father and preferred not to mention the pogroms, as if then they would go away. For the details of what life was like in a shtetl in those days, listen to the recording of *Fiddler on the Roof,* but only the original with Zero Mostel. In the later version, Topol played Tevye with a British accent, as if he expected to be knighted for being Jewish. Shlemazl!

Oscar became a successful pharmacist in Guttenberg, New Jersey—only a little better neighborhood than Minsk—and his son, my late cousin Marty, later took over the business there and in Westwood, N.J., before retiring to Florida to play golf, which he was not very good at. My Uncle Eddie also became a pharmacist—and the inventor of the cure for the common cold, but, again more of that later. My Uncle Bill became a doctor in Revere Beach, Mass., a suburb of Boston, possibly to keep his brothers, the pharmacists, in business. Dad helped support Bill through medical school when Dad was struggling to make his own living, but he never felt that was important enough to mention. He was proud of Bill's considerable accomplishment. There was another relative, Jake, whom Dad was also supporting, but without realizing it. Apparently, Jake became my dad's business partner in Brooklyn and got caught with his hand in the till. I don't know which was considered worse, stealing or getting caught at it, which marked you as a schlemiel, but we never talked about Jake. Once in awhile my mother would use the word "momser," and my sister Elsie and I would know whom she meant. Another relative, Michael (Mikhail?), was something of a rebel. He owned a motorcycle and climbed on it one day in Brooklyn when I was very young, hit the throttle and was never heard from by the family again. In my opinion, he escaped and became Elvis Presley, but I hope not.

My Aunt Ruth lived into her 90s, in Santa Monica, and kept in her room her portrait, painted by the famous artist James Montgomery Flagg, one of her many lovers. Flagg is perhaps best known today for his WWI poster of Uncle Sam pointing his finger and saying, "I want you for the U.S. Army!" I don't think Uncle Sam was pointing at Ruth, but I'm certain Flagg did, many times. I will not repeat the stories I have heard of her romantic life; she was so beautiful in Flagg's portrait of her, she must have gotten into the family by mistake (like Mikhail), and she made the most of it. She later married a poet, Dennis Hartman, who made a living publishing poetry by high school students, thousands of them, all of whom won an award and were obliged to buy Dennis's book to prove it. It made for a hell of a good living. Dennis was the most interesting of all my relatives; he was an intellectual who had read every classic ever written, and had known most of the authors. He had a collection of first editions, and copies of the *Paris Review* containing the early work of Hemingway, Henry Miller and Gertrude Stein, including "Pigeons on the Grass, Alas," from Gertie's "Four Saints in Three Acts," which didn't make much sense to me, but it did to Dennis. Somewhere in his later years, he and Ruth divorced, and Dennis started answering girls' letters in the Lonelyhearts columns and making dates. His son, Bobby, remonstrated that this was dangerous, because Dennis mistrusted banks and kept every dollar he possessed in a money belt under his pants; one of the girls he picked up would certainly take it from him. Dennis assured Bobby that whatever happened, he kept one hand on his money belt. It must have made for an interesting evening.

To get back to the less colorful side of the family, my mother's name was "Shalson." That, I was told, was the Anglicized version of "Shavelson" in England, for she and my father were first cousins. That always disturbed me, although it didn't bother them at all. In Russia, my mother's family name was Chanin. Her mother was Shavelson. I never understood the whole arrangement. Since I was never given a middle name— I haven't figured that one out, except that my mother said I was named for her favorite author, Herman Melville, and he got along pretty well without one—I adopted "Chanin" as mine for awhile, and I even had cards printed, "Melville C. Shavelson." It looked more elegant. To this day, I get requests for contributions from various causes, still addressed that way. I never give them anything.

About 1910, my mother came to New York on a visit, and I assume she and my father fell in love at first sight, which I guess is what you did back then. Both my parents were always embarrassed by sentiment and never mentioned the word "love" in connection with marriage, theirs or anyone else's. Maybe they were right. Hilda (Mom) was always informing Joseph (Dad) that she could have married the Lord Mayor of London, and my father was always asking her why she hadn't. I never heard the answer to that one. Also, she was always telling my father he should have bought that property in Atlantic City when she told him to, and he would have been a millionaire. This was before Donald Trump had the same idea. The fact that my father never had enough money to buy property anywhere but in Spring Valley, New York, never stopped her. He could have found the money.

My mother, as her early photographs show, was an attractive girl, but she was stern and tough, where Dad was soft and forgiving. I can remember her ordering me to take out the water from under the icebox—ice kept the food cold, but it had a tendency to melt, and gathered in a tub underneath. I was small as a child, and I could barely lift the large tub, but I managed, and I can remember fantasizing to myself that I was really a Prince in disguise, who had been placed into this Kosher family as punishment for same royal mistake, and soon I would be freed of the spell and become a Prince again, and all the relatives would be sorry for how they had treated me, and they would bow to me and kiss my feet.

I waited for several years, but it never happened.

Maybe soon.

My earliest memory is going into my father's room when he has very sick and asking him to button up my pants for me. I can place the date, because it was during the terrible flu epidemic in New York in 1918, and I was little more than a year old. Dad was terribly ill, and not expected to live, but he buttoned my pants.

Incidentally, on April 6, 1917, the United States of America declared war on Germany, obviously encouraged by my birth five days earlier. And in 1918, I can remember the huge celebration after my father buttoned my pants. Crowds filled the streets and cheered. Later, I was told it was for the declaration of the Armistice and the end of WWI. But it proved to be a false alarm, so I did not appear in the window and wave. The real Armistice didn't occur until November 11, 1918. My father buttoned my pants that time, too.

My next memory is of climbing over the shelves in the store to reach a toy I intended to steal. Instead, I slipped, and cut my thumb on the edge of a window screen, and carry the scar to this day. I was punished and did not receive a Purple Heart—although I certainly deserved one.

Brooklyn in those days is still fairly vivid in my memory. A streetcar ran down Flatbush Avenue and you could flatten a penny by placing it on the tracks and letting the trolley run over it. I guess it would also have flattened a nickel, but nobody I knew owned one. A lot of the traffic was horse-drawn, so you had to watch your step crossing the street. You could buy a Charlotte Russe for three cents, a delicious concoction of whipped cream piled on top of lady fingers in a paper cup, and sometimes you could have it chocolate-flavored. No dessert in *Gourmet Magazine* has ever equaled it, in my opinion. Two cents plain was just that, two cents for a glass of plain soda water, three cents if you wanted it flavored. Soda water was considered by the family, and for all I know the entire medical profession, as a sure cure for tuberculosis, but only if you belched afterwards. Ralph Nader hadn't been born yet, so everybody believed it.

Girls were stubborn creatures who had to be forced to accompany large boys down the cellar to play Doctor. I was too young to participate, and it didn't strike me as anything worth doing; why would anyone want to take a girl's temperature in a cellar, when she wasn't even sick?

I learned why much later. I was a slow study.

Coney Island was Mecca. Disneyland has always seemed a pale imitation of its glories. Mostly, I was taken to Coney to stare; we couldn't afford the glamorous rides, like the steeplechase horses that shot down and up the rails in the main building. Just being there as part of the crowd, listening to girls scream, was a treat enough. Later, when a measure of affluence arrived, the crowning event was going for one of Nathan's Famous Hot Dogs, seemingly a yard and a half of gorgeous heartburn for a nickel, and, later, when inflation soared out of reason, a dime. We knew then the country was going to hell, and Nathan's was leading the way.

Most of New York's skyscrapers were yet to be built. The Woolworth Building was the tallest structure in the world. Brooklyn had smaller buildings, fewer people, but still, to a child's eye, it was a metropolis, jammed with large human beings, where you were menaced by clanging streetcars and large, unfriendly dogs, as well as gangs of boys set on your destruction. Safety lay only in visiting relatives, like the Chanins who lived in a large brownstone at 1492 St. John's Place, an address I have never forgotten because it was the year Columbus discovered America and decided not to stay. It is not true it was because he met my relatives. The Chanins had kept the original family name; why, I never discovered, and they were a large clan with many children who became my best friends during the Spring Valley Summers, which you probably thought I would never get to. Now seems about time.

The year must have been 1923, when my father's doctor (not my Uncle Bill, he hadn't graduated yet) informed him he had high blood pressure and had to get out of the dirty, hurried, unhealthy city air to the country. Spring Valley, New York, a scant thirty-five miles up the Hudson and in Rockland Country, was soon to become known as Pot Cheese Hollow because of the number of Jewish immigrants who were beginning to settle there. They had come from the farmlands of Russia and Poland and Mittel Europa to the haven of New York City only to learn to hate its sizzling heat and freezing cold and crowded tenements; the huddled masses, yearning to breathe free, made the long trip to Spring Valley and established a defensive ring of Kosher hotels to prevent any Gentiles from joining them. The hotels were only open in the summer, when perspiring fathers deposited their wives and offspring in some haven of tasteless but rabbi-blessed food, went back to the Big City and returned to the hotels every weekend like Jewish swallows returning to their Kosher Capistrano, sometimes to find their wives and the waiters serving each other. Someone would have to supply these with the necessities of life in the wilderness; everything from linoleum to silverware (tin), and whoever did would have spoken Yiddish, at least. My father also spoke Polish, Roumanian, Hungarian, Russian, German, and several other languages I never identified, so he could argue with any of the customers who hadn't paid their bills, which gave him a wide ethnic choice.

Orders were taken in any language, over the telephone, which in Spring Valley, in those days, was a relatively new and feared invention. Our phone number in the store, I remember, was a complicated 592. So there must have been at least 591 other telephones to be served by one harried telephone operator (female, of course) who spoke only Goyish. There were no dials or buttons on the phone, you just spoke to the operator and told her whom you wanted to speak with. You didn't have to tell her their phone number, she knew everybody in town, and could let you know if they had gone to Brooklyn for the day, and save you the nickel on the call.

One reason Spring Valley was selected as Mecca was that the Erie Railroad stopped there, right in the middle of Main Street. The train could take you the thirty-five miles to Jersey City and the ferry to New York and Broadway at incredible speed—two hours, give or take a few cows on the tracks. On the way, it only stopped 16 times at various stations, and 36 at cows. There were no trucks of any size to compete, busses were useless because the roads were terrible, so the Erie RR became our lifeline to civilization, the Kosher Burma Road. The railway station was only a half block from the store my mother, in a fit of inspiration, had named "Shavelson's New York Bazaar." It sold everything that you didn't eat, dishes, "silverware," window shades, linoleum, toys, even bullets and shotgun shells.

When I grew old enough, I clerked in the store, and my father would call me over when there was an argument with a customer, because I didn't speak Yiddish or Roumanian or Hungarian or Polish and they could yell themselves blue in the face and I wouldn't understand a word. You can't imagine how helpful this was.

When we first moved to Spring Valley, we lived in a rented apartment upstairs from a garage on Main Street and a block away from the Volunteer Fire Department There was only one problem with the Volunteer Fire Department: there were no volunteers at first. You ever see a Jewish fireman? Later, they got a few. There was a permanent staff of three local Arnold Schwarzeneggers, and one old fire engine that had to be cranked to get it to start. Then they waited for the volunteers, who sometimes arrived.

Shortly after we moved in—I must have been six years old—a fast-spreading fire broke out in our building. My father raced up the three blocks from the store, burst through the flames to the second floor, and carried Elsie and myself through the smoke to safety. It was only then that someone called the telephone operator and she triggered the village fire siren—2-2-2, EMERGENCY! After awhile, the siren managed to be heard at the firehouse, a block away from our apartment, where it broke up the pinochle game, which was all right because the smoke drifting in had made it difficult to see the cards. The Schwarzeneggers reluctantly cranked up the fire engine. It took awhile to get it started, but still no volunteers had arrived, so they waited. After a long debate, the Schwarzeneggers finally drove the fire engine across the street to our place. By that time the fire had just about burned itself out. Nothing daunted the Fire Department, who bravely destroyed our apartment with fire axes and water hoses before getting back to their pinochle game.

Some time later, ten volunteer firemen showed up. They would have come sooner, but it took them awhile to make up a minyan. If you don't understand that, I'm not going to explain it. That was when Dad decided it was time to build a house of our own, as far from the Fire Department as possible. He figured it would be easier to get insurance.

Dad had found some land outside of town on the Old Nyack Turnpike, a rural area so remote it was rumored the wolves wouldn't venture out unless they held hands. Together with the Chanins, my parents bought a small piece of property. Thirty-six unspoiled acres. True, part of it was undrained swamp, but most of it was lovely virgin woodland. I didn't realize how significant the virgin woodland was until much later, when I learned that two miles further up the Old Nyack Turnpike was Spring Valley's only House of Joy, called that, I presumed, because the roof didn't leak. I learned better. After I was bar-mitzvahed, Dad once ventured to take me there, but this was no father-son coming-of-age bonding. We were the only males ever to visit the House of Joy for the purpose of laying the linoleum.

The family's three houses were built in a row, on a private road, one for us, one for the Chanins, and the one in the middle for my Uncle Willie, who promptly rented it out. These occupied only one acre, but my father assured us that soon we would all make a fortune, selling off the other 35 acres to the crowds from New York City who would descend on this earthly paradise like locusts. Today, close to 80 years later, not one square inch has been sold to them, but there are a lot of locusts. The lovely woodland I would tramp through in summertime, with its rare Indian Moccasin wild flowers, and in winter through its snow-covered birches to the beautiful, hidden little lake I loved, because I could skate all alone, the frozen silence broken only by the sound of the snapping of tree branches and occasionally my ankle, has now been transformed into the first toll station on the New York State Thruway.

Progress.

Speaking of progress, I can remember two stories of scientific achievement during my childhood—how my Uncle Eddie invented a cure for the common cold, and how my father invented champagne.

Uncle Eddie was well known for his sense of humor. On one of my birthdays, he gifted me with a box of chocolate-covered garlic. April Fool!

But he was very serious about being the first member of the family to become a millionaire. He had a drugstore in New Jersey that had a large soda fountain, which I patronized almost out of existence, and he figured that I owed him about 200 sodas and therefore could be put to work in his mammoth enterprise. It wasn't easy to invent a cure for the common cold, but Uncle Eddie had done it. It was a medicine called "Chexol," which he proudly advertised as the result of years of research. Chexol, incidentally, consisted of three small powders which had to be mixed together before taking. It contained aspirin and two harmless drugs which neutralized each other when mixed, with a lot of fizzing and bubbling. This left only the aspirin. That might seem to you like a waste of time, but it was quite impressive. Mix the three powders together, instantly FIZZ! Voodoo Medicine! If you think this is any different from many medical wonder drugs on the market today, you haven't tried them. Will any of them cure the common cold?

My job, at the tender age of eight, was to travel with Uncle Eddie in his old Buick. He would park around the corner and I would go into a drugstore and ask the pharmacist if he carried Chexol. When he said he didn't, I would inform him my mother and all her friends wouldn't think of using anything else, it cured colds instantly, and he would be wise to stock it in the future, or he would lose a lot of good customers. I was the first live commercial. This procedure was repeated until it was time for me to be revived with another chocolate soda. In the afternoon, Eddie would visit the same drugstores and try to sell them his marvelous product.

He never became a millionaire. It turned out that after tasting Chexol, many sufferers preferred making a trip to Lourdes.

When I was a little older, my cousin Marty told me the story of a young man who bursts into a pharmacy in a panic, shouting to the man behind the counter, "You've got to help me! I've had this terrible erection for two days and I can't get rid of it! I've already had three girls this morning and it won't go down! What can you give me for it?"

The pharmacist thinks a moment and answers, "$2,000 and the drugstore."

And now for The Night My Father Invented Champagne:

I remember it was 1930, because that was the time the cows had their hooves sticking up in the air and I became Bar Mitzvahed. It was a happy time for me and Holsteins. The cows had their moment first. I was crossing the pasture that was a shortcut to our house when I saw them lying in the lush grass, on their backs, hooves waving in the air. I ran to tell my father—it was Sunday, the store was closed. Our house, by the way, was located almost exactly on the state line separating New York from New Jersey, a crucial point, although I didn't realize it until later.

Dad took one look at the cows and ran into the house to get a huge glass jar we kept in the cellar for making pickles. His fondest hopes had been confirmed.

The farm next door had been sold to a mysterious family some months earlier. We saw them occasionally, a family consisting entirely of hard-faced Italian men, who didn't seem to know too much about the cows that were kept in their huge red barn. A lot of workmen had been occupied in that barn for weeks, we never could figure out why. Certainly cows didn't require indoor plumbing, but from all the pipes and boilers being delivered at night, they could have been building a bovine replica of the Ladies Room at Radio City Music Hall.

The compost pile outside the barn took on a pungent aroma. The cows' condition immediately confirmed my father's suspicion: the compost was no longer compost, it was mash, the residue of a huge distilling operation, which the cows had obviously been feasting upon and had begun dancing in the meadow, vine leaves figuratively in their hair, drunk as skunks and happy as larks.

For my father, it was a religious experience. Prohibition had made it difficult for him to worship God in the manner God demanded at Passover. The sacramental wine that was an integral part of that holiday was almost impossible to obtain, and tremendously expensive. The usual vintage, which we referred to as Manischewitz Holy Water, was now illegal. Since near our home there was an abundant supply of choke cherries and elderberries, my father had considered it to be his religious duty to make the wine to supply the relatives in Brooklyn every year, so that the Exodus from Egypt and the parting of the Red Sea could be properly celebrated with the traditional Biblical hangovers. But Dad's wine never quite compared with Mouton Rothschild '27, although, as the relatives were quick to point out, Baron Rothschild was equally Jewish. He must have gone to Temple more often than my father.

In our family, the Hebrew prayer for wine was usually accompanied by an invocation for a rapid recovery from drinking Chateau Shavelson '30.

Dad kept trying. Every summer, we children would be put to picking baskets of the tiny black choke cherries from the trees that lined our driveway. Dad would carefully put the cherries down in oaken barrels in the cellar, a layer of sugar, a layer of cherries, and so forth. Then he would cork the barrels and let nature take its course.

Within a month, without fail, the result was 20 gallons of Chateau Shavelson vinegar.

Since the Bible doesn't mention much about drinking Holy Vinegar, obviously something had to be done. Every year, the Chanins in Brooklyn would send out the patriarch of their family. We called him "Zaydeh," although he really wasn't our grandfather. But he looked like a Zaydeh, He was a dignified old man with crisp blue eyes and a manicured white beard, always dressed in a black frock coat and carrying a brown valise and a malacca cane. He would step off the Erie Railroad train at our little station like the Messiah himself—I secretly believed he was, and I had a sneaking suspicion he did, too—and climb into the Chevrolet delivery truck beside my father and me for the trip home.

Once in the house, he would put on his prayer shawl and his tvillin and pray mysteriously to his God for help. After all, if Jesus could turn water into wine, couldn't Jehovah turn vinegar into Mouton Rothschild?

Having finished his prayers, Zaydeh would then repair to our basement, open his brown valise, and take out the most complete and compact still I have ever seen, one he had manufactured himself to precise tolerance so it would fit in the valise and leave room for several gallon jars of the finished product. It included a series of Pyrex glass retorts, tubes, and Bunsen burners designed to distill the product in my father's wine barrels into the high-powered, 100-proof schnapps the Lord really preferred to Manischewitz. The trick was to catch the wine in the barrels just before it had transformed itself into salad dressing.

Science always met its match in Chateau Shavelson wine. The timing was never quite right. All the still ever produced was schnapps vinegar, if there is such a thing. It would take the lining off a stomach without achieving any of the agreeable side effects so apparent in the cows later to be found cavorting in the nearby meadow. After a day or two of fruitless distilling, Zaydeh would sadly pack his paraphernalia, fill a gallon jar with the awful results, just to show the relatives what a shlemiel my father was as a winemaker, and depart hastily on the Erie Railroad—shouting an occasional epithet in Hebrew—for the thirsty, religious throng waiting in Brooklyn.

That is why my father leaped immediately into action when I told him about the cows next door. He carried the huge glass pickle jar over to the neighbors' house, with me tagging along, and immediately borrowed a gallon of pure grain alcohol, 200-proof. No vinegar in the world could resist this additive. The relatives would learn soon enough who was the real Baron Rothschild!

Until this moment, we hadn't met our neighbors, but Dad had the ability to make instant friends in any language, and he even knew a smattering of Italian. In no time at all, they were our lantsmen, our friends and brothers. Their spokesman was a tough but vaguely graceful man with a keen sense of humor and, apparently, a love of children. There were women in the house, women who did the cooking and the washing, and I'm not sure what else, for the men, but there were no children. I wasn't sure why. The Italian Capo—I guess now that was his official position, although I didn't know all that in those pre-Brando days—promised to help me with my baseball career, which I told him had languished since the time I had mistakenly tried to steal first base.

On the way home, my father explained that these men were all momsers, gangsters, bootleggers, and dangerous, and that I should stay away from them. I didn't believe him, of course. The alcohol, generously added to the homemade wine, produced a potent blend that resulted in a schnapps that lifted Zaydeh's beard and forced him to clap a hand to the top of his yarmulke, when he sampled it later. The family switched my father's status from Shlemiel to Messiah. But he wasn't satisfied. No, Dad was determined to do more than rival Rothschild; he would better him, in fact. He would be the first of our family to make his own champagne. Someone had told him that if he bottled the now-potent wine, and added raisins before corking the bottles tightly, the fermentation of the raisins would create a bubbly champagne unmatched in the civilized world. So Dad tried it. We must have put down about 30 quart bottles, richly raisined and tightly corked.

A few nights later, I was awakened by the sound of explosions. BANG! BANG! BANG! We all rushed down to the cellar, where the ceiling and the walls dripped with alcoholic vinegar and the concrete floor was littered with shattered glass. While my mother hollered at my father and we started to clean it up, we heard BANG! BANG! BANG! again. But there weren't any bottles left in the cellar. BANG! BANG! BANG!

We learned later that war had broken out. The New Jersey police had crossed the border in force to collect a missed payment of protection money. They were searching for the Capo, who had disappeared.

Two Italian men brought him over to our house at midnight, my friend, who had been teaching me baseball, his hip shattered by a bullet, with blood dripping from a wound in his cheek, and they asked my parents if they would hide him until the heat was off.

My mother shouted, "No!" But for once, my father was the man of the house. I remember the Italian was hidden in the second house in our row, and a doctor arrived who asked no questions. Our neighbor was patched up, but unable to walk. We hid him for weeks.

After all, Dad said, how can you refuse a friend who let you borrow a gallon of his best alcohol to celebrate the holy Passover? And that's how my father invented champagne. The best in the civilized world.

Chapter II
Growing Up

Childhood, as anyone who has managed to live through it can attest, is not necessarily the happy days of innocence we pretend to remember. I recall my own childhood through cracked, though rose-colored glasses. I was small for my age, and often set upon by older and larger schoolmates. I can recall once when I was alone, minding the store for my parents, two bullies approached the entrance and dared me to come out and fight them, the last thing in the world I intended to do. But the store was my responsibility. I ordered them away, and they only laughed.

So I picked up a BB gun from a counter—we sold the Daisy brand—and aimed it at one of them, who continued to laugh. I was under the impression that the gun wasn't loaded. Isn't that always the excuse? I pulled the trigger, hoping the noise would frighten them (a BB gun coughs when it is fired, and so do I). To my horror it was loaded. The tiny pellet hit under my would-be tormentor's left eye; a half-inch higher and he would have become Popeye the Sailor, Jr.

I was petrified with fright, but my fear was nothing compared to that of my two macho assailants—they hightailed it away down Main Street, certain that they had run into a small, natural-born killer. Thereafter they gave me a wide berth at school, where word spread quickly and I was treated with the respect that fearless murderers were accorded in the Fifth Grade in those ancient times. Today, of course, drive-by shootings and drug warfare on school playgrounds have inured school-age children to violence, which they also view regularly on TV, a form of entertainment which didn't exist in those uncivilized days. BB guns are relics of a gentler, prehistoric past. Radio programs then had their share of violence, too, but you couldn't see the blood, which rather limited their entertainment value.

One fact is impressed on me in these modern times. During my childhood, the planet Earth was inhabited by less than 50% of the human beings who now populate and pollute it. And today's population is scheduled to double within the next ten or fifteen years. When I was growing up—or trying to—small towns like Spring Valley were common; and you could know most of the inhabitants by sight, and almost too much about them. For instance, we all knew that Mrs. Harris, who was a lawyer or an accountant or something weird like that, and wore men's clothes, was the town's token lesbian. It never occurred to us that there must be another lesbian in Spring Valley, or what would Mrs. Harris do with her Saturday nights? But that seemed too much to expect from our straight-laced community. Perhaps Mrs. Harris was an immaculate lesbian, and never practiced her calling. After all, my Catholic friends believed in the Immaculate Conception, and that seemed even more unlikely to me. I'm not sure there was a Mr. Harris. If so, he wisely kept out of sight. Maybe he wore dresses. You must understand that in my very young days, sex itself was an impenetrable mystery. I didn't know what you did with a girl or how you did it. This was in the days long before cable TV. What got me mad was that dogs seemed to know all about it and never confided in me. I used to spend stolen moments looking up dirty words in the Oxford Unabridged Dictionary, but the definitions were very unsatisfactory. Any dog would have sneered at them.

Also, we all knew strange facts about our friends' parents, and about every girl in town. Most of the interesting allegations were imagined, but it made for lively conversations after school. Now, of course, it is understood that every girl over 13 does it, but back then there was often room for delightful doubt. I remember my school pals and I would break into hilarious laughter when we saw a pregnant woman on the street. It didn't matter that she was married. At least it proved she did it.

What has happened now to naive, somewhat innocent, Spring Valley, New York, healthful haven for a small group of Jewish European immigrants fleeing New York City? Of course, if you wanted to go back to the original residents of Spring Valley, you would reach the Jackson Whites, some of whom still existed when I was small. They were the descendants of a native Indian tribe who united, to put it politely, with deserters from the Revolutionary Army of George Washington, and they lived, unwashed, in the Ramapo Mountains nearby, and descended occasionally on our town, which they looked on as their town. They largely disappeared years ago, with their long hair and unkempt clothes, and I never saw them again until 400,000 of them unexpectedly showed up at the original Woodstock. Or at least a lot of teenagers with hair like theirs.

A recent story in the *New York Times* brought me sadly up to date about Spring Valley today:

> "Unemployed men stand on street corners awaiting offers of jobs as day laborers; young men walk the streets peddling drugs. And violence—including the killing of three people in recent months—is on the rise…The steady arrival of the new immigrants, mainly from Haiti, Jamaica, Guatemala and El Salvador has given the village new energy and a cosmopolitan flavor…
>
> "In the heart of Main Street there are Haitian political and social clubs, a law office specializing in immigration, and restaurants and groceries offering spices, jerk chicken, curry goat, oxtail, and beef patties.
>
> 'Trafe!' the old Zaydeh would have shouted, meaning non-Kosher. 'What happened to pastrami and pickles and stuffed derma? To helzl and gribbiness? Gone! Gone with the wind!'"

That wind of change blows everywhere but in my heart. You can't go home again, Thomas Wolfe said. Of course you can't. But in my mind I can see the little town that was a haven to my father after the pogroms of Minsk, it was a small country crossroad where the fresh air blew away all the filth of New York City and seltzer water was a sure cure for tuberculosis. The fresh air would also cure the high blood pressure that had sent him here, he was told; alas, it didn't, even though his brother Bill was now the best doctor in the Western Hemisphere (at least), but Bill could not prescribe for Dad the drugs that hadn't been discovered yet and that could so easily have saved his life. And so Joseph Shavelson died in his little island in the future, but not until he had lived many years in the fresh country air, reading the *Jewish Daily Forward* every day, and managing, somehow with his wife Hilda, to raise three children during the depths of the Great Depression and see that each one of us received the college education he had never been able to afford. I think my proudest moment was standing beside him in Shavelson's New York Bazaar and telling him, "Dad, I won the State Scholarship to Cornell University!" And he said, "Such good news! Already I feel I'm going to get better!" And I think, for awhile, he did, long enough to see his daughter Elsie graduate from Ohio University, and his son from Cornell. He never saw his youngest child, Geraldine, nine years my junior, enter Northwestern University. A long, long way from the ghetto in Minsk. And one day he could take a trip to Hollywood all by himself to visit his son, while Mother had to stay at home to open the store every day at 8:00 a.m. Dad even visited a foreign country, Tijuana. Ironical that Tijuana is what his beloved Spring Valley now seems to have become.

Chapter III
Radio Days

I must have been about 12 years old when I began my career in radio broadcasting. It was an auspicious debut, one long remembered on the Old Nyack Turnpike, where both my family and the Sam Rutchik Estates existed, although the audience was rather limited, consisting of Sam and my parents and my older sister Elsie. Geraldine wasn't born yet.

The Sam Rutchik Estates was a collection of tiny bungalows rented out in the summer to visitors from the city, located at the far end of the Turnpike, about three miles from our home. Mr. Rutchik was inordinately proud of his units, because they consisted of *kuch alains*, or however that might be spelled in Yiddish, meaning they were "cook-alones," consisting not only of a bedroom but also a tiny kitchen with a stove, where each wife could prepare indigestible kosher fare for her family without the indignity of a neighboring wife telling her what she was doing wrong. At the top of the economic strata were the hotels, which served kosher meals at least four times a day, or until the guests were comatose. They also had shows every night, with social directors who stole all the Broadway hits and translated them into Yiddish, before being forced to dance with the wives on vacation from their husbands. A step lower was the hotel without meals, and somewhere below them were restaurants where you could get a kosher meal without having to spend the night.

At the bottom were the kuch alains, where you cooked your own meals, made your own beds, and your mother was the social director. But to Rutchik, they were the ultimate; he believed in the freedom of the individual, and his cottages gave each individual complete freedom to starve. At heart, he was a Socialist, as was most of Spring Valley's Jewish population, but Rutchik was also a part-time Communist and a fervent

Anarchist, which he combined with being a Capitalist by being opposed to all taxes. In truth, he gave Anarchy a good name. But his kuch alains were his pride and joy. They produced a profit.

In our living room, we had a battery-operated Atwater Kent radio with which I often sat up until past midnight, vainly trying to tune in KDKA in that distant, exotic foreign land known as Pittsburgh. Sometimes I could make out the music between static crashes.

On this occasion, my Uncle Eddie had given me a birthday present that didn't contain chocolate-covered garlic. Maybe in penance for his sins, he had given me a kit from which you could, if lucky, build an honest-to-God telephone. I was fascinated and spent long hours putting it together.

One evening, Mr. Rutchik was visiting the family, and they were all seated in front of the Atwater Kent, listening to the Metropolitan Opera, I believe, on the loudspeaker of the radio. After a great deal of experimentation and a few exhilarating electrical shocks, I had found a way to feed that telephone into the back of the Atwater Kent, and had run a long wire to a closet, where I hid that night with my invention.

While some tenor was attacking "Riggoletto," I threw a switch and announced: "We interrupt this program to bring you a news bulletin! Flash! Fire has broken out at a kuch alain in the expensive Rutchik Estates on the Old Nyack Turnpike and is threatening to destroy all the uninsured buildings! The Spring Valley Volunteer Fire Department is speeding to the scene of the terrible blaze!"

I heard a shriek from the other room. Rutchik leaped to his feet and almost had a heart attack. It wasn't the fire, but the thought of what the Spring Valley Volunteer Fire Department would do to his expensive cottages; for the moment, he had turned 100% Capitalist.

At the same time, I shrieked as I touched the wrong wire and got a well-deserved jolt of electricity.

For awhile, pandemonium reigned. I was pulled from the closet while I tried to explain it was all a joke, but Rutchik was already out the door and into his Model T. Radio itself was such a mystery in those days, it was frightening to all of us to hear how it pulled voices out of thin air. That the voice it pulled out had been mine was impossible for Rutchik to comprehend.

He raced up the Old Nyack Turnpike to his beloved Estates at breakneck speed, 25 miles per hour, and when he arrived he couldn't understand why his beloved bungalows weren't in blackened ruins from the terrible fire. There weren't even any volunteer firemen smashing windows and furniture in his kuch alains. How could a voice that came from out of the sky tell a lie?

And that night, in a sense, modern news broadcasting was born.

Today, we have learned not to believe anything it tells us.

I was some 65 years ahead of Barbara Walters.

I suppose my great success as a newscaster led me to look for new worlds to conquer. The next logical step would be to play a leading role on Broadway. However, since I was only twelve, I knew it would be awhile before audiences would accept me as Hamlet or Macbeth, although I had no doubts about my ability to play either role, although I felt some of the dialogue could be improved.

That reminds me of the story playwright S.N. Behrman tells in his autobiography. A group of the greatest playwrights of his era, including Eugene O'Neill and George Kaufman, organized the Playwrights Company to put on Broadway shows with their own money and prove they didn't need the help of the Theatre Guild and other run-of-the mill producers.

Behrman was seated next to O'Neill when their initially under-rehearsed (to save money) production, *Hamlet*, had its first out-of-town tryout. On opening night it was so unutterably terrible that O'Neill nervously leaned over to Behrman and whispered, "Aren't you glad you didn't write this one?"

Of course, contemplating a future on the stage was a little frightening to me, because I was still a little shy—unless I was broadcasting from a closet. Not really as certain of my own abilities as I pretended to myself, I decided to start in a small way: Spring Valley High School was putting on its annual Minstrel Show, and they were trying out end-men. I had to force myself to go through an audition, but somehow I managed, and to my surprise, was selected as one of the traditional four who flanked the Interlocutor.

In our somewhat enlightened age today, the whole idea of a Minstrel Show, where the end-men were whites who blacked up to play comedy as black men, is so racist that the form ceased to exist decades ago. But it was in blackface that such stars as Al Jolson and Eddie Cantor and, yes, Bob Hope, began their careers. In Hope's case, he arrived at the vaudeville theater one night too late to apply his black makeup and the manager shoved him out on the stage anyway. To Bob's amazement, his nose played funnier in white-face; the laughs were so big he never went back to burnt cork again. Besides, it was cheaper without it.

But in those days, blacks were not considered to have feelings that could be hurt. I can still remember how startled I was when a black laborer, who was working on digging up the street near our store, gave me some change to buy him a Coke; he couldn't be served at the candy store nearby. He was large and very black, and occasionally wiped the sweat from his face with a red bandanna. When I brought him the Coke, he gave me a dime tip. It had never occurred to me that anyone with a black skin would be rich enough to give away a whole dime; the Coke itself at that time was only a nickel. I wasn't sure I would be dishonored as a member of the ruling white race if I accepted that much money from a black man. But then I remembered I was Jewish and wasn't a member of any ruling race. I accepted his dime and neither one of us felt at all dishonored. We smiled at each other, both knowing that prejudice played a part in both our lives. We were brothers.

But that didn't affect my performance when trying out for the Minstrel Show. You had to read dialogue with a heavy Negro accent to make it sound funny, the heavier the accent the funnier the joke to white audiences.

I developed quite an accent, sounding like a soprano-voiced Louis Armstrong, if you can imagine that.

To give you an idea of the level of humor, here is one of the jokes I remember:

INTERLOCUTOR (*he was always in white-face, wearing a stylish tuxedo, to contrast with the end-men, who wore old sweaters and torn and patched pants*): Rastus, where do all the bugs go in the winter?

RASTUS (*me, wearing burnt cork; scratching myself*): Ah dunno, Boss. You can search me.

Laughter. Honest.

I believe we did four performances on the stage of the high school auditorium, with packed houses (all white) rocking with laughter each night. I felt I had received the equivalent of the Academy Award when I heard part of the audience discussing the performance later.

"The little nigger on the end was the funniest," one said. And the others agreed.

I swelled with pride. I was that "little nigger." It never occurred to me that it was anything but a compliment.

Or that my friend who had given me the dime was not allowed in that school auditorium unless he had a broom in his hand.

Chapter IV
Far Above Cayuga's Waters
1933–1937

There is a heartless story about a Jewish boy who returns home from his first term at a Yeshiva, a Rabbinical school, wearing a black hat, a prayer shawl, braided hair, and a long beard, to be greeted at the door by his brother who shouts, "Mama! Look who's here! Joe College!"

Cornell is no Yeshiva. On the contrary, the outfit I wore on my first return to Spring Valley consisted of the boots and uniform of the United States Army's Cavalry, since every male Freshman automatically had to join the ROTC. And learn to ride a horse. Or at least learn to climb on one. Getting off was no problem; the horse usually took care of that. Why horses would be needed in modern warfare, nobody ever figured out. When war finally arrived a few years later, the horses never were ordered into battle, while several of the frightened New York City Freshmen, clinging to the saddles that first morning, were. Two of them didn't make it past the landings at Guadalcanal, among the first casualties of a war we didn't know we were rehearsing for.

The horses were the smartest ones of all. They were too old for the Draft.

That first freezing Ithaca morning, our four-legged friends were feeling their oats, as they say, and several of them suddenly bolted. Their horrified riders clung helplessly to their saddles and hollered, "STOP! WHOA! HALT! YOU BASTARDS!" and other colorful New Yorkese, as they bounced helplessly in the air and searched desperately for the brake pedal, stirrups lost, heels banging against the flanks of their energetic mounts, who seemed to believe they were being encouraged to win the Kentucky Derby. The rest of us turned to the Drill Sergeant and asked what he could do to save the lives of our comrades. He told us not to worry, the horses always returned to the stables at feeding time. Whether our comrades would be with them didn't seem to concern him.

I recall dimly that the second time I mounted up for training, we were unceremoniously told we were going to learn to jump. Apparently, they had forgotten to inform my horse, a huge creature called "Rocket," because of his propensity to become gas-propelled; he raced with me up to the first jump, eyed it in surprise, and paused to consider. As I flew over his head, he decided to do a standing high jump, and almost landed on top of me.

I recall nothing of the rest of my military career, except that we were supposed to be part of the Field Artillery, and drilled regularly with 75mm cannon, relics of a past war. We didn't realize it would one day be referred to as World War I. I remember being horrified when I learned the shells we were loading into the 75s contained thousands of steel balls which were supposed to burst over the heads of enemy troops and wound or kill them by the hundreds. This deadly, random death struck me as somehow unfair; wasn't a single fatal explosion enough? Then I realized that the enemy, whoever he was, would probably be using twice as many steel balls and an even larger cannon against me, and I stopped worrying about fairness.

Later, as a reporter on the *Cornell Daily Sun*, I covered meetings of a campus pacifist organization known as the Veterans of Future Wars, and realized my ROTC training had made me look favorably on pacifism. The VFW was led by a particularly fiery card-carrying Communist named Fanny Hill, whose fierce espousal of the Cause was only matched in my later life in a memorable encounter with Vanessa Redgrave. Fanny was no Vanessa, and not the most popular coed on campus.

I reported one of their mass-meetings in "The Berry Patch," the supposed humor column of the *Sun*, under a banner headline, "Peace at any Price Except Fanny Price!" This was later corrupted by my then-friend and housemate Artie Levine, later to become famous as Arthur Laurents, in a film he wrote starring Barbra Streisand in a role obviously based on Fanny. That headline was switched to, "Any Peace but Fanny's Piece!" Better, but it would have been censurable in our college newspaper, one of whose editors had been thrown out of school for reporting the dedication of the first Ithaca landing strip by Cornell President Livingston Farrand, under the glaring headline, "President Farrand Breaks Wind for New Airport!"

I almost followed that editor into exile when, as one of the founders of the Cornell Radio Guild which presented weekly programs over radio station WESG from a campus studio, I came up with a sensational idea for a program to be broadcast from outside the studio, something almost unheard of in those days. I arranged to carry a microphone on a long cable into the street in front of Willard Straight Hall, and interview survivors of the previous night's Junior Prom. The program was titled, informatively, "The Man in the Gutter," and indeed some of the interviewees were still a little unsteady on their feet under the influence of what passed for Scotch whiskey in those final days of the Noble Experiment. I thought they were all amusing and informative, but apparently President Farrand thought differently. Somehow, little WESG, with its puny 500-watts of power, had been heard loud and clear by parents of Cornell students throughout the civilized world. They were apparently outraged to learn that alcohol was available to their children on the ivy-covered Cornell campus and wrote letters expressing their horror directly to President Farrand, who promptly invited me to his office to discuss the matter. Rather, he discussed, and I just cringed, waiting for him to break wind. I was given the choice of cancelling future "Man in the Gutter" broadcasts, or leaving my Alma Mater immediately. Thus ended my promising career as a newscaster. At Cornell, I did get to announce the basketball games from the Drill Hall, and Polo games from the indoor Polo field, sitting in the enclosed press booth, which was as close as I wanted to get to a horse again.

I once broadcast a football game from Cornell's Schoellkopf Field by telephone to a gathering of the Cornell Club in Philadelphia, which was a little difficult because I didn't know the names of the players on the visiting team, so I just made them up. No one seemed to notice. I also had the distinction of covering Cornell's Big Red team for the *Sun* the only year in its history it didn't win a game.

In my Freshman year, I wrote a short story for an English class in the style of Damon Runyon, then at the height of his popularity. Except with my English professor. I received the story back with a D- and every grammatical error circled in red. When I explained to the professor that the errors were deliberate, as I was imitating the famous Damon Runyon style, he asked, "Who is Damon Runyon?" Recovering from the shock, I explained exactly who Runyon was, and Professor Monroe absorbed the information calmly and said, "Oh...another imitator of Ring Lardner," and refused to change that D minus.

I was disturbed enough to send the story with its red chicken pox of grammatical corrections to Runyon himself, who was then writing a column in the *New York Journal-American*. I told him what had happened and complained he might have caused me to flunk English II, or whatever it was. To my surprise, I got a letter back from Runyon in which he wrote, "I'm sorry your Professor Monroe never heard of me, but I never heard of him, either, so that makes it even. Since you obviously have a flair for writing, don't pay too much attention to the collegiate methods but tell your story in your own way." I followed his advice and treasured that letter for years, until it got mislaid somewhere in the dim past. But I have saved one scrap of paper on which I had written:

"I've fallen in love with a public accountant

And what am I going to do?"

Those were the first lines of a poem I inflicted on the Girl from Jersey Shore. We met on a blind date in my Senior year, and I found poetry the only way to express what I was feeling. She was not only beautiful, but her mother was also beautiful, and I figured, wisely, that Lucy would only improve with age, like fine wine or Roquefort cheese.

Our meeting was entirely accidental. Well, not entirely. Her friend, Joan, was a member of the Cornell Dramatic Club, and she appealed to David Heilweil and myself, also Drama Club members, for help. She made the startling revelation that the worst thing had happened to her that could ever happen to a girl. After ruling out every interesting possibility—Joan didn't look pregnant—we learned that two of her girlfriends were driving up from Williamsport, Pa., and she was expected to find them two sensationally handsome men for the evening, and all the handsome men she knew were occupied, so could she prevail on us?

As I recall, neither David nor I was busy that night, or the night before, or the night before that, so we eagerly accepted without demanding further information. That they were girls was enough. Also, they were driving up in a car. We didn't know any girls with cars. Girls didn't take boys out in their cars unless the rumble seat had well-oiled springs. These girls became immediately desirable.

David and I were to pick them up that evening in front of Sage Hall, the women's dormitory they had been sentenced to sleep in.

Lucy and her friend Sally came hesitantly down the steps of Sage, as David and I waited below, with some trepidation, to see what kind of dogs we would be stuck with that night. Obviously, no girl accepted a blind date if she was not a real dog.

We were startled. Both young ladies, in our eyes, surpassed anything available on the Cornell campus, or even at Ithaca College. About 19 years old, beautiful, well-clothed, eager, they started down the steps. I noted immediately that one of the beauties possessed boobs, but the other didn't. My fate was sealed.

Lucy and Sally, in their turn, paused to look us over. What kind of dogs would they be stuck with that night? No man accepted a blind date if he didn't have to.

David was a rugged, devil-may-care-type, who seldom combed his hair or bothered dressing for a date. I had prepared by putting on my best—and only—suit and tie. Like slaves on the auction block, we waited for the ladies to make their choice.

Later, Lucy revealed that she had said to Sally, "I don't know which boy you want, but I want the one with the tie."

Fortunately, our choices coincided.

I don't remember much of the evening that followed in Sally's car, and that's probably all for the best. I know it was a convertible, and we wound up on the shores of Lake Cayuga near dawn, steam rising from the lake and from us. It was an evening of what was described in those days as "heavy petting." In that age, Good Girls Didn't, although the boys always boasted they Did.

Well, these girls emphatically Didn't. Not the first time out of the starting gate. You see how I was still thinking about horses? Sally and David never saw each other again. I didn't know if Lucy and I ever would. Or how deep our feelings ran. How deep is the ocean?

On the Pennsylvania farm owned by Lucy's cousin Clifford, our romance grew. There were long walks on country lanes, and I had the good sense to read her poetry by A.E. Housman and Dorothy Parker, instead of relying on my own. I thought my campaign was working. Of course, my goal was not permanent commitment. One rumble seat doth not a marriage make. Or if that was a possibility, I didn't dare mention it to anyone. Especially Lucy.

And then I heard that she had become interested in another Cornellian, a talented and offbeat actor with an air of mystery about him, Peter Hancock. Tall. Good-looking. Intriguing. He always wore sandals, which I considered in some way an indication of his lack of morals. And in an Ithaca winter, of insanity.

I panicked. Throwing caution to the winds, I telephoned Lucy and proposed. I thought it was Lucy on the phone. It may have been her mother, Emmy. At any rate, whoever answered the phone accepted my proposal. I hadn't yet graduated, I had no money, but I was accepted.

Lucy came to Spring Valley and met my mother, who wasn't too thrilled. After all, Lucille was a half-shicksa Jewish-Presbyterian, an unlikely combination. My father liked her, but he didn't have a vote in our family.

That's how matters stood when I graduated from Cornell and came to Greenwich Village to share an apartment at 16 Gay Street with my sister Elsie. It was a tiny rat warren on New York's tiniest, but picturesque street, only one block in length, and I had a tiny job writing for a radio show called *We, the People*, and another radio show called *The Bicycle Party*. Both jobs came as a result of my inviting a network radio program called *The Pontiac Varsity Show* to Cornell, where I helped the producer, a friendly, bespectacled and overworked network type named Jack Roche, write the script. The MC was John Held, Jr., the famous cartoonist who almost single-handedly invented the Flapper. What a cartoonist was doing as the MC of a radio show where no one could see his cartoons, I never understood, any more than I understood the success of a ventriloquist named Edgar Bergen who had a dummy named Charlie McCarthy, whom the audience couldn't see, either. Since they also couldn't see Bergen moving his lips, the show became an unprecedented success.

Show business. It has no explanation. That may explain how I was allowed into it.

At any rate, Roche took a liking to me—he later became my neighbor in North Hollywood—and helped me get the jobs. Each paid $35 a week, and I felt I was worth it until I was fired from both a few weeks before Christmas. But the experience was invaluable. I'll never forget my office at Henry Souvaine's on the 36th floor of the RCA Building, where I wrote the shows and an occasional bit of poetry for *New York Daily News* columnist John Chapman, and the friends I made, including Nelly Miller and Tom Stix and the others, who introduced me to the strange new world of network radio when its Golden Age was in its infancy.

After being fired from the shows, I didn't know how I could continue to help Elsie with the rent. Lucy occasionally visited from Williamsport and never mentioned an engagement ring, which I would have hocked if I could have afforded one.

And then Opportunity knocked, in the shape of my cousin, Carl Hartman.

Carl, or Bud as we called him, had been working for a Broadway press agent named Milt Josefsberg, writing jokes for Milt's clients to be placed in their name in the various Broadway columns. Bud found the assignment rather wearing, because he didn't like jokes and considered them beneath him; he was a born journalist, and, when he was offered a job with the Havas News Agency, he bequeathed me his position and left immediately. He hasn't written a joke since. Or before.

Milt had a tiny, dingy office on Columbus Circle in New York in the old General Motors Building, which was later torn down in his honor. After considerable negotiation, he finally agreed to hire me on my cousin's recommendation at a salary of $13 a week, a considerable comedown from *The Bicycle Party* and *We, the People*. However, with marriage looming somewhere in my future, I was in no position to haggle. Although I tried.

When haggling proved unsuccessful, I accepted and Milt ordered me to write some jokes for Walter Winchell and Sidney Skolsky to use in their columns, under his clients' names, and left immediately to lie in the sunshine on Manhattan Beach, having become Management again.

When he returned at 6:00 p.m., considerably rested and tanned, I handed him 20 pages of jokes.

He read them and asked, suspiciously, "Where did you get these?"

And I said, "I wrote them while you were getting that sunburn."

And Milt said, "Your salary is now fifteen dollars a week."

Coming from the master of the punch line, it was the greatest compliment I was ever paid. You must remember that in 1938, $15 a week was more than Milt gave his wife Hilda for food, rent, laundry, and a down payment on her new fur coat, which only a month before had been eating carrots.

It was the beginning of years of working together and laughing together. Milt was a master of comedy who worked solely by instinct, and his instincts were not only for fun and games, but for generosity and honesty and integrity and all those other ethical things that have now gone out of style.

One week after I started on the job, Milt suggested we write some scintillating material for a promising young comic who was appearing at Loew's State on Broadway, and was about to start his very own half-hour radio show in Hollywood, glamorous, glorius Hollywood, a town neither of us had ever visited, never having gone further west than Lindy's delicatessen on Broadway. It's difficult to realize that back in those uncivilized times, no bagel had been that far west either. Milt knew James Saphier, a handsome and ambitious cigar-smoking young man who was the comic's agent. Jimmy was the first Jewish golf hustler I ever met. He learned the game so he could lose heavily to his clients, especially the comic, so they all hesitated to get rid of him.

Saph suggested we prepare some hilarious material to show his client. Milt and I spent a day writing a comedy spot together. Halfway through he anjnounced we were now equal partners in everything except his wife, Hilda.

The young comic at Loew's State read the material and invited us up to his suite in the Hampshire House on Central Park, to look at the view and discuss finances. We wouldn't have been so pleased if we had known the gentleman we would be negotiating with, known as Lesley Townes Hope, or Rapid Robert, would, half a century later, own more real estate than the United States Department of the Interior. When we arrived at his suite, it was like throwing two frightened herrings to a barracuda.

I appointed Milt to be my representative in the negotiations, since at the time he outweighed me by a hundred pounds, most of it ketchup,. his main diet.

Hope greeted us warmly, holding our script in his hands, and his first friendly words were, "How much do you guys expect to be paid for writing this shit?" And Milt, without blinking an eye, said, "We usually get a hundred dollars a week." I almost fainted. So did Bob. When he revived, he said, "*Each?*" Milt, who had another business to fall back on if necessary, said, "*Each.*"

A long pause, which in later years Milt wrote often for Jack Benny. And Bob said, finally, "That's a little rich for my blood."

We left.

On the way down in the elevator, I tried to dissolve our partnership on the basis of temporary insanity. Nobody in my family had ever been paid a hundred dollars a week, unless they had faked an injury on their disability policy. But Milt didn't seem worried at all. "We'll get it. We were with him for half an hour and that comic didn't say one funny thing. He needs us."

After three weeks of struggling with his better judgement, Bob finally bit the bullet. We got the money, the job, and a contract drawn up by his lawyer, Simon Legree. Under its terms, I think I am still obliged to deliver monologue jokes whenever he calls. The fact that Hope is no longer around to place those calls hasn't registered on my yet. Even in the Hereafter, Bob would find a way to phone. Collect.

We left for Hollywood by train. Even though Bob was paying, we actually had berths.

I wasn't married to Lucy yet, but Hilda came along because she didn't trust Milt with starlets, Indian squaws, or, for all I knew, Pullman porters.

Chapter V
Never-Never Land

When I was trying out for "The Berry Patch," the humor column of the *Cornell Sun*, I signed the material I submitted with the pen name of "Allison Wonderland." I remember my father was a little confused when he saw that signature, until I assured him that Allison was a boy's name. But I felt like the original Alice when I stepped off the Union Pacific Challenger at the Los Angeles railroad station that August morning in 1938 and realized I was in the Wild West. After Spring Valley and Greenwich Village, everything looked curiouser and curiouser. And still does. I had been startled earlier when the train stopped at Albuquerque and we were attacked by a war party of fierce Navajo Indians. Things calmed down when we found out they were selling Navajo blankets. I felt that no one would need a blanket in sunny Southern California, but I feared I would be scalped if I didn't buy one. Since I didn't have the money, I put on a hat to protect myself. General Custer didn't bother, and look what happened to him.

Hollywood didn't have Indians when we arrived, except at Central Casting, but the feeling of the Old West was almost palpable. From a drive up into the Hollywood Hills I could see the beginnings of the Mojave Desert and the blue foothills of the Sierra Nevada. I knew Gene Autry must be out there somewhere, riding a horse and singing, something I never managed during my entire career in the Cornell Cavalry. It all seemed like the impossible dream come true: here I was in Never-Never Land, all of twenty-one years of age and earning an unheard-of one hundred dollars a week. I figured that in five or ten years I might be earning two hundred.

My introduction to Show Business, Hollywood-style, came the very afternoon I arrived. I had rented a tiny apartment near Franklin Avenue in Hollywood, and Milt had bought or rented or stolen a car and we man-

35

aged to find Paramount Studios, where Bob Hope had left a pass for us at the gate. We both felt very important when we were allowed through and directed to his dressing room. Bob and Shirley Ross had scored a hit together in *The Big Broadcast of 1938* with a new ballad written by Robin and Rainger titled, "Thanks for the Memory." No one knew it would live as long as "The Star Spangled Banner," but Paramount thought enough of it to use it as the title song of Bob's first starring vehicle, again opposite Shirley. Bob greeted us warmly when we arrived, possibly because he was pleased to know we had used the money he had advanced us for train fare to actually take the train.

His dressing room was small but well-furnished, befitting a rising star who would soon order it completely redone once he had risen. He was in costume and makeup for his role, looking almost too handsome for a comedian. Only his nose was funny. The Glory Days were just beginning. He was relaxed and friendly, although he seemed a little concerned that we had spent the whole morning of our arrival without writing a line. I explained I had been apartment-hunting and had only now found a place. Later in our careers I would learn it was unwise to show up at a story conference with Hope sporting a tan, indicating a wasted day at the beach to his expert eye. I would have to excuse looking healthy by saying I had been working in the sun in my backyard, on my portable typewriter. I'm not certain Bob ever believed me, especially when he asked me to take off my shoes to see if sand fell out of them, but he didn't make a Federal case out of it if the jokes were good.

This first day he was in a good mood. Movies were almost as new to him as they were to us. He was enjoying a medium in which he could tell jokes without worrying about the audience coming up to get him. He was thrilled at the moment, because Leo Robin and Ralph Rainger had written a new song for Bob and Shirley, "Two Sleepy People." He insisted on singing it to get our professional opinions. I felt perfectly competent to be a music critic. After all, as a child I had spent three whole weeks practicing the violin until the neighbors threatened to burn our house down. Then I took up the French Horn, an instrument Danny Kaye later described as, "An ill wind that no one blows good." My high school music teacher insisted I keep it pointed into a ventilator during an orchestra competition. After that, I learned to whistle.

Bob performed "Two Sleepy People" as if Milt and I were a paying audience. We both declared it was better than "Thanks for the Memory," and would last just as long. We only missed by about 54 years, not bad for two tone-deaf comedy writers.

Bob agreed with us. He got a call to the set and bade us farewell, but as we got to the door he asked me if I was married, like Milt was. I said, "Not yet," and that seemed to please him. There was no one to share my apartment with me that lonely evening? I thought he was planning to move in with me, perhaps to save rent, but then I realized he had a large rented house and an unrentable wife in the San Fernando Valley, so there must be some other reason. Then he said, as if I were not brand new to this side of show business, "You won't mind if I borrow the key? I'll leave it in the mailbox when I leave around midnight."

Fame and fortune passed me by when I failed to recognize this as the plot for a blockbuster movie. Billy Wilder did, some years later, and won an Academy Award for *The Apartment*. Jack Lemmon played the schnook who gave the key to his apartment to his employer, Fred MacMurray, so his boss could play footsie with Shirley MacLaine. I was a perfect schnook, but I didn't get an Oscar.

Having only arrived in Hollywood that morning, I had no place else to go that night. Milt was occupied with Hilda, and I figured Bob was probably in my apartment, playing footsie with Greta Garbo or some other girl above the title. I wandered the unknown streets trying to figure how long a tryst between two romantic movie stars was liable to last, and realized the answer was discouraging. But I knew Bob had to be on the set early the next morning, so it was still possible he would keep his word.

I returned to my apartment exactly at midnight. The key was in my mailbox. It was still warm. I entered the apartment and saw two sets of wet footprints leading from the shower to the unkempt bed. One set was large, the other dainty. So she couldn't have been Garbo, who wore a size 12. I undressed and wearily got into my own bed for the first time. It was as warm as my key.

I never found out who she was.

I had certainly found out who Bob was, though, and he didn't disappoint me in the next half century. It never occurred to him to be embarrassed or guilty. This was Show Business. He was a star enjoying his stardom. All men would do the same with his charm and opportunities. Still, he valued his marriage and we writers and the press protected him until there was no need to protect him any longer.

Let he who is without sin…

It was now time for Milt and me to join the rest of the writers who had been out-negotiated into joining Bob's staff to help him start the Pepsodent radio show and launch the Golden Age of radio comedy, most of the gold being his. That first indentured group numbered eight writers. At the end of the first option period, Bob fired five of them and hired five new ones, but since he had to give the first five two weeks' notices, for a period of time there were thirteen writers writing one half-hour radio show. And each writer or team of writers had to write an entire show. Then we had to read our jokes aloud to the others, gathered in the living room of Bob's rented Navajo Street home, and if anybody whose job depended on lack of appreciation could be persuaded to laugh, Bob checked the joke. It was the end of the Depression years, and laughter did not come easily. That was when I developed the symptoms of my first ulcer, later to be improved on by my association with Samuel Goldwyn, the legendary producer of some of Hollywood's most prestigious films, some of which I wrote.

It didn't help much that at the end of every week with Hope, all the writers gathered at the foot of the circular staircase that led to his office. Bob stood at the top and made paper airplanes out of our checks and floated them down and watched us jump for them. He claimed he did it because it was the only exercise we got all week. Since I was one of the five writers whose option was picked up, I bought a car for $25 (a Model A Ford convertible) and invited Lucille to come out and get married. For some reason, she came.

Lucy arrived on the last day of October 1938, and we spent the evening alone together. It was the night of the Orson Welles broadcast of *The War of the Worlds*. We were the only ones in the entire United States who weren't frightened out of our wits. We didn't hear it.

The next day Milt and Hilda were driving us to the Temple next to the Hollywood Knickerbocker Hotel for our wedding ceremony when Lucy asked, casually, if I had the wedding ring. Since I had never bothered with an engagement ring, that small item had slipped my mind. Hilda made us stop at the first Woolworth's and she and Lucy went inside to the jewelry department. I had told them to spare no expense, so they bought the best wedding ring in the store. It cost thirty-five cents. When the Rabbi was delivering the service, he asked me for the ring, held it to the light, and intoned, "May your love be as pure and unalloyed as the gold in this ring…and may it sparkle as brilliantly as these diamonds. Amen." Milt rolled on the floor with laughter, as did our Best Man, Bill Watters; Hilda stuffed a handkerchief in her mouth to keep from breaking up, and Lucy and I just clung to each other and howled with laughter. The Rabbi never figured it out. He refused to go on with the service until everyone got off the floor. I saw him the next day in the bank adjoining the hotel, and he refused to recognize me. I didn't blame him.

Later, when Lucille played Bridge or Mah-Jongg with some of the more affluent ladies in our group, they would sometimes slip off their wedding rings and compare their worth. Lucy would always tell them I had made her promise never to take hers off. They would clean the gold rings in ammonia, and she was afraid hers would dissolve. I recently found it among the jewelry she left behind, carefully wrapped, although the gold has grown green and proud with age. Never have thirty-five cents bought so many years of happiness.

Chapter VI
The War Years

It would take several hundred pages of laborious prose to detail my five years of indentured service on the Pepsodent radio show that followed, so I will spare you all but a few of the gory details. Bob Hope had made the transition from vaudeville, where a single routine lasted a full year, and he realized radio required a year's work for every weekly show. Therefore, unlike most of the comedians now flocking to radio, he spent a large part of his income hiring the best writers, who could concentrate on the news events and the happenings of the time with jokes written right up to airtime, and on some occasions even during.

Bob Hope became the first comedian of the instant joke. And in those days, the only one. With a cast of comic specialists like Professor Colonna, Brenda and Cobina and Vera Vague and singers like Judy Garland and Frances Langford, the *Pepsodent Show,* with its large staff of eager and talented—and starving -writers, pushed its way toward the top of the network radio heap.

Those first years from 1938 to 1943 were critical in the history of the United States, encompassing the start of World War II in Europe, the early days of the Roosevelt era, the first peacetime Draft, the attack on Pearl Harbor on that "Day of Infamy," and America's entrance into the war and the army bases and bombing scares and the shortages and rationing and casualty lists that became part of our everyday life. More than that, we Hope writers had to make them the basis of comedy, the monologues and sketches and songs of the Bob Hope *Pepsodent Show.* The laughter helped us endure it all, and kept the true horror of the Great War in the background, until Bob started making overseas trips to entertain American troops and saw too much of it when he, Jerry Colonna and Frances Langford visited military hospitals. Every radio show had a brief moment of reality to balance the insanity we were writing in monologues and comedy sketches, while the war in Europe threatened at any moment to cross the Atlantic. One serious word, and then on with the jokes.

Some fifty years later, I realized that the jokes we were writing to earn a living while others were dying, had a deeper significance than we knew at the time. I was seated with Arthur Pine, my supercharged literary agent, on the porch of his Long Island home one warm spring day in 1989. Artie was trying to get me to write another book because he needed the money. It didn't matter much what was in the book, as long as it had a naked girl on the cover. I told him, "No." I wanted to write a history book. Artie looked at me as if I were insane; history books were written by professors, all of whose literary agents were starving. Since Artie liked to eat, he suggested I write a novel where everybody was screwing everybody else and then murdering their mothers. Couldn't miss. Would probably win a Pulitzer. I told him he didn't understand. I wanted to write the history of the last fifty years of the United States of America as told through Bob Hope's monologues. I knew Bob kept every joke ever written for him in a vault in a building beside his home in Toluca Lake. I would drive by at night and imagine I could hear the laughter sealed within the time capsule of his files, trying to escape. Every memorable moment of a nation at home and at war was recorded in the monologues his writers sweated over through years of toil and worry and jumping for their checks. They made those decades seem hilarious, when usually they were just the reverse. History through laughter was my goal. Bob Hope's name would get the book read by a generation that had grown up believing life began on this planet with the coming of the Flintstones. The level of intelligence of the American public could be measured by a recent poll, which showed that 35% of them believed Joan of Arc was Noah's wife.

And a young studio executive recently turned down a story about World War II by declaring that nothing that happened before he was born could have any relevance to his life.

Well, it was all relevant, kid. And all of you had better learn the lessons of the past, or all the nations of the world we have defeated in wartime will continue to defeat us in the classrooms and the laboratories of the future. That was the point I wanted to make.

I could see Artie's eyes widen at the mention of Bob Hope's name. George Burns was making publishers rich with *Gracie—A Love Story*, which Artie didn't represent, and this looked like a way to get into bed with a billionaire, which Hope supposedly was. Of course, a lot of ladies had had the same idea before Artie, and it did them no good, but Artie figured a book was different. He asked me to approach Bob and see if I could get the combination to the joke vault.

I spoke with Hope and he liked the idea of what he planned to call *Bob Hope's Comedy History of the United States*. We would share credit on the cover and on the publisher's advance. Of course, he would take the lion's share, since he was the lion.

Artie flew out for a joint meeting. Hope, of course, had written—or, rather, had written for him—many other books. One of them, *I Never Left Home*, had a tremendous circulation, since it was given away free with a tube of Pepsodent. Hemingway didn't do better. The other books were received mildly, mostly by Hope fans, and Bob never collected much of an advance or royalty from them. So it was with some surprise that Artie and I, when we met with Bob at his home, heard him say, "Phil Donohue just got a million-dollar advance for his new book. He's on daytime television. I can't take less. I'm Prime Time."

Artie and I left, somewhat disillusioned. That price was four times what Bob had ever received before. His writing ability would have to improve astronomically. Since I was expected to do all the writing, I figured this was the end of history.

Then the phone calls started. Artie had returned to Manhattan and had presented my manuscript -I think it consisted of the title and two sentences—to various publishers, and they started calling me for a few more sentences. The price frightened most of them off, except for Phyllis Grann of Puttnam's. She was only frightened by the title. If I could persuade Bob not to call it a history, Putnam's would meet the price. I quickly assured her Bob would happily change the title if money was involved, and we had a deal.

I was wrong. Bob steadfastly refused the title change; he wanted to be known as the author of a history. It took months before I finally got him to accept *Don't Shoot, It's Only Me* as more saleable. I'd like to say the book appeared and shot to the top of the *New York Times* Bestseller List, but it only got to number two. Phyllis had expected Hope to plug the book on the Bob Hope TV show the week of publication in May, but he had promised the date to the U.S. Army, and refused.

When the show came on again in the fall, Bob had a change of heart. He had met somebody who had read the book. Bob had a wonderful idea: why not do a TV program about it?

I helped, with Bob's giant writing staff, consisting of Gene Perritt and Martha Bolton, downsized from the thirteen of earlier days. The show was a blend of nostalgia, film clips, and performers like George Burns, Danny Thomas, Milton Berle, and Frances Langford. A little of history managed to creep in, and a lot of Bob's career from vaudeville through the Gulf War. My original idea was to have the four living ex-Presidents appear in person as a tribute, but they all seemed to be giving tributes elsewhere. We did, however, secure the services of that sterling comedian, Henry Kissinger, whose accent brought back memories of Weber & Fields, whom I would have preferred if they had been available. Kissinger was cooperative and tried hard, but his timing was as bad as that of the show, which was now too late to be of any help with the book sales.

But the presence of Frances Langford brought the past back to me vividly. More than just a vocalist, Frances has become a symbol of World War II. The image of Langford as a young girl, a slight, shapely figure singing her heart out against a background of steaming jungle outposts in the South Pacific and thousands of cheering GI's in the blistering desert heat of the North African campaign, has remained with me and all those fortunate enough to be around then, all through the years.

There is a story about Marilyn Monroe, when she was married to Joe DiMaggio, entertaining our troops in Korea, and telling Joe, breathlessly, on her return, "It was so thrilling! I stepped out on the stage and 50,000 men cheered and shouted my name! You've never heard anything like it!"

And Joe said, quietly, "Oh, yes, I have."

The divorce followed later.

For me, World War II began when I saw Lucy wearing only a towel, damp from a shower, standing on the front lawn of our home in Toluca Lake as I returned from a meeting with Hope. She shouted at me, "The Japanese have bombed Pearl Harbor!" Of course, I paid no attention. She was always misinterpreting things she thought she heard on our radio, a shiny Scott All Wave Superheterodyne she really didn't know how to tune. So I calmly left for the football game at Gilmore Stadium. It was only when the announcer called out, "All men in uniform are ordered to report to their units immediately!" that I got the message. I realized he wasn't referring to football uniforms when every soldier and sailor in the stands got to his feet and hurried out.

A bigger game than the Rose Bowl was kicking off. Lucy had heard the radio correctly. For once.

For those legions too young to have been there, and those other legions who never read *Don't Shoot*, some brief quotes from the book will give you an idea of how a whole nation was as confused as I was:

"At 3:00 a.m., December 7, 1941, Lt. Commander Kanjiro Ono was listening to Bing Crosby singing, 'Sweet Leilani,' on the all-night musical program from KGMB in Honolulu. He wasn't really a fan of Der Bingle. What he was waiting for was the weather report, which was obligingly provided at regular intervals. 'Partly cloudy, ceiling thirty-five hundred feet, visibility good.'

"'Domo arigato,'" said Kanjiro. Thank you very much.

"Commander Ono was in the radio room of the aircraft carrier Okagi, at the head of a task force including six carriers, 353 planes, and 34 submarines. Nobody had spotted them, except for some tuna who wound up as sushi. The Japanese were some 250 miles northwest of the Royal Hawaiian Hotel, which they have since bought for $100 million, but at that time they were hoping to get it for nothing.

"What happened after that would have made a good routine for Abbott and Costello, if the results hadn't been so tragic. Who's on first? The Japanese Navy.

"Gunners from the cruiser *Argonne* shot down the 14th Naval District radio tower.

"Forty U.S. shells hit downtown Honolulu.

"A coast artillery bugler realized he didn't know how to blow the call to arms. So he blew pay call. It worked even better. The entire unit came out in twenty seconds.

"Tuesday, December 9, NBC made the announcement, 'The Bob Hope Pepsodent Show will not be heard tonight.'"

The President of the United States took Bob's place.

He didn't get many laughs.

Hope soon become a national hero with his overseas tours to entertain at the fighting fronts, and the show shot to number one on the rating charts. Bob had found his career, and never abandoned it. It was said that if there wasn't a war on somewhere, Hope would start one. But the risks he took in bringing his show to the fighting fronts were real. So was sympathy for the wounded he met in the hospitals, where he and Jerry Colonna would break up the gloom by jumping on hospital beds and chasing the nurses around the wards.

Bob always joked about his exemption from the Draft, claiming he had tried to enlist as a hostage. Bob told me, when I was working on *Don't Shoot* with him, that he and Crosby were exempted from the armed forces by direct order of FDR. I can remember on the very first Army show we played, at March Field, Bob Waterfield, formerly quarterback for what was then the Los Angeles Rams, and now a First Lieutenant, told us all to stay out of the army at all costs; what we were doing was much more important. In hindsight, I'm not certain he was right.

By this time, my lovely wife Lucy was no longer so lovely; she was considerably pregnant.

When her time was drawing near, Emmy, her mother, came from Pennsylvania to be at her side, and I asked her to stay awhile. She did. About eight years. Since she always took my side in family arguments, I didn't mind.

I was out on the road with the traveling Bob Hope Army Camp Show when the crucial date approached. Lucille and I had arranged things so I could be present at the birth of whatever it was she was carrying— this was before the day when medical science could determine the sex of an unborn child and took all the fun out of it. Well, almost all the fun. We were planning to trick Hope into believing the baby would be born a week before it was actually due.

We were in Indianapolis at the time; Lucy was supposed to telegraph me that she had been taken to the hospital for the birth, and sign Emmy's name to it, telling me to come at once. "At once" meant three days and nights on the Atchison, Topeka, and the Santa Fe, since civilians seldom got airline space.

When the wire arrived, I showed it to Bob and he somewhat reluctantly gave me his blessing to leave. I had to go to Chicago to catch the train for Los Angeles; from Chicago, I phoned my mother in Spring Valley to say goodbye and she said, "Mazeltov on becoming a father!"

I said, "No, no, it was a trick to fool Hope"—and then I realized Richard Shavelson had fooled all of us by arriving a week early. I was so excited, I immediately wired Lucy a dozen roses. At least, that was my intention.

For some reason, the war effort had caused a sudden shortage of roses.

The brand-new mother found her hospital room decorated with a large geranium in a large flower pot, as a token of her husband's undying love.

C'est la guerre.

All the joy and excitement of becoming a father was negated when Rich developed a serious problem on his first few days after Lucy brought him home…It proved to be a blockage of the intestine whose name I will never forget—pyloric stenosis – and we suffered more than he did through the operation. Fortunately, the surgeon knew how to spell it, and the future Dean of Stanford's School of Education came through successfully.

Shortly afterward, I got a polite note from the President of the United States, inviting me to join his armed forces. When I showed it to my employer, Bob told me to ignore it; he would have me declared essential and I would get a temporary deferment. By this time, I had wearied of writing jokes; here was a chance to go over the wall and escape forever, and perhaps have some small part in a great adventure for a great cause. So I refused, not quite as gallant a gesture as it might have been if I didn't suspect that the stomach ulcer I had developed—a gift from Bob in those hectic years since Navajo Street—might disqualify me from saving the Free World.

It did. I was out of the Army. But I was also out of a job. There now were several mouths for me to feed, including Lucille's mother, Emmy, who was much too beautiful to be a mother-in-law, but she managed.

But the responsibility of supplying food for all of them didn't make for peace and tranquility.

I was still young enough to be an optimist. I sat down at my little portable Corona typewriter and wrote a screenplay I titled *Madame Boss* because it concerned a young woman who took over as head of a defense plant when the owner was off to war. It preceded Woman's Lib by a decade. I should have waited. Jimmy Saphier, suddenly my motion picture agent, called me one day to tell me he submitted it to Samuel Goldwyn, and Sam had turned it down. But Goldwyn had offered to sign me to a writing contract if I was available. If I was available? At last I could call myself a screenwriter, and be free of Bob Hope forever!

Well, not quite forever, Saphier informed me. Just until next week.

Goldwyn was about to film *The Princess and the Pirate*, starring—who else?—Robert Hope, and they just wanted me to back up the real screenwriters, Don Hartman and Everett Freeman, by supplying them with some typical Bob Hope jokes.

Considerably deflated, I agreed. I was even more deflated after my first meeting with the indomitable Sam Goldwyn, author of such profound statements as, "Include me out" and "Take everything he says with a dose of salts." In the past, Hope had given his radio writers the screenplays of all his movies in advance. He told us that the studio would pay him $5,000 for us, to have us "punch up" the scripts. We were happy to divide all that loot for an afternoon's work. We all "improved" such films as *Road to Singapore, Road to Zanzibar, The Cat and the Canary,* and many others. Bob would hand our jokes to the film's producer, who would promptly reject them, and then Hope would slide our pages of jokes between those of his screenplay and "ad lib" them in front of the cameras. He got quite a reputation for spontaneous wit.

Bob Hope also became number one at the motion picture box office, at the same time that he was number one in radio, an achievement no one else ever matched.

I was always pleased when I went to see the films I had worked on, and heard some of my lines getting laughs, whether they advanced the plot or destroyed it. Either way, I felt the studios had gotten their money's worth for what they had paid Bob for us.

At my first meeting with Goldwyn, Sam remarked, pleased with himself, "Now I got my own Hope writer working on his film, I won't have to play the son of a bitch that $10,000 for their jokes."

It was a lesson in how to become a billionaire without really trying.

Don Hartman became my mentor in screenwriting. Don, with Frank Butler, created the *Road* pictures for Hope and Crosby. They were more than films; editorials were written in newspapers throughout the country on how their inspired insanity lifted the morale of a nation fighting a terrible war for its survival. You have to realize that at the beginning, the Nazi armies seemed invincible; we had no doubt Hitler had some terrible weapon that could destroy all of us, especially those of us who had been circumcised. We tried to minimize our fears with laughter; we had no idea there was such a weapon as an atomic bomb, and that Hitler's scientists were feverishly working on it.

So the *Road* pictures took our minds off reality by not recognizing reality. We and Bob were constantly throwing in asides that would have destroyed any other film. When a gentleman in immaculate evening dress walked through the dirty boiler room of a freighter they were shoveling coal on, no one was surprised to learn he was taking a shortcut to Stage Three. Or, when Bob married Dorothy Lamour at the end of one film, that their son looked exactly like Bing. In fact, it *was* Bing.

The camaraderie onscreen and off, the fictional rivalry that had Crosby selling his bosom pal, Hope, to be eaten by cannibals, or worse, had its parallel in real life; the two were always competing with each other for laughs, and Crosby sometimes secretly paid us to write jokes for him to top Bob when they "ad libbed" in front of the cameras. We writers were, in effect, double agents, and Hope suspected the truth, but it was all part of the game. The result was sometimes close to chaos. Don Hartman told me he once walked on the set at Paramount where they were shooting, and Bob called to him, "If you recognize one of your own lines, yell 'Bingo'!"

And Don retorted, "Keep quiet or I'll put you back in the trunk."

Don was warm and talented and egotistical, and a pleasure to work with. He had once been a songwriter. He told me of the time he bought a new Capehart record player, a huge instrument in those days, that not only changed records, but turned them over. It created a sensation, and one night Don invited his important Hollywood friends to watch it perform its miracle. He surreptitiously slid a few of his own recordings in amongst the Gershwins and Rodgers and Harts. They all sat enthralled as the Capehart turned each record over, but every time it came to one of Don's compositions, it threw it out of the machine. It wasn't a phonograph, it was a music critic, and Don was humiliated and angry. It wasn't until all the guests had left, with suitable comments, that he realized his records were older, and therefore thicker, and were automatically rejected for size, not talent. At least, that was his theory, but I noted he never wrote another song after that. Machines were developing too much taste.

Don and I got along so well together that when he had some sort of disagreement with Everett Freeman, who left the project, Don promoted me to be his full writing partner. We would share writing credit equally. With Milt Josefberg, it had taken me two weeks to become his partner, with Hartman, a month.

I was slowing down.

That was the start of a happy collaboration that lasted through my Goldwyn years. I would awaken every morning, eager to get to work. Because, unlike most writing, it was not "work." In Don's spacious den in his home on Rexford Drive, we would laugh and tell stories and pace and occasionally write a few scenes for Jerry, his secretary, to transcribe. *The Princess and the Pirate* was my first screenplay. Don and I had so much fun inventing it and acting out scenes for each other, I couldn't imagine any reason why we wouldn't win an Academy Award hands down.

But the Academy was like a larger Capehart. Our screenplay and the picture got thrown out without so much as a nomination.

Goldwyn had signed a brand-new talent out of Broadway, Danny Kaye, and Don had written *Up in Arms* for him just before I arrived. Now the two of us started on *Wonder Man*, one of many films where Danny played a dual role. In this case, one of him was dead. Special effects played a large part in the comedy, in the days before special effects took the place of story and dialogue.

But we soon ran into difficulties. Don claimed Goldwyn had promised he could direct the picture, and when Sam told him it was not to be, Don walked out and filed a lawsuit.

Goldwyn threw a big party at his home for some reason that escapes me. He invited everyone in Hollywood of any consequence, meaning I didn't get an invitation, but Don did. At the party, when the guests were growing mellow over cocktails, Sam Goldwyn took Don aside and put his arm around him.

"Don," he asked, plaintively, "why should we be enemies? Forget this crazy lawyer business. In my thirty years in the movie business, you're the only one whoever sued me."

And Don said, "Sam, look around. Over there is Teresa Wright – she's suing you. Next to her is Niven Busch—and he's suing you. And on the other side of the room is Ben Hecht, and he's suing you, too!"

Sam didn't blink. "Present company excepted," he said, the matter finished.

Somehow, they settled their differences out of court, as Don knew they would. He knew very well Sam Goldwyn would never take the witness stand where his accent would be exposed; he had too much pride. And not enough English.

It was about this time that my daughter Carol-Lynne arrived. As soon as she could talk, she dropped the "Carol" and the hyphen, and went on to shoot documentaries in China and Russia. A little later.

There were no complications with Lynne's entrance into the world, except that I spent several anxious hours pacing the maternity ward while Lucy was doing the work. I suffered considerably from sympathetic labor pains, but the doctor refused my request for anesthesia. I survived.

Back at the ranch—the Samuel Goldwyn Studios—Danny and Sylvia Kaye became our friends, an association stretching far beyond the

Goldwyn years to Paramount, where I directed Danny in the screen-plays Jack Rose and I wrote for him, *The Five Pennies* and *On the Double*, which Jack also produced. Danny could be warm and funny and com-plicated at the same time. He and Sylvia had a troubled relationship. Her talent and judgement were the foundation of his career; he knew it, and at times resented it. For awhile, the marriage split up.

During that time, Danny had a private telephone line in his dressing room that all of us were given orders not to touch. Eve Arden had been in *The Kid from Brooklyn* with him at Goldwyn, and the rumor was that she had his number.

Danny also hinted he had a relationship with a certain Princess of the British royal family; in the light of recent history that is no more impos-sible than taking a short cut to Stage Three.

There was no *National Inquirer* then, so none of this was public knowledge. But times have changed. One recent sensationalized biogra-phy goes so far as to state that Danny and Sir Laurence Olivier had a homosexual affair. Two years ago, I worked on a tribute to Kaye televised in England, and when the producer came over to interview Jack Rose and myself, Jack asked him point blank if there was any truth to that story. The producer hesitated, and then said, "There might be."

And Jack inquired, "Who got top billing?"

I don't know where the truth, or the participants, lay; it never came up in the days we worked together. Danny was a unique comedian, so talented in so many ways he almost overdid it. He could sing, he could dance, he could mimic; he had a warmth that children picked up on immediately, and gave him the career with the United Nations Childrens Fund to which he devoted the last years of his life.

He had no formal education or training. Yet he became a skilled jet pilot and a black-belt Chinese cook, as well as the darling of royalty in Britain and what passed for the intelligentsia in the United States. He never achieved the size of the audience that followed Bob Hope for de-cades; Kaye was an acquired taste, a little too whimsical for the general, or beer-drinking, public. And he refused to change. He was still trying to be the little boy on the outside he felt himself to be on the inside, and it didn't work when he couldn't escape being 50 years old.

As an actor, he worked completely on inspiration and instinct. Di-recting him was usually a joy, because he gave more than he was asked. However, he believed completely in spontaneity, which doesn't work on film, where the same scene must be shot over and over again, and from different angles. He would object to more than one take, and he would ad lib while it was being shot, which caused chaos.

It was Sylvia who took up the cause for me. She knew just how to handle him. She said to her somewhat carefree husband, "Danny, I know you feel you lose something when you do a scene over and over, so you ad lib a few lines to give yourself a sense of freshness. But, Danny, how do you expect the other actors in the scene to know what to say when they don't hear their cues? They're not you; they can lose their jobs and their reputations. Are you a professional, or a child?"

Danny stopped being a child for awhile, although it was difficult for him. He loved to tease Goldwyn, whose accent he could imitate perfectly, sending all of us, Goldwyn included, into paroxysms of laughter. He would make faces, and Goldwyn would be laughing so hard he would forget why he was reprimanding Danny for some minor crime.

Once, Danny was in New York, and he called Goldwyn on the phone and said, "Sam, I'm making the fish face," and Goldwyn almost fell out of his chair with laughter.

My memory of those days has improved them from reality; I remember that I was unhappy with the salary I had accepted when I would have accepted any salary to be called a screenwriter; each time my option was picked up by Goldwyn, I would ask for my release. One day I was visited by Pat Duggan, the story editor, who told me that Sam was disturbed because I had again asked for my release after being granted a large raise, and Goldwyn wanted me to know he was giving me my release, but, said Duggan, "Only in a fit of pique." Immediately, I said, "If Sam will repeat those words to me, "I'll stay." Well, of course he didn't, and I went over the wall.

How do you categorize comedians? I've worked with too many of them over the years, and in a strange way, I loved them all. Laughter was their life, and there was nothing about those lives they took seriously. They all had their faults, and you had to have a sense of humor to endure them. They weren't always gentlemen or caring, or moral, or a lot of other things mortals are subject to, but inside all the inflated egos there was always a clown with a slapstick, beating them over the head to remind them that life is too serious to be treated with anything but laughter. Their most important gift was their ability to laugh at themselves. I wish we all had it.

Bob Hope, Milton Berle, Danny Kaye, Danny Thomas, all had one thing in common: me. At least for a brief period of time. Hope fashioned a career and a fortune that lasted over half a century. He was the sharpest, with an enjoyment of jokes and life and its pleasures that sustained him all those years. Perhaps what he enjoyed most of all was money; in second place was applause. He lived for both. The only thing to match them in importance to him is—or, sadly, was—the opposite sex. But in his public persona, he seldom used a four-letter word or an obviously soiled joke. Perhaps he became irrelevant, in a world where both have become so common, but he got his laughter the hard way: he earned it, through humor. I applaud him for it, and as long as someone was applauding, Bob Hope was happy.

Milton Berle lasted almost as many years as Hope, but Milty was Hope's opposite, the King of Vulgarity. Anything for a laugh was all right with him, and, like Hope, he couldn't live without laughter. I don't know if he had any natural wit, because he didn't need it. The computer memory in his brain had an unending store of jokes and punch lines, most of them adopted from someone else. But he was so brazen in his demand that people laugh at him, they did. The fact that people laughed at Berle, and with Hope, is a distinction that probably never registered with him.

Danny Kaye, as detailed above, was the most spontaneous. As a child, he was in a troupe in Japan, where he had to develop his own method of getting laughs without knowing a word of the language. Only later did he, with Sylvia's help, twist words like the names of the Russian composers into hilarious routines.

With no education, he was determined to learn to fly. I was with him when he realized he could never get a pilot's license without any knowledge of arithmetic; so he had his daughter, Dena, teach him addition and division, and he went on to be licensed to pilot commercial jets, but not with me aboard. I had one experience after he got his first pilot's license that cured me. He took me out to Van Nuys Airport, where he had a Piper Cub, and explained to me that the pilot was responsible for the lives of his passengers. It was the pilot's duty to keep the plane in shape. Danny carefully checked the landing gear, the engine, the controls, everything he could think of, before he allowed me to climb in beside him. Then he took the little single-engined plane off the ground expertly, and we headed toward Palm Springs. It was a terribly bumpy ride and I prayed our safety belts would hold; fortunately, they did, and we bounced through San Gorgonio Pass and landed safely at Palm Springs Airport, where, for some reason, we had been unable to contact the tower. The airport, I noted, was strangely deserted. No other planes were in the air. Only then did we discover that weather conditions were so dangerous that all light aircraft had been grounded. In checking his Piper Cub carefully, Danny had neglected to check his radio. It was on the wrong frequency.

I went home by bus.

Danny Thomas? The greatest of them all as a storyteller and stand-up comic. He was once described as the kind of guy who cries at basketball games. Yes, he was solid schmaltz, but it wasn't a pose. When he was told he had to have his nose changed or he would never succeed in front of the cameras, he refused. He wanted to remain his own man. Who would recognize him if he were handsome?

Audiences believed his jokes. Would a face like that lie to them? No matter how outrageous his stories were, he made them sound plausible, like his famous "jack" story, about getting a flat tire on a deserted road and walking miles to find someone with a jack so he could fix the tire, growing madder and madder at his fate, until he finally reached someone who offered him a jack and Danny promptly punched him in the nose. He could stretch that one out for ten minutes of continuous laughter. Sometimes more.

One calamity that actually did happen to him became one of his favorites. Many years back, in his radio days, he starred in a half-hour comedy program for Shredded Wheat. When, as often occurs, the sponsor cancelled the program, Danny had one more broadcast to make before joining the unemployed. Since, in those days, the star delivered the commercials, Danny had an irresistible opportunity.

This was his closing commercial:

"Eat Shredded Wheat! Tastes wonderful with strawberries and cream!" A short pause. "My mattress tastes wonderful with strawberries and cream!"

End of commercial, end of job.

His career continued at a low ebb, consisting of occasional nightclub dates and a minor contract at MGM, until Lou Edelman, the only loveable producer at Warner Brothers in those days, or possibly ever, interested Jack Rose and myself in the story of songwriter Gus Kahn, lyricist for a dozen of Tin Pan Alley's greatest hits, including "It Had to Be You" and "Making Whoopee." Lou's approach was a fresh one: In his eyes, the real story was Grace Kahn, Gus's spirited wife, who was his intelligence and inspiration behind the scenes without Gus realizing it. Doris Day was emerging as a big box office star then. Jack and I had written a film for her and Gordon MacRae based on Booth Tarkington's *Penrod* stories, titled *On Moonlight Bay*, which became one of her first big hits, in spite of the fact that Jack Warner hit the ceiling when we told him we were using Tarkington's books, which Warner Brothers owned, as the basis for the film. According to Warner, they had made a series of *Penrod* films over ten years before, and the exhibitors still couldn't get the smell out of their theaters. Change all the names so the exhibitors wouldn't know!

We objected to changing character names that had been famous for a generation, but Warner insisted. The three to be changed were Penrod, his friend Sam, and their dog, Duke. We changed them in the screenplay to Harry, Jack, and Albert—the names of the three Warner Brothers.

There was an explosion in the front office when J.L.—everybody called Jack Warner "J.L.," including, I believe, his mother—learned of it. Reluctantly, we changed the names again, this time to Wesley (Penrod), Jim (Sam) and Max (Duke). But to us, they were always Harry, Jack, and Albert.

Understandably, we had no immediate assignment after that, so when Lou Edelman offered us the Gus Kahn story, we jumped at the opportunity.

The writing took longer than usual because Lou was constantly on the phone to us with story improvements we didn't need. Finally, I installed a speaker phone so we could listen to him on the telephone while we continued to work. We called the phone the "Edelman Equalizer."

As the story developed, we based much of it on real people, characters we knew, so that the dialogue and the events would have a base in reality. I told Jack about my friend, David Heilweil, intelligent but seemingly clumsy, who had been with me on that memorable blind date at Cornell. David had started his career in the Cornell Dramatic Club as a carpenter, building sets and bashing his fingers, and had later fooled all of us by marrying a poetess—Eva Wolas—and becoming a Broadway producer. Still waters run deep, I've been told. David seemed to embody what we saw in the real Gus Kahn. His widow, Grace, supplied us with much of the information about who and what her husband was.

When the screenplay was finished, it had one great drawback: no leading man in Hollywood wanted to play an uneducated, rough-hewn songwriter, whose wife ran his life for him. No matter that it was a true love match, reflected in the lyrics he wrote, and that he was much more intelligent and sensitive than appeared in his rugged features. Forget it. Pass, they said.

But Danny Thomas, languishing at MGM, had in real life all the characteristics we had written into the character of Gus Kahn. While Jack Warner hesitated on pairing an unknown shlemiel with one of his most valuable box office stars, Lou convinced him to make a test with Danny. On seeing it, Warner immediately suggested Danny have a nose job. Danny refused. But when Doris voted for him, nose and all, Warner relented and the film was made. *I'll See You in My Dreams* became one of the most successful musicals in Warner Brothers history; it was the last black-and-white musical film to play Radio City Music Hall, and photographs in the press showed a double line running for three solid blocks around the theater. Homeliness suddenly was box office.

I would like to say it launched Danny Thomas as a leading box office star and made the movie public forget Errol Flynn and Clark Gable. But it was not to be. Danny was immediately thrust into another picture by Warner, a remake of the first talking film, *The Jazz Singer*, that had opened the sound era with Al Jolson singing "My Mammy," but it was not to be. The story of a Rabbi's son who became a Broadway singing star foundered when sound was no longer a novelty and people began listening to the dialogue.

One additional problem. The religious sequences were photographed in an Orthodox Jewish Synagogue and Jack Warner had a battle with his brother, Harry, over whether the extras should wear the traditional Orthodox Hebrew yarmulke at the services that were an important part of the film. It was Jack who won the battle of hats on or hats off, voting for hats off. However, when the film was finished, he was visited by a delegation from the Temple who threatened to sue. The contract for the use of their Synagogue contained the restriction that no religious laws would be violated; since this was an Orthodox synagogue, only "hats on" were acceptable. Ditch the yarmulkes.

Jack Warner ordered the director, Mike Curtiz, to reshoot all the Temple sequences, hats on, at considerable expense, to assure that no Hebrew law was violated. When Curtiz followed instructions, there was a slight contretemps when the company broke for lunch.

The caterer served ham sandwiches.

The extras ate them with their hats off.

Danny's movie career languished after that. One day, Sam Weisbord, one of the William Morris Agency's most eager talent agents (he represented me as well as Danny) came to me with Danny's latest version of the Jack Story. Thomas was growing angry with Weisbord, his MGM contract, and the entire motion picture industry, and was also rapidly growing broke. Soon he would punch somebody, probably Sam. But there was a new medium called Television that was just emerging from its diapers; Lucille Ball and Desi Arnaz had recently started a television program called *I Love Lucy*, and it was actually making money. Sam predicted it might last three whole seasons.

This was a new and uncrowded field, because nobody knew anything about it. Suppose, God forbid, Television happened to catch on and the Morris Office wasn't collecting commissions? Danny Thomas, with his radio and nightclub background, seemed their best bet to break into this new electronic show business. Sam had come to me because in 1947 I had written the first commercial television show ever broadcast West of the Mississippi— I don't want to take the blame for the whole country—when Paramount's experimental W6XYZ became KTLA at the conclusion of World War II. I had written a 90-minute special for Bob Hope and all of Paramount's stars. Sam figured I might know how to write a television pilot. Of course, I didn't, but nobody else did, either. Catch 22 was that Danny Thomas had no money, and the Morris Office didn't want to risk much of their own on a client who wasn't bringing in any. So I was offered an unheard-of proposition: if I would write a pilot script—the name had just been coined—I would be paid half my usual weekly salary. If the show got on the air, I would subsequently be paid a weekly "royalty" without writing another line, and if it stayed on for thirteen weeks, I would have broken even.

Fortunately, I had the foresight to agree to what eventually became the first residual. *Make Room for Daddy* stayed on the air for eleven years and I received a check every week for approximately 429 weeks. I put the money into the purchase of my home, where I have lived ever since on three magnificent acres of lawn, orange trees, swimming pool, and tennis court. It was the best—and only—decent real estate deal I ever made. I think I went to Temple the 429th week to celebrate. Hat on.

Danny was always grateful. When I would show up in the audience when the TV show was shooting, he would ask me to take a bow as its creator, and add, "It's easy to skate when the ice is firm."

The story of how one of the earliest situation comedies for television was born is part of history now, meaning it is almost forgotten. Let me briefly record how it began, as well as I can remember it - or anything else—after so many years.

With Lou Edelman, in a day when, if you were Gentile and out of work, you were unemployed, and if you were Jewish, you were a producer, Lou was authentically a true producer, meaning he had the talent and knowledge and ability to be part of the creation of a film or a television show.

At a meeting at Danny's house, anxiously called by his agents, the William Morris office, to find a way for Thomas to earn money for them, the infant industry known as Television was hesitantly introduced. Everyone came up with unworkable notions until Danny deperately informed us that he had to find a way quickly to come home from night clubs and get to know his family in Los Angeles. They called him "Uncle Daddy", he complained. He came home so seldom he didn't know any of their clothes sizes, and that was little better than a telephone voice. Even their dog sometimes attacked him. That's when I jumped up and announced, "That's it! I could write that overnight!"

Nobody knew what I was talking about until Danny's wife, Rosie, who had been standing in a doorway, agreed loudly, and announced it should be called, "Make Room for Daddy."

She explained that when Danny was away, the two girls slept in the bedroom with their mother.

The dresser drawers were filled with girls' underclothes. When Danny came home, it meant they had to empty the dresser drawers of their panties, stockings, etc., to make room for his shirts and underwear. Make Room for Daddy.

That pilot script, my first, was completed in forty-eight hours, some of them sleepless, and turned over to the ABC network, which immediately approved it. We were in business.

The film was shot in front of a live audience in one frantic evening, and Danny got laughter so great in the days before canned laugh tracks that we had to take some laughter down. The total cost, including his salary, was somewhere around $30,000.00.

It was the network that was laughing loudest. "Make Room for Daddy" stayed on the air for eleven years.

Years later, to fulfill a promise he had made to the Lord, Danny Thomas founded St. Jude Hospital for Children and turned it into one of the leading cancer facilities in the nation, because he honestly loved children, including his own. It was a Catholic hospital, and Danny was a devout Catholic who always wore a crucifix around his neck so he wouldn't forget.

When Hillcrest Country Club, the posh Jewish golf club across from 20th Century-Fox, was accused of being racist because it only admitted Jews to its membership, it decided to open its rolls to all denominations.

The first name suggested was that of Danny Thomas. He was immediately blackballed, on the grounds that if Hillcrest was to admit a Gentile as a member, they wanted him to look Gentile.

Danny was sincere in his Catholic beliefs. When he built his first house in Beverly Hills, he hired an artist to work for months carving an image of The Last Supper into a twelve-foot slab of redwood, which Danny then hung in his dining room. Harry Crane, one of the great Hollywood wits, was employed by Danny as a writer at that time, and Danny stood him in front of the huge carving and turned on a spotlight, which pinpointed the face of Christ.

Proudly, Danny proclaimed, "It looks so real, you can almost hear what Jesus is saying."

And Harry said, "Yeah. 'Separate checks.'"

One more rose-colored memory. Loveable Lou Edelman had come to us at Paramount with a story he thought would interest us as a vehicle for Bob Hope. Comedy was out of Lou's area, at least Hope's comedy, and he was offering it to us out of the goodness of his heart. In Hollywood, any such generosity is looked on with deep suspicion. There is the story of Norman Brokaw, head of the Morris office, who found the Devil sitting on his desk one day. The Devil offered to deliver to him as clients Barbra Streisand, Robert Redford, and Arnold Schwarzenegger. But in return, Brokaw would have to give the Devil his soul, his wife's soul, and his daughter's soul. Brokaw thought for a moment and then inquired, "What's the catch?"

With Loveable Lou, there was no catch. His friend Bryan Foy, producer of many of Warner Brothers B movies, was trying to peddle the story of his family. Bryan was one of the original Seven Little Foys, and had been delegated by the other six to make a quick buck by selling the rights to their father's life story. Since all seven Foys had assisted in making that life miserable, they felt entitled to a decent profit from it. Bryan, as the filmmaker in a family that included comedians Charley Foy and Eddie Foy, Jr., was given the privilege of wringing the last buck out of their father's sacred memory. We discovered that Bryan's asking price was a little steep, but in his haste to cash in, he neglected to ask for a piece of the profits, never dreaming there would ever be any. The picture eventually became such a hit that Paramount couldn't hide all the money, and Bryan was drummed out the family for having been the Irish equivalent of a nudnick.

Be that as it may, we got Paramount to buy the rights to the Eddie Foy story, and then we went to corner Hope in his chateau-cum-pitch-and-putt on Moorpark Street in Toluca Lake.

It was now some years after we had left his benevolent employ. Both of us had continued to write jokes for him on the cuff over the years, not being certain if the Fourteenth Amendment applied to Jewish writers. Much of this writing was done for Bob when he appeared annually as the MC of the Academy Awards, an occasion, he said, known in his home as, "Passover."

We brought a peace offering of a quart of vanilla ice cream to impress Mr. Hope. In the first, hectic days of the Pepsodent Show, Bob used to have the youngest writer, Sherwood Schwartz, whose name once inspired the witty Hal Kanter to identify him as "Robin Hood's Rabbi," leave our heated joke-reading trials in Hope's living room on Navajo Street to buy him a similar quart of vanilla ice cream. Then Bob would devour the entire quart in front of the mob of starving comedy writers, without offering anyone even a taste.

Jack and I handed him our frozen peace offering and were happy to see success hadn't gone to his head. It was the same old generous Bob. He forgot to thank us for the ice cream, put it carefully in his refrigerator, and never offered to share it. Nice to know there are some things in this life that are eternal.

We told Hope the story of comedian Eddie Foy and his marriage to an Italian girl who died after bringing seven children into the world, and how Foy finally faced up to his fatherly duties by taking them all into show business with him. Vaudeville never recovered from the act known as The Seven Little Foys, but we thought the story would make a warm and funny and only slightly saccharine comedy about the long-lost days of vaudeville, where Hope had gotten his own start. Bob was sold immediately; he would commit to it as part of his deal at Paramount, and we would write it.

And then I told him, "Bob, there's a catch. You can't have the story unless I direct it and Jack produces it, and neither of us have ever directed nor produced anything in our lives." He thought about that for a moment, and then he gave us the ultimate compliment. "My last picture was so lousy, you guys can't possibly do one lousier," he told us, encouragingly.

In those days, it was almost unheard of for writers to direct their own screenplays; only Preston Sturges and Billy Wilder were among the few who had achieved it. Writers were kept in a closet where they couldn't annoy the director or the actors by explaining what their dialogue meant.

Today, of course, it is so commonplace. Anyone who can create a saleable script is considered a director; otherwise, why would he waste all that time merely writing?

Bob Hope, at that time, was king of the theatrical box office, the number one comedian in motion pictures. With success came the power to turn a frog into a prince—or a writer who had never directed into a director, which was more difficult.

I was a willing frog.

Jack and I then wrote the screenplay. That process is always glossed over in a sentence, no one believing the emotional and intellectual effort it entails. But it is the heart and soul of every movie, good or bad, and the most difficult part of its creation.

In the process, we wrote a scene to take place at the Friar's Club in New York, where Eddie Foy is given an award as Father of the Year by George M. Cohan. This historical event was a complete fabrication, as was most of this almost-true screenplay, but it gave us the opportunity for the best-remembered moment in the film. Years before, Jimmy Cagney had won the Academy Award for portraying Cohan in the classic *Yankee Doodle Dandy*. He was on the Paramount lot for another film when Jack and I visited him in his dressing room and asked if he would play a cameo role as Cohan and perform a challenge dance with Bob Hope as Eddie Foy atop the tables at the Friar's Club.

Cagney didn't hesitate a moment.

"I'll do it on one condition," he said.

I looked at Jack. A movie star was about to kill the deal.

"I'll only do it if you don't pay me."

Fortunately, nobody had a feather to knock us over.

"When I was a starving chorus boy on Broadway," Cagney explained, "Eddie Foy used to take me to his farm in New Rochelle on Sundays, and feed me up so I could get through the next week. I never said thank you."

"But, Jimmy," I told him when I could talk, "you're going to have to do a complicated dance routine. It'll take a lot of practice, and we're shooting soon. When can you start?"

"I have my dancing shoes in the car," Cagney said. "Where's the rehearsal stage?"

Jim started rehearsing with choreographer Nick Castle the same afternoon. Hope got so frightened when he heard about it, he showed up on the rehearsal stage himself and worked out for an exhausting week.

He'd almost forgotten that he, too, had once been a dancer in vaudeville. Not in Cagney's class. No one was. But when they performed their challenge dance in front of three cameras—I figured there wasn't enough adrenalin in the world for retakes—Hope did well enough to almost hold his own.

At least, he didn't fall off the tables.

I had on-the-job training as a director on that film. There weren't any film schools then to turn out embryo Hitchcocks and Fords by the dozen. All I knew about that obscure art I had learned by hanging around the sets listening to directors swearing at their cameramen for taking so long to light a scene. But I knew my superior intelligence was equal to the task. I showed that intelligence by immediately hiring a film editor named Hal Kern to tell me what to do. Hal had won the Academy Award for cutting a little film called *Gone With the Wind*. If there was anything about filmmaking he didn't know, no one dared challenge him. Hal was older, wiser, warmer than anyone I ever met in the business, and we worked together for years. When some actor would ask me which side of the camera he was supposed to look—not as simple as it sounds—Hal, at my side, would point either to the right or the left. Even if he was wrong, the actor never challenged him. Neither did I.

That picture was a watershed in what passed for my career. All of us, Bob Hope included, worked for nothing, deferring our salaries—Hope for the first and last time—to be paid back out of the profits, if the studio admitted there were any. *The Seven Little Foys* was so successful, Paramount was too surprised to lie. To buy out our rights so they would keep all the picture's future earnings, Jack and I were offered a contract to write, produce, and direct a series of films for the studio. Part of the deal included a hefty chunk of Paramount Pictures stock. I later sold my stock, much too soon, it turned out, but I didn't mind. For a short time, I had been a minor mogul.

Another perk that started with the *Foys* was the opportunity to become a world traveler at a studio's expense. And the ability to take the family with me. Those were the days when most film studios still had monies frozen in foreign countries because of wartime restrictions that continued long after World War II. One way for a studio to cash in their box-office returns in England, France and Italy, was to make a film in the country, using frozen pounds or francs or lira, and then recoup in dollars when the films played the good old U.S. of A.

In the case of Italy, it was even more simple. You merely made a deal with the Pope. More precisely, the Catholic Church. The Pope was not considered a good businessman, so he delegated the deal making to some Bishops, who were. When they took a vow of poverty, they meant yours. The Church would take all the lira a film earned in Italy, and reimburse the studios with dollars collected in America, after a considerable Holy discount. There was considerable praying on both sides.

Part of the Foys' story was set at La Scala in Milan, but it was decided to build La Scala at Paramount, and shoot everything in Hollywood. Perhaps as an apology for this lese majeste, the studio sent Jack and myself to Rome, to scout for an Italian leading lady. It was a memorable trip, quite short, but we met a lot of beautiful actresses and the even more beautiful city of Rome.

From the screen tests we made of Italian actresses, Bob Hope chose Milly Vitale, who was not only beautiful and a favorite in Italian Cinema, but her father was director of the Rome Opera; more important, he shared a common passion with me—he was also a ham radio fanatic. So she understood insanity.

On that first trip, Jack and I also met Pilade Levi, in charge of Paramount's Rome office, and established a lifelong friendship. Pilade was Mr. Rome, an outgoing, effusive, completely Italian male who undertook to make Italians out of all of us, and succeeded brilliantly with Lucy, when she later arrived in Rome. She became so Italian, she learned how to make spaghetti and to drink a doppio—a double espresso—every night at midnight, and sleep like a baby. She drove our white Jaguar like an Italian, ignoring traffic lights and "No Parking" signs, which were in a strange language anyway. She became known to the carabinieri as "La donna alla Jaguar bianca," meaning, "Don't screw around with this broad, she knows Pilade Levi, Jewish friend of the Pope." (He was. He was given Papal dispensation later to be married in a chapel of St. Peter's.) Lucy never got a traffic ticket, only polite notes printed in English, "Welcome to Rome! Since you are a visitor and this is your first offense, you are forgiven."

Lucy had several dozen first offenses in her Roman driving career. Only in Italy would virginity be allowed so much repetition.

Pilade introduced us to every facet of Italian life, and to Carol Guadagna, the young and beautiful casting director he married in the Vatican with the Pope's blessing. The wedding had to be performed there because Pilade was Jewish and Carol is Catholic, and in Italy a Jewish bridegroom must stand outside the bar during the wedding ceremony in a Catholic church. Pilade would have none of that; since the Vatican is a sovereign state not part of Italy, he asked the Pope's dispensation. Lucy and I were invited to the ceremony in St. Peter's, and I was most impressed by the small room adjoining the chapel where a Priest served as bartender, and the liquor was a wine known as Lachrima Christi, The Tears of Christ. They must have been tears of joy; it was a very happy marriage until Pilade's untimely passing. Mr. Rome is no more, and the city has never been the same without him.

Of many fond memories, I remember Pilade introducing us to a wonderful Italian restaurant—they were all wonderful then—near the stockyards, which served the best steaks in Rome. It was so crowded that night that they moved some of their outdoor tables onto the streetcar tracks. Pilade assured us the streetcars didn't run at that late hour.

In the middle of demolishing some wonderful steaks, we heard the insistent clanging of a streetcar bell and looked up to see an outraged trolley bearing down on us at high speed, filled with shouting passengers calling out colorful Italian epithets. Not waiting for a translation, we picked up our table and ran with it to safety, just in time to escape total destruction.

But we never stopped eating.

When in Rome…

What else can I tell you about Roma in those days? It was a city filled with marvelous old architecture and old flowing fountains. Every time they started digging the new subway, they came across ancient ruins more beautiful than any place the subway could bring you to, and had to stop tunneling for a few years while they uncovered and admired the remains.

The Via Veneto was graced with lovely sidewalk cafes, which still had lovely prices, and lovely parading prostitutes, whose prices weren't that lovely. The City Council had made the grave mistake of allowing a woman to join its male membership. Her first official act was to have the Roman brothels, some of which dated to the time of the Caesars, whose names could sometimes be found on the ancient guest lists, closed forever. The hard-working horizontal employees immediately moved their business to the Via Veneto, which was akin to Tiffany displaying its jewels on the sidewalks of Fifth Avenue. On the Veneto, this resulted in a lot of window shopping as the merchandise paraded past, temporarily vertical, and feverish bargaining went on all night. A trip I made to the ruins of the famed houses of joy in Pompeii, where marble plaques over each room announced the specialty of the lady within, convinced me that nothing new in this area had been developed since Vesuvius erupted and wiped them all out in the middle of the business day. In the rooms advertising the more interesting positions, the occupants had probably been too busy to notice before the lava arrived.

The only modern difference is that today the ladies advertise the same ancient wares on the internet.

Plus ca change, plus la meme chose.

In Rome, everyone took a three-hour siesta in the middle of the day. It didn't seem to matter. No Roman took work seriously anyway. The windows of the hotels on the Veneto all had iron shutters that could be closed against the sunlight, so a midday siesta with a wife, a mistress, or anything in between, occupied as much of the three hours as could be spared from eating spaghetti. Both major Italian appetites could be indulged to the full.

Today, unfortunately, no Italian can afford to live in a hotel on the Veneto or in a house al centro, in the center of the city, so families all live in the suburbs. In the three hours allotted, it is now impossible for a starving husband to drive home and back in today's mad Roman traffic, consequently, many things previously available at home have to be rented in the city. Fortunately, they are always available.

On the Via Veneto, the iron shutters on the hotel windows get a lot of use during siesta these days. It saves petrol.

While we are on the fascinating subject of Italian mores, the saga of my first encounter with Vittorio De Sica deserves to be included. De Sica, one of the most handsome and cultivated of Italian actors then, and also a world-class motion picture director, had played a large part in getting Sophia Loren to accept a role in *It Started in Naples*, a project Jack and I had prepared at Paramount to follow *Houseboat*. Sophia felt the story was too trivial. De Sica assured her that, for an Italian, there was nothing trivial about making money; in fact, the story was quite charming, and he himself was accepting a role in the film. Since Vittorio was like a father to Sophia—"Unfortunately," he admits in one line of dialogue—she finally agreed to make our film, to be shot completely in Rome, Naples, and Capri. The fact that Clark Gable had committed to play the lead may have had a little to do with changing her mind.

Since the Cinecitta studios had been constructed during the days of silent films, Italian producers had never bothered making them sound-proof. Consequently, they rarely attempted to shoot sound in them, pre-ferring to dub all the dialogue later. Sophia herself, in Italian films, had never been considered enough of an actress to dub her own voice, so a real actress was always hired to do the job.

But this was an American production, and I was determined to keep it realistic by shooting sync sound. Sophia's voice, and De Sica's voice, would be recorded live, as they performed. We had hired a British sound crew who had a bus filled with recording equipment shipped from Lon-don. The bus had to be parked in a hallway outside the stage while we were shooting, since there was nowhere to put it onstage. Therefore, the sound engineer was not able to see the action.

He called me over frantically the first day and asked, "Who's playing De Sica's part this afternoon?"

"What do you mean? De Sica, who else?"

The sound man shook his head.

"He's pulling a fast one. It's another voice entirely."

And he played back a recording of a scene we shot with De Sica in the morning. Bright, cheerful, energetic. And then one recorded that afternoon. Two octaves lower.

I confronted De Sica on the set and asked him what the hell was going on? Did he have a double?

He laughed.

"You Americans! You will never understand Italians."

"What do you mean?"

"I am married for many, many years. My wife and I, we have two wonderful children, now full grown. But I also have a wonderful mis-tress, fortunately not full grown."

"So?"

"She is Italian, too. So we have two children of our own. Young children, going to school. My wife knows all this. She is Italian, too. So she understands."

"Then what's the problem?"

"The problem, my innocent friend, is that my wife insists I sleep at home with her and keep all my clothes there. And my mistress insists I must be in bed with her when the children come into the bedroom in the morning to say 'Good morning' to Papa before going to school.

"Now, you insist I be at the studio by eight o'clock every morning. So I must awaken at my wife's side at 5:30, jump into my clothes, drive to my mistress, take off my clothes, jump into bed with her, and wave to the children when they come in on their way to school. 'Good morning, children!' 'Good morning, Papa!' Then I must jump out of bed again and jump into my clothes once more to arrive at this studio at the ungodly hour upon which you insist.

"And you must know that, in Italy, jumping in and out of bed with a woman, even your wife, is considered bad form if the man confines his jumping only to jumping."

"I understand."

"No, my innocent American friend, you really don't. You see, today I also had to have lunch in my dressing room with my new girlfriend. She is eighteen and at lunch, she has a tremendous appetite."

After that, I shot all of De Sica's closeups and dialogue in the morning. The afternoons were devoted to long shots and vitamin pills.

About Sophia. What can I say? She was about 21 and one of the most beautiful women in the world when we met in Hollywood for the start of *Houseboat*, but I already knew a great deal about her. In a desk drawer in my office I kept a publicity photograph taken of her for an Italian epic about the Emperor Nero. It was a costume picture, but Sophia wore no costume. At least, not above the waist. The whole Roman Empire was gloriously on display. I would often review it for inspiration.

We would never have met if it were not for a family film, *Room for One More*, that Jack and I wrote at Warner Brothers for Cary Grant and his then-wife, Betsy Drake. Cary played the father of two children, until Betsy adopted two more, who were both difficult problem children. Our problem was to make Cary Grant, whose movie image had been the reverse, into a credible father figure. He was the most popular star in Hollywood at the time, the handsomest man in films, in demand at every studio and prominent in every female's fantasy, when the small but fearless Henry Blanke, who had arrived from Germany as assistant to the great Ernst Lubitsch and had then produced such classics as *The Story of Louis Pasteur*, had the chutzpah to send Cary our screenplay, in which he would play a faithful husband and father.

The timing was perfect; Grant was getting a little bored with his image as a male sex symbol – imagine! – and longed for a complete change. He also saw the opportunity for Betsy to play opposite him, as his wife. So, to everyone's surprise including his own, he accepted.

One of the reasons, Cary later told me, was that he had never been able to win an acting award, because he played his suave roles with his hands in his pockets, and audiences couldn't tell he was acting. Then, as a coal miner in *None But the Lonely Heart*, the director allowed him to scratch his ass. The audience immediately could see he was acting, and he won an Academy Award nomination.

In *Room for One More*, he played a typical middle-class father with a family he could barely support, and he could logically scratch any place that itched him. Stanislavsky would have approved. *Room for One More* was a great success; so much so, that years later Warners turned it into a television sitcom; without Grant and Betsy, it sank without a trace.

But Cary had been so pleased with the film, he asked Jack and me to find him another un-Cary Grant role. We nodded and promptly forgot about it. Grant was hitting the heights then with Alfred Hitchcock, and knowing his reputation for unfulfilled promises, we didn't believe a word of this one.

Some time later, after I had become an auteur by directing *Seven Foys*, Cary was making a film at Paramount and came over to Jack and me while we were eating in the commissary and asked why we hadn't yet found a story for him. We promptly told him we had been looking every day and hadn't yet come up with something with sufficient depth and heart to be worthy of his talents.

He said, "Don't worry; I have. Can I tell it to you and see if you like it?"

After about one tenth of a second I said, "I'll look at our schedule. I think we can find the time."

And Cary said, "Can I come up to your office right now?"

Can the mountain come to Mohammed?

In our fourth-floor cubbyhole in Paramount's Writers Building, Cary Grant told us a storyline in which most of the action was confined to a houseboat.

I was polite enough to say, "It's very interesting, Cary. Who wrote it?"

And he said, "Betsy."

Immediately, we both told him it was the greatest idea for a family movie we had ever heard. How much did Betsy want for it?

And Cary said, just as immediately, "Approximately $30,000."

In other words, the two had talked the whole thing over; Cary was acting as Betsy's agent, and we were certain he would collect his ten-percent. A Cary Grant vehicle had fallen into our laps; more important, he couldn't walk out on his wife's screenstory.

We told him we would go down to the front office and see if we could possibly sell the story to the studio. Then we raced down to the office of D.A. Doran, who was in charge of making story decisions for Paramount—we called him, "The tower of Jell-O," for reasons that will soon be apparent—and excitedly told him, "We have a chance to get a commitment from Cary Grant, but you have to buy the story from Betsy Drake for thirty thousand dollars."

"That's a lot of money," the Tower said, "but if Grant has committed to do it, I think we can make the deal."

And we said, "You don't understand. Cary doesn't want Betsy to think you only bought the story because he will be in it. So you have to pay her the thirty thousand before he will commit."

Long, long pause. Finally, D.A. made his usual swift, forthright decision. "I"ll get back to you," he said.

About a week later, he called and said, "Okay, we have bought Betsy's story. Now, get Cary's signature."

We tried. Nothing. We couldn't reach him. He was shooting. He was unavailable. He was out to lunch.

We didn't know what to do.

Finally, Cary came up to see us. He said, "By the way, fellows, I'm going out of town."

"How far out of town," I asked, knowing in my heart he did not mean Cucamonga.

"I'm going to Spain," he said, "to make a picture called *The Pride and the Passion*, with Frank Sinatra and some new Italian girl."

"When does the plane leave, Cary?"

"Tomorrow morning."

Before he was out of the office we ran down to the Tower and told him, "You better be at the airport tomorrow, and you better have the contract and you better get Cary to sign before he gets on the plane, because we're already halfway through the screenplay and we may not have a star."

So D.A. caught him before he got on the plane and told him, "Cary, I hate to do this, but when we bought the story there was the implication that you were going to sign; and if you don't, we're going to have to tell Betsy we only bought her story because you promised a commitment."

Long, long silence, but the plane was getting ready to leave. Cary signed the agreement, and in his haste, he signed in several places. He committed to do the film, he committed to me as director and Jack as the producer, and he flew off to Spain to shoot *The Pride and the Passion*, where both his pride and his passion were soon put to the test.

Jack and I went back to work on writing a screenplay about a typical American couple. Betsy was to play the wife, of course, and Cary her husband, and if you don't consider them a typical American couple, you're out of touch with reality. They settle in on a houseboat with their brood of typical American children.

I was just typing "Fade out" on the last page of the screenplay when we got a call from Cary in Spain.

"Fellows, how are you coming with the script?"

"Fine, Cary." We actually had a start date then.

He paused a moment and said, "You know, I have just met the next Garbo."

"Who?"

"This girl named Sophia Loren. She's going to be the greatest star...more than that, she's going to be something quite wonderful...Fellows, would it be much of a problem to change the leading lady in *Houseboat* to an Italian girl?"

And we said, "Of course not, Cary," and we hung up, tore our screenplay into tiny bits, and I put a fresh sheet of paper in the typewriter and typed, hopefully, "Fade In."

Two months and a hundred and twenty-five pages later, Cary returned from Spain. He called Jack and me and said, "Let's have lunch at Lucey's," which was the posh restaurant across from Paramount. We went there, knowing he never picked up a lunch check. At its best, this would be Dutch Treat.

As we sat down, Cary said, "Now tell me the story of *Houseboat*."

So I started. Immediately, he stopped me.

"Wait a minute! You've changed the leading lady to an Italian girl!"

I said, "Cary! You called us from Spain and told us you'd found the new Garbo!"

"That bitch? I will never work with her again as long as I live! Change the whole thing back or I'm out of this picture."

And he left us with the check.

We asked around a bit and discovered there are no secrets on a movie set, even on a foreign location. The story, as we pieced it together, was that Cary had been having an affair in Spain—with his chauffeur. This was before the other side of his sexuality became public knowledge. As you may well imagine, when he encountered Sophia, he changed from AC to DC. They had a brief, passionate romantic episode, and then Sophia had brought Cary down to earth by telling him she was in love with Carlo Ponti, even though he was a married man, like Cary. Carlo had made her a star and though he was a dozen years her senior, she preferred him to Cary. Grant went wild. You do not turn Cary Grant down. You may turn him, but you don't turn him down. He had never been rejected before, by either sex.

He was absolutely determined never to make another film with the new Garbo.

He went to Paramount and offered them two more commitments if they would let him out of this one. Knowing the trouble they had getting him into *Houseboat*, and already having his signature on the contract, they decided that a Cary Grant in the hand is worth two in the bush any day, and refused. He was forced to make our film, and made my life on the set a living nightmare.

But my problems with Cary were minor compared to Sophia's. She came to me one day and asked, "Doesn't Cary know I am truly in love with Carlo, and isn't Cary a married man, and will you please ask him to stop chasing me? I can't work."

. He wouldn't stop, and finally, in desperation, Sophia married Carlo Ponti by proxy in Mexico City the very day we were shooting her marriage to Cary aboard the houseboat. That marriage was interupted in 1962 by a highly publicized charge of bigamy resulting from the stringent Italian divorce laws. After an annulment, they were remarried in 1966.

But Cary stopped chasing her.

And that's how you make a carefree family comedy in Hollywood.

There is an encouraging coda to this. Cary kept trying to get me interested in "sleep learning," which was having a vogue then. You must understand that Cary was into almost every vogue that came along. He was President of the Los Angeles Chapter of LSD, in the days when it was considered a harmless hallucinatory. He also confided in me that the reason he had married Betsy was that she was the only woman who could hypnotize him. Many times, during the shooting, I wished I had her talent. Also, the week before the film started, Cary told me he was going to have the very visible carbuncle on his forehead—you may remember it from his earlier films—removed surgically. When I protested it would be impossible to photograph him until it healed, and that would take weeks, he merely smiled at me condescendingly and said, "I'll think it well." I hate to report that he did; there was no sign of it when he reported for the first day's shooting.

That's when Cary tried to get me interested in another item in vogue, sleep learning. He was learning French in his sleep, he told me, by placing a tape recorder under his bed and having it repeat French lessons while he slept. Since Lucy had a friend who was a Naval surgeon, and had reported to us that the Navy had spent millions using sleep learning to train new recruits and found out they had learned as much as they would if they fell asleep during a lecture, I was not convinced. Cary grew very angry when I refused his advice, and things became more difficult than ever on the set. He was even accusing Harry Guardino, playing a typical Italian handyman in the film, of sleeping with Sophia nights after the shooting. He had actually put a private detective on Harry's tail, which made Harry, a great performer in his first big film role, exceedingly nervous. Guardino, who became my great friend, told me later that the detective had seen him driving into Sophia's house many times; but the truth was, Harry was sleeping with her maid.

As the situation on the set grew more tense, my sound man came over to me on day and said, "You don't have to worry anymore. My brother is a radio repair man."

"Why don't I have to worry?"

"Betsy Drake is one of his customers. Yesterday, she brought in the tape recorder Cary uses under their bed. It wasn't working, but there was a tape still in it; when my brother took it out and played it, you know what was on it?"

"I haven't the foggiest."

"The voices of Cary and Betsy, saying over and over, 'Cary Grant, you are the greatest actor in the world. Cary Grant, you have nothing to worry about. Cary Grant, stop worrying. '"

I felt a little better after that. But I didn't bother learning French.

In spite of her beauty, Sophia decided to have her somewhat Italian nose fixed after *Houseboat*, but no one had ever noticed her nose when the rest of her was onscreen, I can remember little eight-year-old Charlie Herbert, one of the children in the film, who watched with me while

Sophia modeled several too-revealing bathing suits to be used in the picture. I saw the way he looked at her, and I asked him, "Charlie, you have an older sister at home. Does she look anything like that in a bathing suit?"

And Charlie laughed and said, "Even worse!"

Of course, in a later scene when Sophia picked him up and held him close to her breast, he seemed to be enjoying it too much. She never held him to her breast again.

In that regard, some years after that, when I was in Rome, I phoned Sophia when she was making a film in Carlo Ponti's studios in Livorno, and she asked me to come north and see her. After all, she told me, Livorno was very near the historic city of Pisa, which I would enjoy exploring.

"Why would I want to go to Pisa?" I inquired. "There's nothing in it but one old tower, and that one's leaning."

"Yes," Sophia told me, "but the natives say when I walk into town, it straightens up."

Sophia was completely unspoiled and still enjoying her new life as a sex symbol, and was able to laugh at it all, in those early days. She told me she learned her English listening to American rock music, which I found incredible, I didn't know there was any English in rock music.

But she was much wiser than her years. Shooting *Houseboat*, I would note that her makeup kept getting darker and darker as the day progressed, and I would have to have her wipe it off and start over. Then I learned why. Cary Grant never used makeup, because he didn't want to get to the studio an hour earlier every morning to have it applied; he preferred to sleep. So, instead, he sat under a sunlamp regularly, and developed the famous tan that identified him. He was several shades darker than Sophia when the day started.

In Italy, however, if a girl has a good tan, she is thought to be a member of the upper classes, the only girls who have time to spend in the sun. Sophia figured Cary was trying to show her up as a girl of the streets, by appearing on screen darker than she was. She kept applying tan makeup during the day until she was darker than he was.

In *Lualda*, the novel I wrote about an Italian movie star, I have been accused of using Sophia as the basis of the main character; Lualda is portrayed as having begun her career on the streets of Rome's Trastevere district. (I didn't base it on Sophia, it was a highly fictionalized account of my own fantasies.) It may well be that Sophia read the book and misinterpreted it; I haven't heard from her since its publication. Someone I did hear from was one of my—and America's—favorite novelists of that day, a writer I had never met: Robert Nathan.

He took the time to write me: "I want to congratulate you on 'Lualda.' I not only enjoyed it thoroughly, but admired it, too; it's such a marvelous picture of a writer-director in Hollywood—the old Hollywood, and the new—written with wit, with a hard, bright mind, and a generous heart..." He went on and on, but I never bothered reading the rest. I have it tattooed on my chest.

The novel began when I made a deal with Donald Fine, of Arbor House, for an advance of a magnificent $5,000 on the as-yet unwritten book. Since this sum was almost enough to cover the rent for three months in Rome in those days, I quickly accepted, and prepared to leave for Rome.

I remember I ran into an old friend of mine at that time, a screenwriter who was also starting to write novels. We exchanged a few notes about our work, and both wondered whether this meant a new career for either of us. Even then I considered him amazing. He had written an entire television series completely by himself, as well as a couple of excellent films, and we wondered if either of us could make a living in the future by writing novels.

I think he managed. His name was Sidney Sheldon, and at this date the number of copies of his novels in print approaches 300 million. Mine? Let's say, less.

I'm happy to say Sidney liked my story, so I went back to Donald Fine with renewed confidence. But Fine is not a trusting soul. He had often dealt with authors who made a deal with him and immediately left the country. This became a problem when I went to Rome. Regularly, I would send him a chapter by airmail as soon as I finished it; it would never arrive at his office in New York. Disgruntled Italian postal employees, seeking higher wages, were diverting all first-class mail to a warehouse in Milan, holding it hostage for months while negotiating with the Italian government for more liras. That was a problem, too, because in Italy in those days, the government changed every few weeks or as soon as it got dusty, and negotiations would start all over again.

Carol Levi suggested we should send our mail from the Vatican (as previously noted, a separate country) which had a postal service which had a reputation for being gruntled, as opposed to disgruntled. Lucy would dutifully carry the book's chapters to St. Peter's Square, where the post office was so busy, part of it overflowed onto a bus, and mail them carefully to New York from there.

They never arrived, either.

We were then informed that each package used a great number of Vatican stamps, which were considered works of art by stamp collectors, some of whom were mailmen. These mailmen promptly steamed them off their envelopes and sold them to tourists as souvenirs.

Finally, Carol was called to New York on business and I entrusted her with all the chapters that had gone astray, and she delivered them to Donald Fine by hand.

It was only after the book was published that I discovered I had used the wrong address for his office. All the chapters mailed from Italy had been returned. But since the Italian postal department had more important things to do than read a return address, they promptly wound up in the warehouse in Milan, where they are still waiting for the postal workers to get their raise.

Maybe the next Italian government.

While in Italy, I'll backtrack a bit to Sophia, not a very difficult thing to do.

Houseboat had helped make Miss Loren a star, and had made Italians out of Jack Rose and myself, a much more difficult task.

In Hollywood, we plotted and schemed for a way to get back to Rome at Paramount's expense, ever since first visiting it to scout actresses for *Seven Little Foys*. Naturally, we decided the easiest way to do it was to write our way back.

That reminds me now of my good friend, Isobel Lennart, who was once in Philadelphia struggling with the libretto of the Broadway musical *Funny Girl*, starring Streisand, much as I later struggled with the book for *Jimmy*. Isobel later made an all-night round trip by train from New York to Philadelphia to lend me moral support during my struggles with the play's director, for which I am forever grateful. Poor Isobel was later killed in an auto accident, but I'll never forget her kindness and understanding. And hatred of directors. And, while we're at it, of producers and stars, as well. Isobel Lennart was an Equal Opportunity hater.

Ray Stark was the producer of *Funny Girl*, and while it was in tryout in Philadelphia, the second act was in terrible shape, according to Ray and Barbra Streisand, One night Isobel returned to her hotel and found Norman Krasna, an old friend and talented screenwriter who was living in Klosters, Switzerland at the time. They encountered each other by accident in the lobby. "Norman! What are you doing here?" she inquired, surprised. And Krasna, who had just arrived and didn't know what she was doing in Philadelphia either, replied, "Ray Stark sent for me to save *Funny Girl*." Isobel went up to her hotel room, and, she told me, "I wrote him back to Switzerland."

So Jack and I had determined to write our way back to Rome. An opportunity came in the form of a story by Michael Pertwee, a fine British screenwriter, about a fisherman on the island of Capri trying to raise the orphaned child of his sister when an aunt arrives to take the child from him. In the blink of a Hollywood eye, the fisherman became Sophia Loren, a dancer in a Capri nightclub, and the aunt became an uncle who was a Philadelphia lawyer. Our great plan hit an iceberg when we took our version to Sophia and she coldly turned it down. She didn't want to play what was, in essence, a girl of the streets, something on which her career had been launched in the wonderful Italian film, *Gold of Naples*.

And then the greatest agent in the world, Herman Citron, who was later to perform the miracle of getting a Jewish movie financed in Hollywood, solved the problem. His client, Clark Gable, searching for something light to do before plunging into *The Misfits* with Marilyn Monroe, was handed our story by Herman, and told to like it. That was Herman's method. He was in charge of his stars' careers; therefore, he made all their decisions. The fact that he also got them enough money to bankrupt their studios made his method even more attractive. He was known as "The Iceman," because he was so cold when closing a deal. Gable liked the story of what was to be *It Started in Naples*, so named because someone in the secret department at Paramount that thought up idiotic movie titles felt it would fool people into thinking it was the Gable of *It Happened One Night*. It didn't. Herman told Sophia of Clark's decision. Citron knew that Clark was still Rhett Butler in her eyes. In Italy, great movie stars never grow old. Sophia couldn't resist what might be her last opportunity to play opposite a legend. She signed, with one caveat: we would get her friend, Suso Cecchi d'Amico, one of the Italian cinema's foremost writers, to help us in "Italianizing" her role. We said, "Yes," and made the acquaintance of one of the most charming and witty Communists we had ever known. Many Italian screenwriters, we discovered, were Communists. In Italy, it was a badge of honor. The Communist Party was the second largest in the country. Of course, everyone knew they didn't mean it.

The power of agents in Hollywood was then greater than ever. Citron represented me for many sucessful years, and a few not so successful, but I also leaned on many others in Hollywood at various times. Help came mainly from the William Morris Agency, still one of the largest, and two of their best who risked their reputations representing me. One was Sam Weisbord, who spent much of his time advancing a fellow named Danny Thomas and keeping him employed in the days before Thomas became a multi-millionaire in spite of—or perhaps, because of—his nose, which he refused to change; and Norman Brokaw, who had risen from the mail room to become a leader in much of the work of the Morris Office for many years, and was always there when I needed help, which was most of the time.

After finishing a first-draft screenplay, Jack Rose and I left for Italy to polish the script and our appetites for pasta. There we ran into another problem: the siesta. Our Italian secretaries, who typed and transcribed our messy notes in our office off the Via Veneto, did not work during siesta, from noon to three p.m. What the girls did during those three hours we never inquired. They never asked us.

However, Jack and I were so attuned to our Hollywood working schedule, what we did during siesta was work. We couldn't stop. We grabbed a sandwich—sacrilege in Rome—and continued writing against our deadline.

Our secretaries returned at three, but they didn't leave the office again until 8:00 p.m., again Roman hours. Jack and I could hardly quit while the girls continued to work; so we started with them at nine in the morning and worked until they left at eight o'clock at night. American plus Italian-style hours.

Afterwards, we were too exhausted to enjoy Rome; but, somehow, we managed.

Suso Cecchi d'Amico was a great help. We would go to her apartment, where she would greet us with great warmth, and then sit with a portable typewriter on her lap, typing away, cigarette dangling from her lips, as we all discussed story and improvised dialogue. It was only when I got a chance to see what she was typing that I realized it was in Italian.

"Suso!" I cautioned her. "This screenplay has to be in English!"

She puffed at her Italian cigarette—the worst—and said, "Oh, this is not your movie. I am also writing one for Rossellini."

It didn't matter. Suso could write two movies at once. Sometimes, three. She said it kept her from being bored.

When it came time to go to Naples to start shooting, Suso asked us, "Who is your Company Thief?"

I told her I could name a few, unofficially, who were involved in the production in Rome, but she said, "No, those are amateurs. I am talking about professionals. When you go to Naples, you will need a real thief, to get back what has been stolen from you the day before."

When we looked blank, she explained, "Of course, they will steal from you. Cameras, film, whatever they can, and sell it the next day in the Thieves' Market. You will need it back immediately, and only a professional thief will know where the market is being held early that morning, because it is moved every day. For a price, you will have your cameras and other things back in time for the day's shooting. I can put you in touch with a very reliable thief in Naples, who has worked for both MGM and Universal, and comes highly recommended."

So we employed the thief of her choice, who was so good he often got us back watches and jewelry that had not yet been stolen.

When we did begin our first day's shooting, at the Naples railroad station, the final shot was on the exterior, where Clark Gable and Vittorio De Sica, as his Neapolitan lawyer, were hurrying to De Sica's tiny Fiat Cinquecento, on the way to locate Sophia.

As I was lining up the camera for a tracking shot, I noted a huge iron ball hanging from a cable, which started smashing into the station as we prepared. I was informed that the station had been damaged by continued bombing during WWII, and after all these years was finally being torn down so a more modern railway terminal could be built. For some reason, they had decided to start the destruction exactly where I had placed the camera and dolly track. When I asked the cost of stopping the destruction while we made the shot, it appears there was a price list for stopping, smashing into the station for one hour, two million liras. After all, we were from Hollywood, where silence is golden.

I refused their kind offer.

Instead, I went to Clark and Vittorio and explained the situation, and asked if they could do the scene in a single take, while there was station left to photograph. They promised to try, and I rolled the camera. As it pulled back ahead of them and their dialogue, I could hear the iron ball smashing into the stone walls behind me, closer and closer. The two pros, Gable and De Sica, never faltered; they completed the dialogue without missing a beat, squeezed into the Fiat and drove off just as another segment of the wall was smashed to the ground behind us.

When we returned from our Capri location a month later, the iron ball was hanging from its cable exactly where we had finished the shot, waiting for another gullible Hollywood movie company.

Not another inch of the station had been touched.

See Naples and die.

One reason Jack and I had chosen Capri as the setting for the exteriors in the picture is that weather charts rated it as having the most continuous hours of sunshine of any spot outside the Sahara Desert.

Murphy must have laughed at that. When we got our outdoor sets finished and prepared to shoot, Capri was hit by the most violent hurricane in decades, winds toppling trees in droves and cutting off electric power.

But the show must go on. We had generators and a cover set inside a building that was more or less intact. But it was down at the harbor, and Clark Gable had been installed in a lovely house in Anacapri—at the very top of the Capri Alp. No roads were passable. But somehow, Rhett Butler found a way to hike down to the Marina Grande, studying his lines as he clambered over fallen trees, and arrived at our makeshift set letter-perfect in his dialogue.

I have found, in my more or less illustrious career, that the greater the artist, the worse the temperament. Most of my work as a director has consisted of sessions as psychotherapist with male and female performers unable to go on performing. Or, in some cases, living. The reason was once capsulized by playwright Moss Hart in his description of the egotistical columnist Alexander Woollcott: "There, but for the grace of God, goes God."

Clark Gable epitomized the reverse. He was as big a star as a bizarre industry has ever produced, but he didn't care for the role. If truth were told, he didn't really care for any role. Acting had been more or less thrust upon him by his rugged good looks. Although Jack Warner had once rejected him because his ears were too big that never seemed to bother the women in the movie audience, for whom he was the ultimate macho image. His ears and their size were not what women were interested in.

He was, inexplicably, almost apologetic about his stardom. When Sophia came to me terribly unhappy one day, because she felt Clark was deliberately upstaging her so his good side would always be to the camera, Clark laughed and said he didn't have a good side; she could stand wherever she wanted to. After that, they became the best of friends.

My relationship with him was equally comfortable. I was the director, he was the actor, and he would make suggestions, but ultimately take direction. He enjoyed making the film, and brought his wife, the former

Kay Spreckels, to Capri, and they seemed to enjoy the sunshine (when it finally showed up) and the wondrous Italian food and the camaraderie of a movie company on a foreign location.

We discovered, however, that camaraderie with the native population was a little less salutary. Perhaps it was the proximity to Naples that had rubbed off on them.

One night we were shooting a difficult scene in the central Piazza, a colorful and noisy gathering place for all the tourists. I had set up a long track for the camera to precede Gable as he made his way in and sat down at a sidewalk table at one of the cafés. We had bought out all the cafés for that night, to simplify shooting, and brought over a lot of pretty girls and attractive young men to act as tourists and give the gaudy Piazza a little class. When we were finally ready to shoot, I found our extras had been elbowed out of the way by the regular tourist population. When we complained to the café owners that we had bought them out, they told us of an obscure Italian regulation which stated you cannot buy a street; and since the tables were set up in the street, we couldn't tell anybody not to sit at them. When we asked why they had not informed us of this before we paid them, all we got was a pained expression, in Italian.

The dolly track had been set up to end at a table we had placed properly to the camera for the scene with Gable. When we prepared to shoot, we found a company of German tourists seated at it, their cameras at the ready to photograph Clark when he sat down with them.

When we asked them politely to take another table, they refused to move. Italy was a free country; they were entitled.

Rather than risk World War III, I reset the dolly track and set up another table on blocks, for Gable to use. When it came time to make the shot, an assistant director came to me and told me, "There's a guy standing on the dolly track and he won't get off. And he doesn't seem to understand any language we know."

So I crossed to the immoveable tourist and said, "I don't know what language you speak, but if you don't get off that track, in thirty seconds half a ton of camera will roll over your feet."

He got off.

I thought my troubles were over.

In the scene, Gable is annoyed by all the noise and music around him, and asks his waiter—an old Italian character actor—"Does this go on all night? It's after one a.m. How are people supposed to sleep on this island?"

And the waiter replies, reasonably, "Together."

At least, that's what he is supposed to reply. After hiring the old actor, I had been informed that he was deaf, but needed the money. That made good Italian sense, unless the scene depended on his hearing Gable's straight line. I arranged the shot so the waiter was facing Gable and could read his lips. Done, I thought.

But the waiter did not speak English. He had never heard the word, "Together," and couldn't remember it. Then a friend of his came up with a solution. They both knew an Italian director named "Togazzo." All the waiter had to do was remember his friend, and associate his name with "Together." They rehearsed several times.

Happily, the actor informed me he was now ready for the shot.

"Action!"

"... How are people supposed to sleep on this island?"

"Togazzo!"

Eighteen takes later, he got it right.

Although Clark was always professional and did his best, at that moment in his life he was dependent on alcohol. I noted that his hand trembled—as soon as the camera rolled. Recognizing his problem, he had inserted a clause in his contract stating that he could not be photographed after 5:00 p.m., when the trembling was most noticeable. In return, I gave him every possible piece of business using his hands that I could think of; in that way, I felt he might overcome part of the problem, and for awhile it worked.

We were shooting the big trial scene of the film, in which Gable is attempting to win custody of his brother's child from Sophia, when another problem arose. In an Italian court, there are four judges on the bench, and no jury, possibly because the judges preferred not to share the trial money with ordinary mortals. The first day, I had completed the master shots, and on the second day was about to move in for the close shots. Bob Surtees, my cameraman, who had just won an Academy Award for shooting *Ben-Hur*, was at my side when my assistant director informed me that the Chief Judge had not shown up.

"Why the hell not?"

"He got a better job."

I almost exploded.

"He can't do that! I've already photographed him in the scene!"

"He told me to tell you not to worry. He sent his brother to take his place."

And while I suffered a mild coronary, I heard Bob Surtees murmur, "I wonder if Gable has a brother who'll work after five?"

Later, I met the missing actor in the commissary, and asked him how he could be so unprofessional as to walk out on a role after he'd been established?

"Signor," he explained to me, reasonably, "in that scene, you have Clark Gable, Sophia Loren, and Vittorio De Sica. If anyone notices it is my brother instead of me on the judge's bench, you must have a pretty lousy story."

He had a point. When the picture was previewed in California, it didn't play as we expected it to. The audiences were missing a lot of the comedy. Jack and I decided there was only one way to remedy it: we would have Gable record a tongue-in-cheek narration to carry the audience into the light mood of the story.

Clark was in Palm Springs at the time, on a strict regimen of diet and exercise to prepare for his strenuous role opposite Marilyn in *The Misfits*, due to start shooting shortly. He generously agreed to record the narration for us, explaining he owed us much more.

When I inquired how he meant that, Clark explained that, since he never looked at rushes while a film was shooting, he had not seen himself in *Naples* until the preview. He was shocked by his puffy appearance. Why hadn't I told him about it sooner?

"Clark," I said, "you're a real pro. I figured if that was the way you looked, it was the best you could look."

"Wrong," he said, "I'm taking off 40 pounds for this picture with Marilyn. I owe you fellows an apology. More than that, you have my promise to commit to whatever screenplay you bring to me next."

The tragedy, of course, was that the forty pounds Gable took off too quickly weakened his heart. Clark died a week after finishing the tremendously physical role opposite Monroe in *The Misfits*.

Otherwise, I'm certain he'd have kept his promise to us. Clark Gable was no Cary Grant.

Chapter VII
End of a Marriage

Jack Rose and I had a very long run together, as such things go in Hollywood. After *Naples*, we made *On the Double* with Danny Kaye, our second with Kaye after the highly successful *The Five Pennies* with Danny, Barbara Bel Geddes and Louis Armstrong.

On the Double was inspired by a true story of WWII. At the time of the planning of the D-Day invasion, the British were determined to confuse the Nazi high command. Everyone knew such an assault would not take place without the participation not only of Dwight Eisenhower, but of General Bernard Montgomery, the irascible commander of British armed forces. They discovered an actor with a startling resemblance to Montgomery, and sent him on a much-photographed visit to British forces on Gibraltar, when Montgomery himself was very much in England preparing his troops, The Nazis bought it, and were completely surprised by the launching of the D-Day invasion while Montgomery was supposedly wandering about the Mediterranean.

That's all Jack and I needed as a springboard. It became the story of an American private—Danny—who resembled the British General whom U.S. Intelligence knew German spies were about to assassinate. Danny, playing another dual role, was set up as the General, without being told the true reason, and it was hoped the spies could be successful in knocking him off, thus misleading the Nazis. U.S. Intelligence referred to their plan, hopefully, as "Operation Dead Pigeon."

On the Double was highly successful, with Danny, the pigeon, forced into one life-threatening crisis after the other, in the course of which he had to impersonate everyone from Marlene Dietrich to Adolf Hitler. Only Kaye could have brought it off.

But I had been growing uneasy in the partnership with Jack, and being referred to as "The Boys." I wanted to establish my own identity. I had already done it in television, with both the Danny Thomas series and *My World and Welcome to It*. Jack had never been interested in television, but I felt it was the medium of the future.

I approached him on a practical basis; each of us, alone, could earn as much as the two of us together on a film. Now, while we were "hot," was the time to cash in on what I was certain was our individual potential.

Jack seemed to agree; it was only later in reading his unpublished memoir that I learned how deeply he was hurt.

We had been The Odd Couple indeed; Jack had the acid wit and the jaundiced view of humanity that made life a series of one-liners to him. I was the sentimentalist, the corn in a popcorn world, the believer in the good in all of us, and in happy endings. Together, we balanced each other. I say this only now, in the clarity of hindsight; perhaps our marriage should have continued.

We parted, and Jack and his then wife, Audrey, moved to Rome with their adopted daughter, Melissa. They lived for awhile in Trastevere, the wrong side of the Tiber, where the best child's education was a Hebrew school. Jack loved to tell the story of little Melissa, when she came home from the first day of school and greeted him with, "Shalom, Daddy. That means Ciao."

Then Jack went to England to begin a collaboration with Mel Frank, who had also split with his longtime partner, Norman Panama. Somehow Jack and Mel Frank managed to win a British Academy Award and many other honors for *A Touch of Class*, without my help. They then returned to Hollywood and continued together.

Mel Frank had a notorious appetite. Whenever people asked Jack what had happened to Norman Panama, he would always answer, "Mel ate him."

The years, as they have a habit of doing, passed, and so did Mel Frank. Jack continued the only life he knew, at a typewriter with two fingers, and wrote a play and a few more films. We would see each other occasionally. By then, Jack lived in Santa Monica in an apartment house owned by Lawrence Welk, the old-fashioned bandleader. Jack loved to tell the story of the difference between the Lawrence Welk band and a moose. "With a moose," he would explain, "the horns are up front and the asshole's in back."

Lawrence Welk passed on, and I believe his spirit had a lot to do with persuading the next earthquake to collapse his apartment house on top of

Jack, who managed to survive. Jack moved to Beverly Hills to escape further retribution, but he wasn't successful. It was about this time that he lost his voice—but not his sense of humor—and gained a new appreciation for his family, to whom he devoted himself during his final chapter.

It was with heavy heart and a feeling of some guilt that I wrote the following eulogy for the gathering of friends at an informal service for Jack at the home of his sister-in-law, Nora.

JACK ROSE
A Memory

He would have hated these words as he hated all sentiment. But he really was an optimist at heart. He preferred to look at the world through Jack Rose-colored glasses. As some writer who isn't around to claim credit once said, "He was born with the gift of laughter and the sense that the world was mad." I think he was right.

Jack was born in Warsaw, Poland, the youngest of thirteen children. His father soon moved the entire family to Brooklyn, which Jack always claimed was not much of an improvement. One week, when Jack brought home 20 dollars he had earned writing jokes, his father had Jack's brother, Eddie (who later became an Assistant District Attorney under Tom Dewey), investigate to see if Jack was working for the Mafia, Eddie found out it was worse. Jack was working for Milton Berle.

One of Jack's other jobs was serving as a waiter at Camp Copake in the Jewish Alps, also known as the Catskills. Believe it or not, five-foot-three Jack became one of the stars of Camp Copake's basketball team. They were almost as tall as he was, and later became known as the William Morris Office.

Eventually, in 1939, Jack came west and joined the large platoon of prisoners writing the Bob Hope Pepsodent radio program, where we first met. I had already been locked up for a year on that show, so I was a trustee and was allowed out occasionally, including the two hours off Bob gave me for my honeymoon. According to my Lucy, he was too generous.

In those halcyon days, as I have mentioned before, we all gathered at Bob's house and read our jokes aloud to the other writers whose jobs depended on their not laughing. What a jury! Jack startled all of us because he read so badly, and because his jokes were so good it didn't matter.

Most of us worked in teams, so there was at least one of us laughing at our material, but in those radio days Jack worked alone and he was the only one he could depend on.

In recent years, that became the story and the tragedy of his life. His worst fear these past days was that someone might feel sorry for him. I guess, after two incomplete marriages, he couldn't bring himself to believe so many of us truly loved him. He would have considered that a joke, and waited for the punch line. Well, Jack, here it is: we all did and still do, and now it's too late. Isn't that funny?

We both went over the wall from the Hope Show as soon as World War II arrived. Jack wound up in Armed Forces Radio and I wound up with Sam Goldwyn, for which I should have received combat pay. After the war, Jack went to work for Col. Jack Warner, of whom Wilson Mizner once said, "Jack Warner is the only man I know with rubber pockets so he can steal soup." Rose was also fond of repeating Mizner's other classic, "Working for Warner Brothers is like screwing a porcupine. It's a hundred pricks against one."

Not wanting me to miss such a happy experience, Jack sent me an SOS that he was in trouble, Warner Brothers was in trouble, and there was no reason why I shouldn't be in trouble, too. Would I join him in writing a screenplay?

I did, and that was, to coin a phrase, the beginning of a beautiful friendship.

The main trouble at Warner Brothers was with Dennis Morgan, who had just turned down a script they had sent him and been barred from the lot when Jack Warner found out he could read. The picture, with Jack Carson, had to start shooting in about three weeks because, as was the practice in those happy times, Warner Brothers had already booked it into their theaters and it was scheduled to open within six months.

In order to make that impossible date, Jack Rose had been asked to write an entirely new movie in two weeks; there was no idea and no story, and Jack only typed with two fingers.

But he knew I was a touch-typist and therefore had exactly the right talent for the job.

I joined Jack in his tiny office at Warner Brothers, and it took us almost two days to come up with a story for a completely new movie. Bill Jacobs, an old-timer even then, was the producer, and David Butler, who directed a lot of the *Road* pictures, was sentenced to the job on this one. They both reacted enthusiastically to our story—what choice did they have, even though we hadn't put a word on paper?—and Butler immediately said, "Now we're in real trouble."

"Why?" we asked, innocently.

"Because Dennis Morgan has to agree to do it."

"That's easy," I said. "Have him come in this afternoon and we'll tell him the story."

"We can't do that," David Butler said.

"Why not?"

"Because Dennis Morgan is barred from the lot."

"Okay," Jack said, "we'll go to Morgan's house and tell it to him there."

"We can't do that," Butler said.

"Why not?" I asked.

"Because you guys are writers, and writers can't leave the lot between nine and five, the cops have orders."

Good old Warner Brothers.

"Okay," I said, "we'll tell Dennis the story at 5:30."

"We can't do that," Butler said.

"Why not?" Jack and I felt like a Greek chorus, even though we weren't working for Spyros Skouras.

"Because," Dave Butler said, "after five o'clock, Dennis can't hear. He's flat on his face in some bar."

I hasten to add that Dennis long since kicked the bottle and became a solid citizen, but then it was a real problem. We pondered for awhile until finally Butler said, "I got it! I was at Santa Anita yesterday!"

That made about as much sense as our new story, until Butler explained, "I got a big horse blanket in the back of my convertible! I'll throw the blanket over you guys, we'll drive by the cop at three o'clock, and he'll never see you!"

And that's exactly what we did. We found Dennis at the bar at the Lakeside Country Club, he was still vertical, he listened to our fevered telling of the story and, wonder of wonders, he approved it. Then Butler threw the horse blanket over us again and we drove past the cop at the Warner Brothers gate to save it from bankruptcy.

Now we had two weeks to write the screenplay. There was no time to build sets, so we had written the whole story to take place at Warner Brothers. In return for our ingenuity, we told Jack Warner we needed the services of every star on the lot who was under contract and couldn't get out of it. As a consequence, our cast included, in addition to Morgan and Jack Carson and a young singer just getting started, who was named Doris Day, the following: Joan Crawford, Gary Cooper, Jane Wyman, Sydney Greenstreet, Danny Kaye, Edward G. Robinson, Eleanor Parker, Patricia Neal, and a fellow warming up for the Presidency of the United States named Ronald Reagan, in addition to directors Michael Curtiz, King Vidor, and Raoul Walsh.

We were up in our office in the Writers Building when we heard David Butler on the lawn outside yelling, "Roll 'em!" Jack had to stick his neck out the window and yell, "Dave! Stop! We haven't written the end of that scene yet!"

Who said motion pictures aren't an art form?

Probably everybody who saw *It's a Great Feeling*.

A couple of other quick Warner Brothers stories before I leave Utopia.

Whenever Jack Warner met us crossing the lot, he would always wave and say, "Hello, Boys." Once Jack was crossing alone, and Warner waved at him and said, "Hello, Boys."

One of the big secrets Jack and I kept for years was that Jack Warner asked us to write the jokes he attempted to deliver on various important occasions. He would invariably call us late at night after the event and tell us how each joke played, which we didn't want to hear. It never occurred to Warner that he wasn't exactly Jack Benny, but it occurred to us often. His delivery would have made Henny Youngman sound like Noel Coward.

Left to his own devices, the level of Warner's humor can be judged by the lunch he gave in his private dining room for Madame Chiang Kai Chek and a delegation of top-ranking Chinese statesmen returning from Washington after establishing the first diplomatic relations between the U.S. and the new Republic of Taiwan. Standing up to deliver some warm welcoming remarks, Warner looked at the faces around the table and said, "That reminds me. I forgot to send my laundry out this week." War would have been immediately declared, if Madame Chiang hadn't been forcibly restrained.

Another story my partner liked to tell was the time we were working on the Doris Day film, *April in Paris*, with songs by Vernon Duke and Sammy Cahn. We were in a projection room with them watching a song number they had written when Jack said to me, too loudly, that Vernon Duke's music was not only terrible, but he had stolen the melody from George Gershwin.

On the way out, Vernon Duke leaned over to Sammy and remarked, "Mel is the warm one."

Jack and I wrote a series of hits for Warner Brothers that were so successful, Jack Warner fired us when one of our jokes didn't get a laugh for him at a PTA meeting.

I moved to Paramount, at the invitation of Don Hartman, who was now head of that studio, and called for Jack to join me on *Sorrowful Jones*, the remake of Shirley Temple's *Little Miss Marker*, starring Bob Hope, who didn't play Shirley's role, but Adolphe Menjou's, so he didn't require as much makeup.

That film began the glory years, with Jack producing and me directing *The Seven Little Foys*, *Beau James*, *The Five Pennies*, *Houseboat*, *It Started in Naples*, and a few others that are unforgettable, although I've tried. The happiest and most productive years of my life were spent at Paramount with Jack.

Writing is supposed to be a chore, but with Jack it was an unalloyed pleasure. We would sit in a room with me at the typewriter and Jack staring at the ceiling, and Jack would always come up with the right line at the right moment. His story sense kept us away from most of the treacle I tried to drown our characters in, and his modesty made it possible for me to take most of the credit when the result was good.

Our main purpose was not to write a movie, but to get a free trip to Europe on the studio. That's why we named the corporation we formed "Scribe Productions," after the Hotel Scribe in Paris we hoped to visit some day at Paramount's expense.

Sitting in our office on the fourth floor of the Paramount Writers Building, searching for an inspiration for our next epic, we would look at travel folders and find a country we couldn't afford. We even promoted a trip to Italy on a picture we never made. Hank Fonda was shooting *War and Peace* with Audrey Hepburn near Rome, and we talked Paramount into flying us to Italy so we could talk Fonda into playing Orville Wright in our screenplay about the Wright Brothers. He turned us down, maybe because he wanted to play Wilbur, but it gave us the opportunity to turn down Audrey Hepburn for *Mrs. A,* a movie we were preparing about Gertrude Lawrence, which also didn't get made. To add to our record of brilliant vision, when we were preparing to shoot *The Five Pennies* with Danny Kaye, we needed a five-year-old actress to play his daughter. Judy Garland invited Jack and me to her house to watch her little daughter sing and dance an audition for the part. But the kid had absolutely no talent, and we told Judy to keep her out of show business.

To sum up my experiences with Jack, there was no pretense in him about his work, his life, or the women he loved and lost. The last of these was Betsy Drake, Cary Grant's real-life and also movie-wife when they co-starred in *Room for One More,* which Jack and I wrote for producer Henry Blanke at Warner Brothers a century or two ago, when Blanke, producer of such erudite gems as *The Life of Emile Zola, Of Human Bondage* and *The Treasure of the Sierra Madre,* decided he needed a change from erudition and naturally thought of Jack and me. *Room for One More,* with Cary and Betsy as parents who adopted two problem children into their family, was the result. After Betsy and Cary later divorced in real life—or what passes for it in Hollywood—Betsy waited for some 30 years before dating Jack. They were an improbably odd couple, Betsy with her finishing school accent and bearing, and Jack with the unmistakable stamp of the Bronx. They carried on a strange sort of romance separated by a continent and the Atlantic Ocean, Jack usually in Hollywood and Betsy in London, but they did meet occasionally, like wayward planets. What went on I have no idea, because Jack never explained, and I could never bring myself to ask Betsy. It lasted until the end of Jack's life, which came much too soon.

To conclude this overlong eulogy—too bad I couldn't have handed it to Jack as I used to, and asked him to cut it down— my wife Lucy reminded me of a scene Jack and I had written years ago for *Houseboat*, in which Cary Grant tries to explain life and death to his young son, played by Paul Peterson.

"Why does everything have to die?" Paul asks his father.

"For the same reason everything has to live," Cary tells him.

"That's what I get from my teachers," Paul snarls, "Double talk!"

"Think what the world would be like if no one ever died," Cary explains. "There'd be no room for the new, the young and the beautiful that are being born all the time."

"I'm not making room for anybody," Paul says to Cary. "Let 'em come and get me."

Okay, Jack. They finally had to come and get you. But not until the shortest basketball player at Camp Copake had shown us all how to play the game.

Fade out. The End.

Chapter VIII
The Promised Land

Looking back—something Satchel Paige advised us never to do—I realize that most of the books I've written in a brief literary career have been inspired by films I've directed in various foreign countries. Perhaps I never wanted to leave, so I had to recreate them. These include my very first book, *How to Make a Jewish Movie*, about the filming of *Cast a Giant Shadow* in Israel—as the jacket blurb reads, "with Kirk Douglas, John Wayne, Frank Sinatra, Yul Brynner, Angie Dickinson, Senta Berger, Five Million Dollars, and the Israeli Army," made in the days when five-million dollars was more than the salary of a second-rate first baseman. I don't think Robert Nathan ever read that book, but I have an equally compelling note about *Cast a Giant Shadow* from another recent novelist:

Dear Mel:
    I think it was a good picture. It could have been better if I had paid more attention to you.
                      Love 'n kisses,
                      Kirk

That one hangs on my wall beside the other. As this is written, Kirk has won the battle to regain his health and his life. What he is referring to in his note are the many angry words we exchanged while shooting in the Negev Desert in temperatures approaching 120 degrees. At one point, Moishe, the young Israeli who was my very muscular driver, solicitous right hand, and later a daring Israeli paratrooper, inquired solicitously if I would like him and a couple of his friends to "take care" of Kirk that night. Since there was no replacement within six thousand miles, I resisted temptation.

As a sad footnote, Moishe was later killed in the Yom Kippur War, fighting for his country, just as Mickey Marcus, played by Kirk, was killed on the approaches to Jerusalem in the scene that ended our film. Moishe was "taken care of" by an Arab bullet.

There could be no retakes.

I soon wrote another book with an Israeli theme, *The Eleventh Commandment*, and again to quote the book jacket, "The story of what happens to world politics when Israel strikes oil and the oil deposits of the Arab world drain into the Israeli reserves under Pinsker Street in Tel Aviv." That was a light-hearted treatment of an important theme, and is my absolute favorite among all my books. I had several offers to turn it into a stage musical, but I resisted. Instead, I sent a copy to Peter Sellers, then my favorite comedian, with the suggestion that we make a film where he played all the leading roles, including the irascible 75-year-old hero, Jacob Schoenbaun, and also Golda Meir, Richard Nixon, and Yasser Arafat. Sellers was the only actor, to my knowledge, who could have brought that off, and all for a single salary.

I got a letter back from Peter, who was in England, reading in part:

> Dear Mel,
>
> My wife and I read "The Eleventh Commandment" and thought it tremendous. I really enjoy fine political satire. I feel it's best as a book, in this moment in time. I think the Middle East is a disturbing affair, all too scary and real for an audience, particularly the mongoloid cinema type…The arms race, yes, now that's worth looking into…

And Sellers then gave me the name of a book about the atomic bomb. Peter apparently thought there was more laughter in nuclear war than in Pinsker Street oil wells. He may have been right; the moment of Israel's greatest popularity, which began with its heroic wars against overwhelming odds and later the daring raid on Entebbe, has now been diminished by the struggles of a tiny democracy to stay alive; Arafat emerged as a hero, only to be replaced later, and Schoenbaum and Golda Meir are long forgotten.

The Eleventh Commandment is still my favorite of my own few novels. In England, it won an award as Comic Novel of the Year. In this country, only a request from a Temple in Florida to stage it ever materialized.

Broadway? Forget it.

I wish I could forget Broadway. I had one calamitous experience on that Street of Dreams with my one-time meal-ticket, Col. Jack Warner. (Warner had been appointed a Colonel by Franklin Roosevelt during WWII for making *Mission to Moscow*, and he continued to run the studio in full uniform, which he wore all the time.) Long after the war, the lady hairdresser, who was his constant companion during our Broadway experience, was reported to have asked him to remove the medal from his pajamas. I don't know if he complied.

Warner had recently sold the Warner Brothers studio that he and his brothers Harry and Albert had started after their butcher business. They built it into one of the largest and most successful in Hollywood, home to every big star from Bogart and Cagney to Bette Davis and beyond. Warner once confided to me that he only sold it after his brothers died to prevent it from falling into the hands of his family after he himself passed on. They were all nudnicks, he explained, and would have lost everything.

Richard Gully, the tall Englishman who was his tennis partner and occasional alter ego, told the story of walking with Warner around the WB lot the morning after the sale had been made final. He asked, "Jack, why do you look so miserable? You just made a pot of money, your time is your own, you can afford to do anything you want to, what's your problem?"

And Warner answered, "Yesterday I was Jack Warner. Today, I'm just another rich Jew."

To keep himself occupied, he decided to produce a musical on Broadway. He would be the sole investor. It was to be the story of New York's dapper Mayor Jimmy Walker, as mentioned earlier. Warner figured it was a sure thing for the Big Apple where, in Gene Fowler's affectionate words, spoken by Walter Winchell in *Beau James* (the movie version Jack and I had made earlier), "The memory of him is green. The love for him is warm. He is a legend now, and when you ride in the taxicabs on the streets of New York, if you ask who best typified the heart of the greatest city in the Western world, you are bound to hear the name, 'Jimmy Walker.' And the smile that goes with that name makes you feel warm, and fine, and forgiving, all day long."

You would think his story would be a sure thing on the Broadway stage for a New York audience. You would be as wrong as the man with rubber pockets, which were soon quickly emptied.

The movie, *Beau James*, had been one of the few roles for Bob Hope which required him to act. To my mind, he gave the best performance of his career as James J. Walker, the certainly immoral, and possibly corrupt, darling of New York. Some years after the film was released, when Warner was having trouble with the book for his upcoming musical to be called, simply, *Jimmy*, he ran *Beau James*. Then he called me and asked if I would rewrite the libretto. I don't know if he remembered my connection with the *Penrod* stories, which he had once said had befouled his theaters in the dim past, but if he did, the success of *On Moonlight Bay* had mellowed him. I found that unemployment had also mellowed him into a human being. His Broadway musical was in trouble. Would I help?

I agreed to rewrite *Jimmy* because this time, I reasoned, I would be a playwright, not an employee; every word I wrote would be protected by the Dramatists Guild, and my relationship with Jack Warner would be entirely different, especially since neither of us knew anything about the Broadway theater, as we were destined to soon discover.

My first creative achievement was to get Warner to buy the screenplay Jack and I had written for the Paramount motion picture with Bob Hope. I figured all I had to do was take the camera directions out of the *Beau James* script, and I would have the libretto for *Jimmy*.

Rude awakening. Murphy's Law quickly took over. At first, I was announced as the director of the musical; then I was replaced by an experienced Broadway director, who shall be nameless here. I agreed to his taking over, since I was ignorant of stage technique and I was not so ignorant that I didn't recognize my ignorance. I wish now I had decided to learn on the job, even without a Hal Kern at my side.

I had sent the book of the musical to Gene Kelly, the ideal choice. He called to say it was the best script he had seen in months, but he couldn't face the idea of six performances a week in front of a Broadway audience—or even his doctor. So we were forced to hold extensive auditions for the lead, and decided on Frank Gorshin, an excellent imitator who had never played a leading role. It didn't dawn on anyone, much less Gorshin, that he was not Bob Hope. And that he was not Jimmy Walker. And that imitation is not acting.

Much later Gorshin became successful on Broadway playing George Burns. I assume that, sometimes, imitation does work.

But Jimmy Walker was beyond him. Or my version was.

The music was also a problem. The composer and the lyricist, Bill Jacob and his wife Patti, had only written brief commercial showcases for various manufacturers' products. They were talented, but I think they would have been the first to admit they were not yet Rodgers and Hammerstein, although they certainly tried. Julie Wilson and Anita Gillette sang their score—very well, I thought. But no song became a hit.

However, I was having my own problems with the director, who certainly was having a few with me. Many of the scenes I had adapted from the screenplay simply would not work on a stage, and I was constantly rewriting. But I felt the pace and the spirit of the original *Beau James* were sadly lacking, and that the actors needed an expert comedy hand at the helm. But no one asked me.

We were trying out the show in Philadelphia, that graveyard of hits, when I phoned Warner in Hollywood and told him, "Jack, you're going to have to close this turkey. It's a big vacuum cleaner. Everybody is in it for what they can take out of your pockets."

And Warner said, "Stop worrying about my money. It's only a mil."

A million dollars from one angel was unheard of in those days, but Warner was a gambler all his life, and was not going to change now. I said, "Jack, you can't take this show into New York and expose it to the critics. Close it now!"

I'll never forget Warner's answer. I can still hear his voice: "If I close the show, who'll have dinner with me?" He meant it.

Opening night of the tryout in Philadelphia, an elderly man in the last row dropped dead just as the curtain went up. He was the lucky one.

After the disastrous reviews following the Broadway opening, Jack Warner kept his turkey open for three long months by throwing in another mil from his own rubber pockets.

I was walking down Broadway with Frank Gorshin the morning after the devastating notices appeared. Frank was walking backward, so he could keep admiring his name on the marquee of the Winter Garden Theater, when he said to me, "I think I'd like to have you write a movie for me to star in, when I finish in the show."

I couldn't believe it.

"Frank," I said, "you have a run-of-the-show contract. You may not be available for five years!"

And Frank said, magnanimously, "I'll wait."

So much for Broadway. No wonder my favorite city in all the world is Rome. I never had a musical on stage there. If I had, the Romans might have started throwing Jews to the lions.

Over the years, I filmed all or part of three motion pictures at Cinecitta Studios, on the outskirts of the city, and wrote the novel *Lualda* on a rickety dining-room table in an elegant apartment overlooking the Tiber.

I have a memory of one magnificent dinner Lucy staged there for some of our Italian friends. I can still see the proprietress of one of the many local pizza parlors staggering in with thirteen medium-sized pizzas stacked confidently on her arms. Our guests demolished them almost before she set them down, along with four litres of what some natives called Dago Red, followed by dancing through the night to the melodies from our out-of-tune piano played by a guest who was in the same condition as the piano.

With the novel finally completed, it was time to return home. I was now at last on my own in Hollywood, where, to paraphrase Sinatra's elegy about New York City, if you can make it there, you'll make it anywhere. The corollary: if you can't, you won't.

To hide my own insecurity, I decided that on my next film, without Jack Rose, I would be writer, director, *and* producer. If anything went wrong, it would be my fault. I didn't have a brother to take my place.

I found a whimsical book by Donald Downes, a former OSS officer in WWII. Downes had written a comic novel, *The Easter Dinner*, about the Allied liberation of Rome. It focused on the fate of a group of wayward U.S. carrier pigeons who got themselves eaten by a hungry Italian family on the way to the liberation. It was not only funny, it was based on reality, and had the sting of truth. And it was truly touching.

And equally important, it was set in my favorite city, where I planned to have Paramount pick up my hotel bill.

All I had to do was write a screenplay, get a star to play the lead, get the studio to finance it, and then go to Italy to produce and direct it.

I missed Jack as soon as I started to write it.

But I did start. Again, Herman Citron to the rescue. At that time he represented Chuck Heston, Ben-Hur himself, and also star of *The Ten Commandments*. As I have noted, one of Herman's Ten Commandments to his clients was, "Thou shalt do any film I tell thou to do." Chuck had starred in one comedy, *Major Benson*, and it had been very well received. Herman was convinced Heston now needed another comedy, or he'd be playing Biblical roles for the rest of his career.

Chuck seemed a logical choice to me; after all, I had written the lead role for Bob Hope. All Heston had to do to fit the part was pass a small miracle.

Child's play for someone who could make a living by walking on water.

Herman sent Heston my script and his Commandment. He arranged for us to meet at Chuck's home in Laurel Canyon, not far from my own. Although we are poles apart politically—I think Heston had his own pole—he turned out to be completely affable, intelligent, and the possessor of a considerable sense of humor.

English translation: he liked the screenplay.

However, there was a problem. Any film called *The Easter Dinner* that starred Charlton Heston, would lead an audience to believe the opening scene would be the Last Supper, followed by the Crucifixion and the Resurrection. We didn't have the budget. We might have afforded a decent crucifixion, but we wouldn't have enough left for a good Resurrection. Audiences would be disappointed because there was no happy ending.

In a stroke of pure studio genius, *The Easter Dinner* was retitled *The Pigeon That Took Rome* while I was shooting in Italy and couldn't prevent it.

Shooting that film was pure joy, exteriors in Rome, interiors in Hollywood. No temperament in a cast led by Chuck and including the lovely Elsa Martinelli, the great Metropolitan basso Salvatore Baccalone; and Marietto, the little Italian scene-stealer from *Naples*; Rudolph Anders, as the nicest Gestapo officer you ever met; Brian Donlevy, as a road-company Patton; my good friend Harry Guardino, from *Houseboat* and *The Five Pennies*, as an American radio operator; and Gabriella Pallotta, as the sweet, innocent young Italian girl who suckers him into marrying her while she is just a little bit pregnant by another U.S. soldier.

Of course, Murphy's Law still operated in Italy. The story, which opens with Heston and Guardino smuggled into Rome in the guise of Catholic Priests, required an important sequence to be shot among the Bernini Columns in front of St. Peter's. The Vatican refused permission; the Pope had been upset because he had given Federico Fellini his consent to shoot a scene for *La Dolce Vita* in the Vatican; and Fellini had promptly flown a statue of Jesus Christ by helicopter over the sacred dome of St. Peter's, an aerial sacrilege.

I assured them I had no such intention, but the Pope didn't have the time or inclination to read our script, so we were denied access to the Holy See.

The alternative was to build St. Peter's Cathedral on the Paramount lot, but cooler heads in the Finance Department reluctantly advised against it. My Italian production manager, however, told me we could set up our cameras in the street just beyond the Vatican border, and the Pope himself could not prevent us from photographing St. Peter's Square from Italy. When I pointed out that even our longest lens was not equal to the task of getting closeups at that distance, he came up with a better solution. I was naturally dubious, until he told me his brother worked in the Vatican and informed him the Bishop in charge of illegal filmmakers never arose before 10:00 a.m. If we could get our shot by that time, and get our equipment out, the Bishop would be checkmated.

So at 6:00 a.m. we invaded the Bernini Columns with our cameras, Heston, Guardino, and Barry Fitzgerald's brother, Arthur Shields, who was playing an Irish Catholic Priest, and hastily began to shoot the scene.

The Swiss Guards looked the other way; the production manager's brother had promised them a large, earthly reward. All went well until about 8:30, when the Bishop had to answer the call of nature and happened to stare out of his window. Sacrilege! Disobedience of a Papal order! Vatican police, not the Swiss Guards, started to descend on our company. It was Naples all over again, but no one was demolishing St. Peter's; there was a long, convoluted argument in Italian as our production manager and his brother held the police off until we completed the shot. Then the actors and the equipment were tossed into our trucks and the invasion of the Vatican was concluded. If I had been Fellini, I would have had a few helicopters standing by for the evacuation.

A similar scene took place, minus the Vatican, some days later. We were shooting our final sequence on the streets of Rome. Because of my education on Capri, I had carefully prepared the way with a generous bribe to the Italian Police Captain in charge of the area, so that permission could be secured, traffic could be stopped, and the street cleared for our shooting.

Setting up for the shot with Chuck and Elsa Martinelli, I was startled when Italian Police descended on us and ordered us to leave. It was politely pointed out to their Capitano that we not only had a permit, but had also sealed it with the regulation bribe to the police officer in charge of the district.

"Ah!" said the Capitano. "E ill mio fratello, e sulla vacanza oggi."

Meaning, my production manager explained, that the officer we had bribed was on vacation. It was necessary to start the bribing all over again with the other police officer, who was his brother. The bidding was to start at two million lire, take it or leave it.

Rather than leave it, I had an inspiration. A good friend, Irv Robbins, who was the cofounder with another friend, Butch Baskin, of the Baskin-Robbins Ice Cream Co., was in Rome on vacation and had come down to the street to watch us. Irv was an amateur photographer; he had brought his trusty Leica.

As the furious argument in Italian continued between the police and the production manager, I explained to Irv he was missing a great moment if he didn't photograph this slice of Roman life. He enthusiastically agreed. Of course, I didn't tell him what the argument was about, so he blithely began to flash photographs of the Police Captain with the bribe money in his hands.

Now, everyone in Rome knows how negotiations with the polizia are conducted; however, they do not like to see them immortalized. Instantly, Irv was seized roughly by the polizia, the film yanked from his camera, and then he was shoved into a patrol car where they all joined him, and sped off to the nearest police station, so his frantic protests could be translated and ignored.

I immediately had the production manager chase after them and bribe Irv's way out. This occupied the police while I got the last shot I needed. We had vanished from the streets of Rome by the time the angry polizia returned. I think the Capitano's brother was with them. He had had a great vacation.

Later, when Irv appeared and complained loudly about the polizia destroying his negative, I bought him another roll.

And an ice cream cone.

What are friends for?

Lest it seem I am unduly chastising Italian morals and integrity, there was the incident of the great Italian motion picture *sciopero*—strike—that closed down the entire industry for twenty-four hours, the longest time Italian crews can go without a pizza. We were shooting a scene on the Wedding Cake, the huge Vittorio Emmanuele Monument, the day we were scheduled to be struck. My chief electrician, who had become my friend after he had his brother steal some lights for us from the *Ben-Hur* production that had long finished, came to me and asked how long the light would be right for shooting at the Monument. I told him that by four o'clock, the shadows would make it impossible to continue. "Then, would it be all right if our crew started their sciopero at 4:05?" he insquired. I gave my approval.

But there was an American strike later that was pointedly different. There was a work-stoppage in Hollywood by the below-the-line Unions, meaning those who did the real work of movie-making. In order to avoid the strike and edit the film when it was completed, I had to move to New York City, where Chuck graciously offered me the use of his midtown apartment. Using a Manhattan editing facility, the finishing of the negative proceeded without delay.

Finally it was completed, and it was time to preview. We then discovered that the negative of the entire first reel had disappeared. Frantic searching revealed no clues. The cut negative is the heart and soul of a motion picture; without it, no copies can be made for distribution. Something similar had happened to Danny Kaye in France, where a reel of the negative of *Me and the Colonel* had been hijacked en route from Nice to the Paris laboratory. The kidnappers were holding it for ransom; it was the final day's work and the cast had scattered. The producer refused to pay, reassembled the company from all over—Danny was in London— and reshot the entire day's work at considerable cost.

It was the first scene cut from the picture after previews.

In our case, the reel could not be cut; it was the essential opening of the movie and had to remain. However, *The Pigeon That Took Rome* had been shot in black and white because I wanted to integrate actual black-and-white World War II news footage into the action. This was before colorization was developed and used expensively in *Ike*, the Eisenhower miniseries.

The newsreel companies still possessed their original negatives; it was possible to get them back for that missing first reel of *Pigeon* and use the fuzzy daily prints for the rest of the reel.

The press remarked on the "feel" of the war I had miraculously succeeded in capturing. How had I managed to get that quality of reality?

I modestly said it was nothing. And it was.

Pigeon received some of the best notices of any film I have directed, fuzzy first reel not withstanding. Or perhaps that was the reason.

George Weltner, then President of Paramount Pictures, wired me in Hollywood from New York, "Dear Four-Star Mel"—and enclosed the four-star notice from the *New York Journal-American*, a newspaper which has since disappeared, hopefully for other reasons.

There was also the notice in the now-defunct *New York World Telegram* by Archer Winston, I can still quote from memory—

"*The Pigeon That Took Rome* is the kind of picture that depends for success most heavily upon the sharpness of its producer, the inventive brevity of its director, and the wit of its screenplay writer. Luckily all of these qualities are found in producer-director-writer Melville Shavelson...In a Donald Downes novel, he has found material worthy of his talent..."

The missing first reel was finally found years later when the film lab had its first cleaning. It had been tossed up behind a ventilator by some Union member in sympathy with his striking brethren in Hollywood.

If I knew his name, I would thank him.

After all, strikes were once my business. As President of the feisty Writers Guild of America, West, I had had the opportunity to call the laborers away from their typewriters more than once. We had learned, to our sorrow, that none of the advances we had made in the areas of money and recognition were ever granted by the movie companies out of the goodness of their hearts; we always had to take them away, a sometimes long and nerve-wracking operation that went on for months.

The strike that started in December, 1980, lasted a long 95 days, during one of my turbulent terms as President. We struck the producers and the networks, and the result was the ground-breaking agreement that set the terms of the new world in television and motion pictures.

It is difficult to recall the very first similar strike, about 1963, which WGA settled by turning over to the infant called television all films shot before that date, for a grand contribution of $500,000 to the writers' health fund. The producers laughingly assured us that motion pictures would have little value in the technical curiosity called "vaudeville in a box," which would certainly disappear after its novelty was exhausted. Promises, promises.

We took them up on the offer, and promptly fell into the same trap later when they assured us the DVD was a passing fancy that was too expensive to ever succeed.

Shortly after we agreed, when we came to our senses, at a strike meeting the WGA had called in the Beverly Wilshire Hotel, I was handed a note on the dais that read, "There is a bomb in the building. Get everyone out immediately but don't let them know."

So I informed the audience that the fire department had objected to their smoking and ordered everyone out into the parking lot at once.

When the hotel was cleared, I climbed on top of someone's car and told them all the truth. What the real truth was, no one ever found out. No bomb ever went off, either at the Beverly Wilshire or at WGA Headquarters, where another threat was later received. And there was no note claiming credit, so the villain couldn't have been a writer, to whom a credit is more important than life itself.

There was once a note left by a disappointed screenwriter, after he decided to end it all. The police captain who arrived found the note beside the body, amidst a huge stack of rejection slips from every studio in town. After looking the writing over carefully, the captain announced, "In my thirty years in the police department, this is the dullest suicide note I ever read."

An entirely different crisis occurred when the Guild was negotiating with the Hollywood production companies for a percentage of the gross for films sold to pay television, a brand-new source of income at the time. Gross, of course, is the total money taken in by a film, with no deductions by the studio.

As WGA President, I was sitting across the negotiating table from representatives of the top management of all the movie studios, plus a large array of their most expensive lawyers. A Vice President of 20th Century-Fox, who shall remain nameless because I have forgotten his name, rose to his feet to inquire, "Why are you writers so foolish as to demand a percentage of the gross? You know you'll never get it!"

And I asked—reasonably, I thought, considering we were on strike against all of them—"Then what, in all fairness, do you suggest?"

"Why don't you writers just take a percentage of the net, like everybody else?"

"By whose bookkeeping?" I inquired, as if I didn't know.

"Why, ours, of course. You can trust us. We're 20th Century-Fox!"

There was a slight stirring on our side of the table.

"Last week," I reminded him, "the *Los Angeles Times* carried a story about a Fox picture, *Aliens*, which had three participants in the net profits. Fox announced that the picture had just grossed one hundred million dollars. Not one of the three participants has ever seen a penny of it."

"That's an absolute lie!" the V.P. shouted. "Every one of those people had a check in the mail the day after that story appeared!"

The roar of laughter from both sides of the negotiating table should have knocked him over. But it didn't. Management won the argument. To this day, there is no Guild contract of any sort that guarantees a writer of a film a piece of gross profits. But there is a clause in every writer's contract, which he is obliged to sign, declaring that the studio is the author of the screenplay he just wrote, so management can claim ownership of the author's copyright, sometimes worth millions.

In countries like France, where writers are considered a national treasure, the income from a tax on every movie seat goes directly to the author of the film. When Warner Brothers announces it is the author of a screenplay, and has a signed contract to prove it, there is loud Gallic laughter and, I believe, a large party at which the members of the Societe des Auteurs Francaises, the French Writers Guild, drink up the tax money due the writer to keep it from falling into unworthy hands.

The only writer, to my knowledge, who has received copyright to a film he wrote is Joseph Wambaugh, author of *The Onion Field*, among many others. Wambaugh writes stories based on his experiences as a longtime member of the Los Angeles. Police Department. When he was called to a meeting with a studio to discuss the sale of one of his novels for a film, I was told he took out his service revolver and ostentatiously removed the cartridges and cleaned the gun during the negotiations.

He was allowed to keep the copyright.

So much for Hollywood-style labor relations,

My next adventure in loneliness after *Pigeon* occurred when I was basking in its success, and decided to go all the way: write an original screenplay, no adaptation this time, every word my own, and produce and direct it in the foreign country of my choice. Having worn out my welcome with the Italian Caribinieri, and also the Pope, I felt it was safer to turn my talents to France, where I had no police record. I couldn't think of anything more pleasant than to have Paramount pick up my hotel bills in Paris, including a dinner or two at the Tour d'Argent, which might possibly bankrupt the studio.

My inspiration for working in Paris went back many years. In 1955, Lucy and I were visiting the city where an old friend from my days on the *Cornell Daily Sun,* Jim Nolan, who was then in the Paris publicity department of Air France, introduced us to a young veteran from W.W.II who had returned to more or less civilian life and begun writing a newspaper column for the *International Herald Tribune,* titled, "P.S. From Paris." Art Buchwald was about to leave on a vacation and was desperately seeking volunteers to write his column while he was away enjoying himself. Why he had to leave Paris to enjoy himself, I never did find out, but I did learn a great deal about a newspaperman who became a legend during and even after his life was over.

Buchwald then had a small apartment not too far from the Eiffel Tower, which could be viewed beautifully from his bathroom window, reducing it to its proper importance. Also, Art told me Picasso had once written him a note about a column, and Art had written back that Picasso's notes weren't worth much, but if Picasso would send him one of his paintings, he'd mention it in the column. Picasso did send a painting with the request that Art should put it where everyone could see it, so Art of course hung it over his toilet. It was a very nice painting, if you like women with three breasts, an acquired taste for me. And probably for Buchwald. The toilet itself was just average, except for the view of the Eiffel.

Part of the column I wrote, which he printed and then promptly left Paris, was headed, *"Bonjour Tristesse, ou est l'American Hospital?"* It began, "The Legend rose from his chair and extended a friendly hand. I accepted it warmly, but I noticed that my wife, a romantic creature who was born and raised near an idyllically beautiful coal mine in Williamsport, Pa., looked stunned. Could this be him, the gay, carefree bon vivant, America's most glamorous expatriate, intimate of royalty, gourmet of gourmands? It was. I knew that behind that stubble of yesterday's beard, tomorrow's haircut, and last week's shirt, lay the soul of France. Out cold.

"Buchwald announced he would take us to an obscure little bistro with a quaint menu, a quaint proprietor, and the quaintest prices in Paris. My wife nodded, happily.

"And that is why I am trying to get the American Hospital on the phone at this moment, although the operator speaks such abominable French that I can't understand her...Buchwald had led us to a picturesque café located on a side street...He studied the menu critically, a little furrow creasing his brow, and asked us if we liked poached eggs. I assured him I did, and I also liked Marilyn Monroe, but what did they have for lunch? My wife kicked me under the table. If the Legend was suggesting poached eggs, obviously they would be like no poached eggs we had ever tasted before. Unfortunately, she was right.

"To go with them, he ordered us a bottle of Beaujolais that was ruby red and sparkling with the flavor of some of the finest corks this weary old palate had ever savored. And then came the piece de resistance—*volaille de champignons avec poulets de tetes de veau*, if memory serves me correctly, and I see no reason why it should. I'm not myself today.

"This dish was served with baked beans, at his insistence; he ordered a plate of French bread, finished the beans, and brushed aside my wife's tentative comment that if the *vollaille* etc. was lamb, it was too rare, and if it was beef, it was too well done, and if it was fowl, it must be some bird unknown to the Audubon Society, as it had pigs' feet. He made some comment about French fowl being extreme individualists, then ordered the *patisserie* for us and ate another plate of French bread. That was the end of the meal, except for the check, which occupied him and the proprietor for half an hour of friendly hand-wrestling, and then it was all over. We had had lunch with The Legend.

"We shook hands all around and waved good-bye as Art hailed a taxi for Looey's Delicatessen, which he told us was in the shadow of the Eiffel Tower. Of course, in Paris, everything is in the shadow of the Eiffel Tower. Ask any French real estate office.

"The ptomaine didn't hit my wife until several hours later, so it was probably caused by some underdone Bromo Seltzer she took as soon as we returned to our hotel.

"As for myself, I felt fine. I had another plate of French bread."

As a result of writing that free column, Buchwald never asked me for another one.

I have never understood why.

I will miss Buchwald. But I will never miss that lunch.

With that for inspiration, it didn't take me long to turn out a story for a film.

Some years before, while in Paris with Lucy, I had witnessed the celebration of the Festival of St. Catherine; it was a strange religious holiday, in which the midinettes, who worked in the French fashion industry and still had retained their virginity (they said), paraded through the Paris streets in outlandish costumes and prayed at the shrine of St. Catherine, the patron Saint of all virgins, asking the good Saint to find them husbands. St. Catherine had a small, but select, group of believers.

That was enough of a springboard to get me started. Soon I had finished a storyline about a forthright American girl named "Samantha," whose business it was to sketch and to steal the latest Paris fashions. Her friends called her "Sam" because of her lack of femininity. I had her admit, "I'm a semi-virgin. That's a girl who tried it once, and didn't like it. It's terrible. It's like eating one peanut." She joined the parade to St. Catherine, and the good saint persuaded her to discard virginity, and even semi-virginity, and seek out a man. The result of this Saintly advice resulted in Samantha overdoing it and being mistaken for a prostitute by an American sportswriter in Paris.

It was all to take place against the background of the Spring Paris fashion shows, hopefully with the cooperation of everyone from Cardin to Givenchy. There was also a role for Maurice Chevalier as Maurice Chevalier, for which he wouldn't have to rehearse, and for the annual bicycle race known as the Tour de France. I had thrown in everything except Charles de Gaulle, who was then Prime Minister and probably unavailable.

I turned the "treatment" in to the powers-that-be at Paramount, and promptly forgot about it. It would take the geniuses who ran the studio several months to read it and several more to decide if they could afford it. In the interim, I had more important things on my mind—a greatly-needed European vacation, albeit at my own expense, with Lucy and no children, a very attractive prospect.

We started in London with the delivery of a shiny Jaguar XKS convertible. I was feeling very important until I parked the new Jaguar in London's posh South Audley Street Garage.

The space next to mine was labeled, "Cubby Broccoli. Rolls-Royce Number II."

Not only had I been upstaged, but by a vegetable I hated. I had been humbled by no less than James Bond himself, or rather, 007's amiable producer, whom I later came to know in California when he was up to Bond Film #5, and Rolls-Royce #VIII.

It didn't spoil my vacation. What did spoil it, after the pleasure of driving across Europe on Autobahns, which had no speed limits that anyone noticed, was a five-word cable that awaited us when Lucy and I arrived in Vienna, a city for which I had managed to slow down.

"I read 'Samantha', loved same," the cable informed me. It was signed by the Paramount President in New York, and was followed by a frantic transatlantic telephone call from a friend, Marty Rackin, a former screenwriter now head of the studio operation in Hollywood. He had been attempting to reach me everywhere in Europe, but the Jaguar had outsped the phone calls.

It seems there was a problem. Joanne Woodward. She had read the treatment and had committed to make the picture.

"That's not a problem," I told him, "unless she's also been committed to an institution." I had no experience with actresses who would sign before there was a single page of a screenplay.

But that wasn't the difficulty. Joanne, in her enthusiasm, had persuaded her husband to join her. Since her husband was an actor named Paul Newman, the difficulty still eluded me.

Marty explained, patiently. Newman was the hottest property in Hollywood at the time, Cary Grant having relinquished the title, but Newman was signed to start another movie at another studio within eight weeks. Could I possibly write the screenplay, cast it, organize the production, go to France and direct the film, all within two months?

"No problem," I said, and hung up. It was then that I realized I hadn't heard a word after he said, "Paul Newman." Who wouldn't grab the opportunity? I had all of two months? The difficult we do immediately, the impossible takes a little longer.

There was a story I heard from Bob Hope about a priest in a Catholic church in a drought-ridden Texas town. He had his congregation pray for relief from the terrible dry spell. The prayer was followed immediately by a torrential cloudburst that washed them out of the church and submerged half of the state. The priest managed to battle his way back through a raging river that had overflowed. He got down on his knees as his pulpit floated by him and pleaded, "Oh, Lord, I know we prayed for rain, but Jesus Christ, this is ridiculous!"

This *was* ridiculous. I had promised to write and direct a major motion picture in the time it usually took me to get through to my agent.

But…Paul Newman? And Joanne Woodward as well? I would kill for the opportunity, even if I was the one who wound up as the corpse.

As I hung up the phone in Vienna, I realized the first thing I had to do was to get rid of the Jaguar. Even an XKE would slow me down. The car was loaded aboard a Viennese freight train, which waltzed it all the way to Trieste. There it was placed aboard a freighter and arrived in Hollywood just as I was finishing the movie and vice versa.

With Lucy, I flew to Paris to scout locations for a film I hadn't yet written. Since I had no idea what I was going to write, it took very little time.

Flying back to Hollywood, I wrote the opening sequence in my head. Had this been the age of the laptop, I would have written it in my lap. I had only a rough idea of what should follow.

Back at Paramount, I finished writing the first act—movies don't really have acts, there is no curtain; it's merely a convention to make screenwriters feel more like playwrights. I felt obliged to show it to Paul and Joanne, who had taken me on faith. We were all jittery. I remember Paul telling me he and Joanne had never been successful together in a comedy. He could see the advertisement—"You hated them in *Rally 'Round the Flag, Boys!* Why would you want to see them in this?" But he couldn't have been more helpful or cooperative during the shooting, except for the day he took me joyriding on the back of his motorcycle after he had demonstrated how he had won the U.S. Army's Budweiser Medal for chugging the most cans of beer.

I survived, but it was so hair-raising an experience that I would actually have preferred being on a horse. Even Rocket.

After the Newmans finished reading those first pages, I met with them at Paramount, where Joanne told me it was the dirtiest screenplay she had ever read, and she couldn't wait to start. You must understand that this was in the era of the Hays Office, when Saints didn't discuss virginity in motion pictures and prostitutes had to die onscreen, like Camille, or you couldn't release the picture.

But the rules and public morals were changing fast, and I was pushing the sealed envelope with this comedy about a girl who was a semi-virgin and a semi-prostitute at the same time.

Paul's deadline was approaching, and the Paris sequences had to be photographed immediately. But Newman wasn't available because he was shooting still another film at the time, about which no one had bothered to inform the director.

It was necessary for me to fly to Paris again and start shooting a second unit, with a French crew and doubles for Paul and Joanne, *tout de suite.* Paramount fortunately insisted that Lucy accompany me to see that I retained my sanity. I don't know how she was supposed to tell.

We arrived in Paris completely exhausted and were immediately rushed to our hotel near the Champs Elysee. Those were the days of the Algerian bombings in Paris. Attempts were being made almost daily on the life of President De Gaulle. Police were on patrol everywhere.

We collapsed into bed and I was awakened about midnight by the sound of bombs, followed by machine gun and artillery fire. The room seemed to shake with the noise, but I didn't give a damn; if the hotel were to be destroyed, I prayed for a direct hit, which would solve all my problems. No such luck. The bombing continued for hours, or so it seemed.

It wasn't until the next morning that Mickey Moore, always my First Assistant Director because he was the best in the world and still is today, told us that Darryl Zanuck had previewed his new production, *The Longest Day*, the night before. As part of the publicity, Zanuck had installed powerful loudspeakers atop the Eiffel Tower to play back the soundtrack of the D-Day invasion. That's what had awakened us.

I was a little disappointed at having survived. So was Mickey, later, after we had started shooting all over Paris. He showed up at our hotel suite one evening and worriedly asked Lucy to see the director's screenplay, since he had none, and he had to prepare for the next day's shoot.

I had warned Lucy to stall. There was no screenplay. I hadn't written the Paris scenes yet. But I didn't want the crew to worry. I was handling that.

What I had done was tell my French production manager to get me permits to shoot any place in the city, since I had no idea yet where we would be. With the Algerian bombings continuing, the police had insisted we list every location and diagram every camera position. If I'd known where they were, I'd have been able to write the script. One of the unwritten sequences was to feature the Tour de France, the national insanity. This annual bicycle race was to start in Paris and wind through the entire country. Bicyclists from all nations annually engage in this idiocy, which covers more than 2,500 perspiring miles and involves climbing both the Alps and the Pyrenees. Why, I have no idea. Half a dozen ambulances usually accompany the racers and do a thriving business.

The start of the race would make a colorful sequence; I doubted anybody would be left at the finish, so we wouldn't bother covering that. We would merely insert our doubles for Paul and Joanne during the Paris section.

My expert French cameraman set up our camera behind the fences surrounding the Presidential residence, near the Rond Pont off the Champs Elysee, where 140 muscular bicyclists were lined up for the race's beginning. As we prepared to shoot, I noticed the lens on the camera. Our film was to be in VistaVision, Paramount's answer to Fox's CinemaScope, for which film passed behind the lens sideways, so it was dubbed the Chinese Camera. VistaVision required a very special and expensive lens, which we had shipped from Hollywood because there were none available in Europe.

It wasn't on our camera. Our expert cameraman, who spoke little English and understood even less, finally confessed he had never seen a VistaVision lens, so he couldn't be blamed for its absence.

Frantic, as the start of the race grew near, I phoned our second company, shooting another sequence nearby. They had a lens. A Paris taxi sped from their location to ours and a burly prop man leaped out and raced to the fence surrounding our camera position. There was no time for him to open the gate; the Starter was raising his pistol. The crowd was already cheering. The prop man hurled the $40,000 lens over the fence and into the arms of the Second Assistant Cameraman, who caught it nonchalantly as my stomach dropped with it. He hurried it to the camera, where our expert cameraman substituted it for the standard lens.

"Roll 'em!" I shouted. "Moteur!" echoed my French assistant director. Nobody rolled 'em. My expert French cameraman explained to me that while he was expert on French cameras, he had never seen an American Mitchell camera before. This one had a little door on the film compartment, and he couldn't exactly get it to close. And light would destroy the film image.

Nearing apoplexy, I realized I was wearing a black raincoat, perhaps subliminally as a shroud. I quickly tossed it over the head of the camera operator and the camera, protecting the film from the light as we started shooting. The crowd was cheering again, but I don't think it was for me.

My expert French cameraman called me that night to tell me the report from the lab was fine. The negative had not been damaged by light. I breathed a sigh of relief.

I took the sigh back the next day when I viewed the rushes. The film had indeed been saved by my raincoat. What we saw on the screen was a charming closeup of the rear end of the last bicycle racer disappearing around a corner.

My expert French cameraman had encouraging news. He had found out how to close the film compartment. It was the little lever here, Non?

"Bravo!" I told him.

By this time, we were playing tag with the Paris Gendarmerie because we were shooting streets for which we hadn't had time to secure permits. We had a truck full of bicycles and French bicyclists as we raced all over the City of Light.

The problem was the traffic, which had to be stopped. We had attempted to solve that by hiring a dozen actors and renting uniforms so they could dress as flics and stop all traffic when we needed to get a shot. The real Gendarmes were outraged when they heard about it. We moved fast, but the genuine Gendarmes were only one location behind us.

As we finished each shot, we would throw the bicycles, our cyclists, and our hired "Gendarmes" into our trucks and speed to the next spot.

But for the final sequence we had to photograph our bicycling extras circling the Arc de Triomphe and racing down the Champs Elysee, closing down the busiest street in Paris. Without a permit. With a unit of angry Gendarmes in hot pursuit. It would resemble the last act of *Les Miserables*, without the sewers.

And the Champs had its own contingent of the Gendarmerie, on duty day and night.

With time running out, I asked our production manager to try to make a deal. Offer the Gendarmes on duty at the Arc any bribe to allow us to stop traffic and get our shot. We would pay them whatever we had left in our budget, since this would be our last shot in Paris and we had to complete it before the unfriendly Gendarmerie arrived.

We waited, nervously, as a long negotiation ensued, in French, between our production manager and the local police at the Arc de Triomphe.

The production manager returned. He had closed a hard bargain.

"How much?" I inquired, worriedly.

He told me that each Gendarme on duty would have to be bought a brandy, and allowed to sit at a café, as our fake "flics" directed traffic for them, while they observed how the crazy Americans made a movie.

And what of the other Gendarmes, who were pursuing us with a warrant for our arrest? What did they say about them?

"Fuck 'em," was their polite response, in French.

Traffic was halted on the Champs Elysee, our cyclists circled the Arc de Triomphe three times until the cameras caught the action properly, and every auto on the Champs protested long and loudly.

The last time I saw Paris, the clamor of their squeaky horns was music to my ears.

Once the sequence was completed, we threw the bicycles into our truck, thanked the real and movie flics and our racing extras, and sped off to the Paris airport where Lucy and Mickey and I and our American crew boarded a plane to the U.S. just before the unfriendly Gendarmerie caught up with us, presumably to have us guillotined in the Place de la Concorde, for which we didn't have a permit, although it would have made quite an interesting shot.

Back in mundane Hollywood, we raced to meet Paul Newman's fast-approaching deadline, with a cast that included Thelma Ritter, Eva Gabor, George Tobias, Marvin Kaplan and Robert Clary.

We were all awaiting the arrival of the quintessential Frenchman, Chevalier, who had a key scene and six Chevalier song classics, all to be shot in a single day. The reason was simple; his salary was $25,000 per day, an enormous sum in those times. Maurice had reestablished his fame and his price with *Gigi*. We had only been able to negotiate the deal because he was flying from France to New York City to perform his one-man show, and could stop off in Hollywood on his way.

We didn't inform him Hollywood was not on his way, but some 3,000 miles further. Why deprive him of the geography lesson?

Everything was ready for Maurice, including the set for a party to celebrate St. Catherine's Day with a stage on which Chevlier would perform, and the musical backing to allow us to directly record his singing, since there was no time for the usual prerecording session. All that was missing was Maurice himself.

The morning of the big day arrived. I waited impatiently in my dressing room until there was a knock at the door.

"Who is it?" I inquired, hopefully.

No response. Just another knock.

I threw the door open and there was Maurice, made up and in costume for his role, pointing to his throat. He gurgled something that sounded like "La laryngite," which I cleverly translated as "laryngitis."

I had hired $25,000 worth of hoarse throat.

It was the unexpectedly long plane flight from Paris that had destroyed his voice, but he was gamely showing up to collect his check. All we had to do was figure out how he was going to earn it, since he had to leave the next morning to make his New York opening.

There was only one way; Maurice bravely rasped his way through the festive scene with Joanne, Eva and Thelma, danced a bit, and gargled the six songs. Then he and his check left for the Big Apple, after promising me he would re-record everything when his voice returned.

Two weeks later, I flew to New York and Chevalier and I spent a day with his voice in a recording studio, where he redid it all, the dialogue, the songs, the laughter, back to his image on the screen. It was a difficult task, synchronizing the lip movement and remaining Chevalier.

The next morning I was awakened in my hotel room by a phone call from him. He asked, anxiously, "How were the songs?"

"They were good, Maurice."

"Only good?"

"Yes."

"I will do it all over again. You will pay me nothing more."

I almost fell out of bed. I hadn't realized his pride was greater than his renowned avarice. I had heard of a luncheon he had in Paris with Bob Hope and Mort Lachman, a friend and collaborator of mine, where Hope and Chevalier had stared at the check for hours after it arrived. Neither moved a muscle.

Finally, in desperation, Mort picked up the check and paid it so he could go to dinner.

Maurice recorded the songs again, "Louise," "In the Park in Paree in the Spring," "You Brought a New Kind of Love to Me," and others. This time, they had all the verve of the Chevalier boulevardier style at its best, and we were both more than satisfied.

A year later, in Paris, he invited Lucy and me to his home. We had a wonderful time. For lunch, Maurice served crackers and cheese.

They were delicious.

The song, "A New Kind of Love," became the title for the picture when Billy Wilder abandoned it for a film he was making and gave us permission to use it. I went to Sinatra and asked if he would make a new recording for the movie. I had known Frank since he had co-starred in *Double Dynamite*, a film I had written for producer Irving Cummings, Jr., who became a lifelong friend in spite of it. The movie came at a low point in Sinatra's career, and starred Frank with Groucho Marx and Jane Russell. Howard Hughes had insisted on *Double Dynamite* as the title, hoping audiences would think they were to get a view of Jane's astounding anatomy. They didn't. We had clothed her in dresses that reached to her chin.

Frank agreed to make the record, with one condition. He was just starting his own music publishing company and wanted to establish it in all areas. One of his clients was the great pianist, Erroll Garner, who had written the song hit "Misty." If I would hire Garner to write the score for the film, Frank would re-record the title song. I approved quickly and the deal was made. Garner was a fine composer, and there didn't seem to be any problem. He had composed "Misty."

One problem quickly developed. Erroll Garner did not read or write music, Frank had forgotten to mention it.

This had never interfered with Erroll's self-taught career before, which included many hits. But writing the score for a motion picture is a complicated mechanical process; the music must fit exactly to the length of every scene. Timing is as important as talent. Each note must be written down and fit the action onscreen precisely.

Impasse.

We finally solved it by hiring Leith Stevens, a talented film composer himself, to sit beside Garner as he improvised melodies for the film on his piano. When Leith heard something he liked, he would ask Garner to play it again so he could write the notes down.

Impasse. Inspiration came only once. Erroll couldn't remember the notes he had just played.

So Leith solved that problem with a tape recorder, which could. Then Leith would sort it out, write it down, and eventually we had a film score by Erroll Garner. Published by Frank Sinatra.

Paul and Joanne threw themselves into the spirit of the comedy without looking back. In a sense, we all worked like Erroll Garner, purely on the spur of the moment. We finished, happily, on a tight budget and schedule, just in time to release Paul for his next film.

The critics, who didn't know—or care—how the picture had been made, were mainly pleased by its completely formless informality, the product of desperation:

"Want to laugh until you almost split your sides? See 'A New Kind of Love!'

"The audience at the preview could be heard screaming a block away from the theater, and I was one of the screamers...

"This, my friend, is satire of the most hilarious sort. What's more, it's practically a new kind of picture! ..."—Hazel Flynn, *Los Angeles Citizen-News*

"'A New Kind of Love' is, I must warn you, strictly for the grownups in your family. It is the least inhibited sex-comedy fantasy from Hollywood since 'Irma La Douce,' and not dissimilar in its subject matter.

"Like 'Irma,' it is wacky and witty, acted with enormous joie de vivre...and it reminds us happily once again that Hollywood's know-how is still second to none...

I have, wisely, destroyed all negative reviews of everything I've done, so you won't find any here. Just take my word that they existed.

Looking back, as I find myself forced to do too often these days, I can still feel the exhilaration of writing a film from day to day, freewheeling ideas from moment to moment, nothing too outrageous to try, a freedom usually reserved for the Woody Allens of this business, of which there is only one.

Bob Hope as Eddie Foy and Jimmy Cagney as George M. Cohan "The Seven Little Foys." Cagney danced for free. Hope should have.

The Author, Cagney, Hope, and Jack Rose. We gave Cagney's horse a trailer. Cagney gave us a hit.

The Author and Jack Benny, backstage at "Beau James," proving neither could play the violin.

The Author, the kids, Cary Grant and a jeep. In Washington for, "Houseboat."

Maurice Chevalier, Sylvia Fine, Danny Kaye, and the Author. Only the Author couldn't sing.

Mel, Susan Gordon, Danny Kaye, Louis Armstrong. "The Five Pennies." It took Louis an hour to warm up his lip...but it was worth it.

Vittorio Di Sica, Sophia Loren, Clark Gable, and the Author.
Trastevere standing in for Naples. "It Started In Naples."

Sophia Loren and the Director, who is trying to direct the Blue Grotto.
"It Started In Naples."

Sophia, Gable, and the Director on Capri. "It Started in Naples." And almost finished there when the hurricane arrived.

Prime Minister Nehru, Mel, Chuck Heston, Elsa Martinelli, and the children. Behind the camera near "The Pigeon that took Rome."

The Director, Eva Gabor, and some biting dialogue. "A New Kind of Love."

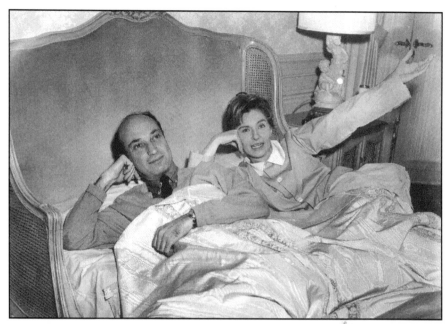

The Director in bed with Joanne Woodward. She is reaching for Paul Newman. "A New Kind of Love." Indeed.

The Director being directed by Kirk Douglas. The Negev Desert. "Cast A Giant Shadow."

Kirk Douglas, John Wayne, the Director. In the Nazi concentration camp that
was built in Rome. After they were thrown out of Israel. But they still
"Cast A Giant Shadow."

Dov Airfield. Frank Sinatra and the author looking for some nice Jewish girls.

The author and Sinatra, who has just remembered he has an insurance problem.

Chapter IX
1964–1966
The Promised Land

I went in a diametrically opposite direction in my next film, *Cast a Giant Shadow*, an attempt at a serious portrait of the Israeli War of Independence. Since that one film encompassed enough outrageous incidents to warrant a book of its own (the aforementioned *How to Make a Jewish Movie*) I'll be mercifully brief here.

Once more to quote a book jacket:

"Anyone who has managed to make a motion picture with Kirk Douglas, John Wayne, Frank Sinatra, Yul Brynner, Topol, Angie Dickinson, and Senta Berger that has not even earned back its negative cost obviously has an important message for the world: stay out of Israel; even if you're Jewish!

"But the true message of this book is exactly the reverse. While ostensibly detailing the misfortunes of its Hollywood writer-producer-director, it is in reality a perceptive, humorous, and warm account of an impossible people fighting an impossible war under impossible conditions.

"'Cast a Giant Shadow' was the biography of a brave and brilliant American, Colonel David 'Mickey' Marcus, who helped lead the Israeli Army to its 1948 victory and was killed on the last day of the fighting...Despite this tragic ending, or perhaps because of it, 'How to Make a Jewish Movie' is more than a behind-the-scenes look at movie-making and movie stars in a colorful, insane country. From this account of nearly three years of comic frustrations and desperation while preparing and shooting the motion picture, emerges an affectionate and vivid portrait of the Israeli people, that entire unworkable, unmanageable, incredible, defiant and, above all, impossible nation which refuses to disappear."

The book was almost as much of a success as the movie was a failure. Except in Israel. The Israeli Army took exception to some sections of the book, in which I printed a facsimile of that Army's bargain price list for use of

its men and weapons in the film, including: "Three tanks for burning purposes, 1,000 IL (Israeli Pounds); soldiers per day, 6.50 IL.; M.G. machine
gun, 34 IL; 9.81 mm mortars, 12.00 IL." Since an Israeli pound at the time
was worth about $3.00US, I can understand their fears that some Saudi
Arabian Prince might buy the Israeli Army as a souvenir. The Army proclaimed that most of the book was a fabrication.

At any rate, *How to Make a Jewish Movie* all but disappeared from Tel
Aviv bookstores, and I was given to understand I would do well to wear a
bulletproof vest (18.00 IL) when I stepped off the next frequent-flyer flight
to Lod Airport.

To my surprise, the Army was shouted down. I received a copy of the
book, mailed from Tel Aviv, that came from Ephraim Kishon, one of Israel's
most respected humorists and filmmakers. He had inscribed the title page,

"Certificate of Kashrit (Kosher)
"I hereby certify that the events listed in this book could, to my
best knowledge, happen, most probably happened, as a matter of
fact they must have happened, <u>at that time</u>.
Signed,
Ephraim Kishon, Chief Rabbi of the
Israeli Film Producers Association"

And the book review in the *Jerusalem Post* by Shimon Wincelberg read
in part:

"Mel Shavelson, one of Hollywood's most distinguished writer-producer-
directors of civilized light comedy, was one of the unfortunates who tried to
make a high-budget American film in Israel at a time when the country was,
you might say, not quite ready for such a bizarre undertaking…

"Strictly speaking, 'How to Make a Jewish Movie' is not a 'How to'
book, but a devastating (just because it is written with tolerance, wit, and a
good Jewish heart) 'How Not To.' Thus it emerges not only as a superb job of
story telling, but also for Shavelson's bruising honesty about all the things
which were his own damned fault.

"All told, the book is funny without being frivolous, and often quite
moving and informative about the 1948 war. Toward the end, Shavelson
even finds it possible to say:

"'But I would gladly do it again…for I had been given an insight
and a pride in my own people, their history and their aspirations,
their stubbornness and their gentleness, their kindness and their irri-

tating aggressiveness, and this had come, finally, to one who had been only vaguely conscious—and resentful—of his heritage.'"

Long after my Israeli adventure had been forgotten, I was reminded of it in the year 2006 by the continuing struggle between the small nation of Israel and the growing forces of the Palestinians, and Hezbollah and others, which had exploded into years of bloodshed, on both sides. What the final result will be by the time you read this, I have no idea. I can only hope that reason and right will at last prevail on both sides, based on my own past experience with an unusual human being while making *Cast a Giant Shadow*. I note the facts here:

> Amid the noisy and happy singing at a loud peace rally on a warm November night, a young law student named Yigal Amir took careful aim and killed the man who had once told me he didn't want to be played by John Wayne. The year was 1995, the scene was King's Square in Tel Aviv, and the victim was Nobel Prize winner, Prime Minister, and former Commander of the Israeli Army, Yitzhak Rabin.

Up to that fatal moment, Israel and the Palestinians had come closer to ending their Biblical confrontation than at any time in the previous 2,000 years. Today they are still far apart, but without the presence of one human being who was trusted by both—nay, by all sides, and wound up with a bullet in his back.

Fade out. The End. Or is it?

As the Israeli Army withdrew from territory won against overwhelming and bloody odds, and Hamas and Islamic Jihad promised a three-month truce where David once slew Goliath, everyone from Ariel Sharon to George Bush to Mahmoud Abbas to Condoleeza Rice and Yasser Arafat waited to see if Yitzhak Rabin's dream would ever come true.

Rabin had once helped me make a money-losing movie because he thought it might help the world understand the young country in which he was born. *Cast a Giant Shadow* was not the best, but the only Hollywood film besides *Exodus* that told the full story of Israel's creation in the face of the hatred that still exists on both sides and seems to get greater every day. Even now, Hollywood continues to show its reluctance to put its money where its heart is—on the big screen.

Today it seems barely possible that Rabin's dream may be more than a special effect. As a writer and director trying to get a film made, I first met him in 1965 as a soldier with a sense of humor in a simple office with no trappings of power or glory when he faced me across a rumpled desk. He was Commander of the Israeli Army and I needed his help. I assured him that John Wayne was not going to play him in the true story about the triumph of the tiny, outnumbered army he had helped lead in the troubled days of the creation of his nation. But I also told him that without John Wayne, the ultraconservative representative of the American right wing, there would never have been a movie in the first place. Rabin was interested in any motion picture that presented a favorable view of his nation to the world—or wherever the movie was allowed to play. I told him I had bought the story from MGM, who abandoned it after they were assured by several Arab nations that all MGM theaters in Egypt, Saudi Arabia, and other Middle Eastern markets would be closed down permanently if they made the film. And so I had taken the story to United Artists, because they owned no theaters anywhere. What's to close down?

Rabin smiled at that, a reflection of the schemes Israel used at that time to get along with its neighbors—they would withhold an Israeli stamp of admission on your American passport if you were going on to Jordan or Egypt, who frowned on any recognition of the country and might stop you at the border. Tourists were necessary to the economy of Israel, so they didn't worry about international formality.

I told Rabin that John Wayne figured in the film I was planning because when I took the story to almost every studio in Hollywood, all the executives turned it down, protesting that they had already given to the United Jewish Appeal, and who wanted to see a film about a Jewish General?

Since I had earlier made a film with Duke Wayne, I had cornered him in his Paramount office and pitched him the story of David "Mickey" Marcus, the American Colonel who helped lead the tiny Israeli Army to its 1948 victory and was the last soldier killed on the way to Jerusalem on the last day of fighting. When I finished, Duke got to his feet and took six and a half months to light a cigarette, or so it seemed. Then he exhaled and I could see my future disappearing in the tobacco smoke.

"That's the most American story I ever heard," Wayne said, "about an American officer who helped a little country get its independence. And gave his life to do it. What's your problem?"

I told him of all the executives who had turned me down, and why. He understood, but said, "I can't play Mickey. I'm too old, and besides, who'd ever believe I was circumcised?"

"I only want you to play an American General in the picture. That would make it Gentile by association."

Duke grinned.

I took his grin to the Mirisch Company at United Artists, and cashed it in. That's what I was doing in front of Rabin's desk that day. I already had signed Wayne, Kirk Douglas, Frank Sinatra, Yul Brynner, and Angie Dickinson. Hollywood, when you got below the executive level, wanted to be part of the film. Israel, in those days, was the darling of the Democratic world. I was told that with that cast, I could have shot the telephone book and made money. Unfortunately, I shot my screenplay instead. But that, as they say, is another story.

All I needed to complete my cast was the Israeli Army.

Rabin had listened to my tale and didn't hesitate. The IDF—the Israel Defense Force—would give us all the cooperation possible—after they read my screenplay.

That Rabin knew all about "script approval" indicated the speed in which he was ready to adapt to any combat situation, where his basic tenet was "Attack! Attack! Attack!" to keep the enemy off balance. If the script did not please all elements of the General Staff, all bets were off. Since, in Israel, the possibility of getting everybody to agree on anything is as remote as marinating a herring without sour cream, I was happy I hadn't torn up the return portion of my ticket on El Al.

But there was more. In the unlikely event that the script should be approved by a group who sometimes questioned the Bible, Rabin continued, all film shot in Israel would have to be reviewed by the military authorities before being shipped out of the country. I breathed easier. Since the film was to be shot in color, and since there was then not a single color processing laboratory in the—until that moment—Holy Land, I decided not to worry about it. Why get upset about a picture that was not going to be shot just because the film wasn't going to be developed? The fact that later, after we shipped the negative out of the country and had it expensively developed in Italy without Israeli interference, very few went to see it, merely emphasizes my point.

General Rabin, a sturdy, intelligent, tanned, and hardy military man, having stated his conditions, then relaxed. His battle was won. Was there anything else he could do for us?

I repeated, almost apologetically, that we would like to borrow his army for the picture. Yitzhak Rabin, in reply, reminisced for awhile about his days as a young officer fighting at Mickey Marcus' heroic side, and admitted the Israeli Army indeed owed the indomitable Col. Marcus a tremendous debt for helping organize and help lead it on the march to Jerusalem. The trouble was, however, that the Israeli Knesset didn't owe Marcus anything.

The Knesset, the Israeli Parliament, was then made up of twenty-six different political parties, none of whom would be caught dead in the same room
with any of the others. And Israel was fighting for its life, as usual, and didn't
have a penny to spare. How could General Rabin go to the Knesset and ask for
the funds so the army could help poor little Hollywood make a movie?

My technical advisor on the film was a small, warm, intelligent Israeli
Colonel named Gershon Rivlin, who had fought gloriously through the war
of Independence and become a close friend of David Ben Gurion, the Jewish George Washington. Everybody, Rabin included, had to listen to Gershon,
because George Washington listened to him. Rivlin had a simple Israeli solution. If the American production paid directly to the army every penny
above cost for everything that was needed, the Knessed need not even be
approached. They didn't even have to go to see the movie after it was finished. (They didn't.)

General Rabin nodded his approval of this end-around play. If we waited
for the Knesset, we would not get an answer until after the next war.

Of course, he didn't know there would soon be an attack launched from
Egypt that would become the Six Day War. Luckily, the Arab nations waited
until our war was over.

But that, too, is another story.

To my surprise, the screenplay was finally approved by General Staff
Headquarters with detailed instructions on how to improve the basic story
and restructure 31 scenes, including the official admonition that, "The love
affair between Col. Marcus and Magda [Senta Berger in the film] is being
exaggerated…The hero is being weakened by a sex-starved woman longing
to have an affair with the great General."

They were probably right. Mickey had become the first general in the
Army of Israel in 2,000 years. I could have skipped the love story and had a
better movie. I didn't.

But I still needed Yitzhak Rabin and the army. At our next meeting, he
understood our production problems—perhaps better than I did—and handed
me a detailed list of what it would cost to rent everything from soldiers in
uniform to tanks for battles and tanks for burning. For instance: Soldiers, IL
6.50 per day, Machine guns, IL 34, Tanks with Crews, IL 200 per hour, fuel
extra, Three Tanks for Burning Purposes, IL 1000. Since the IL (Israeli Pound)
was then worth about three dollars, it sounded like a bargain, but in those
days, it added up to a considerable sum in our budget. After the meeting, one
of my assistants saw the Army list and told me he had been on a Paramount
picture in Israel with Sophia Loren called *Judith*, and we were being charged
double by the Army.

I wanted to go back to Rabin and face him with it, but I was scheduled to meet with the Prime Minister, Levi Eshkol, and immediately seized the opportunity to ask Eshkol why the Israeli Army charged twice as much to play Jewish soldiers as they did to play Egyptian soldiers? In *Judith*, I explained, the soldiers played both sides, since no one cared to issue a casting call to the Egyptian army, but in my film they played only Israelis, and the army had doubled the ante.

Eshkol asked me a simple question: had the *Judith* producers bargained? Of course not, I replied, who bargains with the army?

And the producers paid every penny?

That's right. "So what did you expect," asked the Prime Minister. "Discounts?"

When I looked upset, he finally said, "Mickey Marcus was a friend. Let me speak to Rabin."

When the price lists from the army appeared on my desk the next day, every price had been cut in half. With Rabin's signature at the bottom.

I didn't know whether to thank Eshkol or Rabin. Since I was in Israel, I thanked God.

The picture went on to its stormy conclusion, including a sequence in the Negev Desert, when a line of Israeli tanks disguised to represent the Egyptian Tank Force roared up out of the desert in 120-degree heat and turned in perfect formation, firing their guns over the heads of the director and the cameramen who were photographing them, exactly as planned.

Before the shot was completed, they roared out of the scene. When I shouted my complaint to the Israeli officer at my side, he pointed to the radio in his hand and told me they had just been called up to the Syrian border, where they were needed to play the lead.

The scene was too long, anyway, he said.

The critics killed the film because I had used too many Hollywood stars and destroyed its credibility. How credible would it have been if I didn't have any stars, and the picture hadn't been made? Maybe that was their point.

For years, Yitzhak Rabin survived the film better than I did. He became a world leader in the cause of peace, and winner of the Nobel Peace Prize, and Prime Minister. He fought valiantly and often for his beliefs, but was willing to listen to all, even those of us from Hollywood.

And he received the same fate. Cut down by a critic who declared, "I have no regrets."

Yitzhak Rabin was buried in a hillside ceremony in west Jerusalem. Among those paying homages was King Hussein of Jordan and Presidents Bill Clinton, of the United States, and Hosni Mubarak, of Egypt. Even Yasser Arafat sent a message, "I am very sad for this awful event...I lost one of the most important, courageous men in Israel."

Rabin's 17-year-old granddaughter called him, "A pillar of fire before the camp, and now the camp is in darkness."

I don't know who will come along next to bring the light. I can only hope that those who have replaced him can do the job.

I am only honored to have met him in the course of a Hollywood picture that tried, and failed, to help.

The Israel I visited to shot, "Cast a Giant Shadow," in 1965, was a very different country from today's Israel. In 1965, most of the important men who had helped establish it as a state were very much alive and active in government, business and the army. They were firm in building a democratic state, freedom for all, strong in its alliance with the United States, admitting unlimited refugees from persecution in other states all over the world, turning the memory of Hitler's concentration camps into a country with freedom for all and especially freedom to attack their own government—in Israel, as I wrote, there are three sides to everything, Yes, No and Aha!

They were relatively poor, depending on assistance and contributions from Jews and friendly governments in the West, and offering a military island to the United States in the midst of the warlike Middle East. They fought off numerous wars from enemies who are still attacking them whenever possible.

Since that time, they have prospered, built businesses and exports that help support them, improved their military and their air force, and remained almost the only friend of the United States in the entire Middle East. Meanwhile, Hezbollah and Iran have continually attacked them with overwhelming forces, using thousands of missles launched continually against Israeli civilians. The United States has stood silent, and our press has attacked the Israelis for defending themselves with their air force. The wheel has come almost full circle.

The U.S. government is afraid to aid them too visibly. And oil determines U.S. policy most of the time.

Almost all the visionary founders are now gone, replaced by a generation to whom they have become distant history. Once the darling of the democratic world and easily remembered as victims of Hitler, Israel is now being portrayed in much of the Western press as a confused nation attacking its neighbors indiscriminately. Even their present military and civilian leaders seem confused.

I guess I am, too.

Chapter X
Sometimes I Loved Lucy
1967–1968

I needed a change from warfare to comedy again. I was much more comfortable with laughter than with gunfire, although my experiences with Israel in the War of Independence and Bob Hope in World War II had plenty of both, at times directed at me.

Along came a phone call from the indefatigable Lou Edelman about an impossible project involving America's favorite comedienne, Lucille Ball, actress, ex-wife, mother, director, producer, and studio owner. Lucy was at the height of her television career, but wanted desperately to get back on the big screen, where she had begun. She not only had found a property she wanted to star in, she had bought the rights from *Life* magazine, and also owned the studio that was going to produce it: Desilu, built by the fortune she and Desi Arnaz had made on the original *I Love Lucy*, although Desi's love didn't last as long as the series. Whose would? *I Love Lucy* is still on the air after 40 or more years.

What made the project impossible was its improbable subject matter: a Navy widow with eight children who marries a naval officer with ten. 18—count 'em—18.

Although it was based on the true story of the Beardsley family, Lucy had not been able to develop a script that made it seem credible and real. She had called on Lou Edelman for help. Lou, helpfully, had called on me.

I regarded the whole idea as an open challenge to my sanity and was about to hang up quickly when Lou reported that Henry Fonda was interested in playing the naval officer with ten children. Perhaps raising his daughter Jane made Fonda feel that was only a small problem.

Hank, of course, would bring a reality to the naval officer no one else could. He was one of my all-time favorite performers since *Mister Roberts*. Jack Rose and I had once flown to Italy when he had been shooting *War and Peace* with Audrey Hepburn, to try to talk him into playing Orville Wright in the story of the Wright Brothers we were preparing. He refused, and *The Wright Brothers* never got off the ground, but at least Jack and I had had another free trip to Rome. So I told Lou I would do Lucy's project.

Herman the Iceman negotiated a deal for me in which I would be paid more than ever before to write and direct. When I protested he hadn't also secured a piece of the profits, he told me it was nothing to worry about. None of Lucy Ball's past pictures had earned enough to defeat the studio bookkeeping, and since this time she owned the studio, the books were in her hands. Take the money and run. I did, and held it against Herman later when *Yours, Mine, and Ours* went through the box office roof and made me feel like Bryan Foy. But that, as they say, is another story.

I remember Don Hartman telling me that writers always had to lick a story, or beat it, or struggle with it, or hammer it into shape. The story was a palpable villain that tried its best to defeat you on every page. To help in the battle, I called in my friend Mort Lachman, a superb comedy writer who had survived years of Bob Hope and the Vietnam war Christmas shows, which he also directed. Mort was willing to help me as long as it didn't interfere with his golf.

We licked the story, beat it, struggled with it, and hammered it into shape. Lucy Ball approved the screenplay, and we started to shoot.

I would like to say it was a rollicking, happy experience, *I Love Lucy* with eighteen loveable kids and Mr. Roberts as their father, but it was anything but. Lucy Ball was used to being the whole show in television; she set the camera, controlled the lights, conducted the rehearsals, picked the shots. I wouldn't, or rather, couldn't, allow her to do it. After facing the entire Israeli nation and surviving not only the Arabs but the Israeli Army, I wasn't going to be stopped by one talented, redheaded comedienne.

I remembered the story of Golda Meir's confrontation with President Nixon, when she was asking for more military aid.

Nixon told her, "Golda, you have to understand my problem. After all, I am the President of over 200 million citizens."

"Mr. President," Golda answered, "you have to understand my problem. I am the President of six million Presidents."

So it was a question of who's President here? It was a constant competition. Lucy Ball was a very wise and competent television performer; she understood lighting and camera angles, and exactly what would make her photograph so her age didn't show. This had become necessary because her skin had deteriorated after decades of makeup, and light had to be directed from the front so it filled the wrinkles. I deferred to her in this, but in the matter of movement and interpretation, I insisted on being her director.

There is one key scene in the film, where she and Fonda are courting, and his children have spiked her drink to prevent her from becoming their mother. Unsteady from the alcohol, not realizing her drink was sabotaged, she accidentally spills food over one of the girls at the dinner table and stands up unsteadily to apologize to the man she realizes she has fallen in love with. She finds herself laughing at the situation and crying for herself at the same time, as the room spins about her.

In rehearsals, Lucy informed me no one could play that scene, and asked me to cut the speech.

"Lucy," I said, "you're right. No one in the whole world could play that scene and bring it off. Except you."

She played it. It was one of the outstanding moments in the film. There is no doubt in my mind that Lucille Ball was our greatest comedienne. She lasted a whole generation. But even she needed encouragement and persuasion.

The last shot of *Yours, Mine and Ours* was a close shot of Lucy. When I called, "Cut!" she looked up at me and asked, "Well, how did you enjoy working with me?"

And I said, foolishly, "Lucy, this is the first time I ever made a film with nineteen children." To my surprise, she started to cry. Obviously, she had expected the compliments she always received from her public. She didn't speak to me for months afterward, until the grosses of the picture started to come in. They were astounding. The film became one of the biggest hits of the season, and editorials were written about its successful portrayal of American family life, although a highly-extended family.

When Lucy did start to talk to me again, it was to complain. During the filming, she had sold her Desilu studio to Paramount for a very tidy sum, but she hadn't realized that Desilu owned the profits of the film. They were so great that, in essence, Paramount earned back the price it paid her for the entire studio on that one motion picture.

She had given away Desilu. It was my fault for not telling her the film would make too much money.

It took her awhile to recover, and accept the love of her fans that remained with her beyond her lifetime. *I Love Lucy* is still on the air, nightly. No other performer in history has held onto an audience for so long.

As long as there are televison sets, Lucille Ball will remain forever young.

Lucy herself came to forgive me for the picture's success. When I asked, hesitantly, if she cared to write a blurb for *The Eleventh Commandment*, when my novel about Israel was about to appear, she sent me this puff:

"Only Mel Shavelson could mix politics, religion, sex and the world oil crisis in this outrageously funny book."

My novel didn't enjoy the same success as our movie. Perhaps that was because Lucy Ball wasn't in it.

Chapter XI
James Thurber
My World—And Welcome To It

For those unfortunates too young to remember the days when we all impatiently awaited the next issue of *The New Yorker* in the hope of finding in it another story and/or cartoon by James Thurber to brighten our lives with its wonderful hatred of women, dogs, and children—not necessarily in that order—a brief introduction to one of the great literary figures of our time, who couldn't draw a straight line and made a memorable career out of it.

James Grover Thurber was born December 8, 1894, in Columbus, Ohio. No one else of note was ever born in Columbus, Ohio, except O. Henry, who left as soon as he could walk.

Thurber described his growing up in his pixilated family so accurately in *The Thurber Album* that for years no one in the family would speak to him.

He attended Ohio State University, which now houses the James Thurber Theater, but in those days barely housed Thurber himself. There he met a beautiful coed named Althea Adams, just before World War I interrupted the romance. Corporal James Thurber landed in Paris a week after the Armistice was declared. Peace made Paris even more attractive than usual. The GIs fortunate enough to be stationed there found themselves suddenly irresistible.

"Girls snatched overseas caps and tunic buttons from American soldiers," he wrote, "paying them in hugs and kisses and even warmer coin. A frightened Negro soldier from Alabama said, 'If this happened to me back home, they'd hang me.'"

Returning to Columbus, Jim was startled to find himself married to Althea one careless day in 1922. Althea turned from beauty to Thurber

"That's my first wife up there, and this is the present Mrs. Harris."

Woman almost immediately, forcing Thurber to move back to Paris and write the Great American Novel to support her. Thurber didn't quite manage. He got a job on the *Paris Herald-Tribune* for $12 a week; eventually, Jim was forced to leave for New York without her.

He struggled in Manhattan alone for awhile, until Althea returned to his bed and board—particularly, his board.

Came the day in February 1927, when Thurber met Harold Ross and was hired on the spot for the struggling new magazine that changed his life, *The New Yorker*.

Most of Thurber's best work was written for the magazine, and later anthologized in the books that helped make his fame. By 1935, he and the first Thurber Woman, Althea, were divorced, and just one month later Jim married the second Thurber Woman, Helen Muriel Wismer, who was to stay with him the rest of his life, although she knew there was always the danger she would end up on top of a bookcase.

Thurber has said he tried to draw a staircase with a woman at the top, but found he couldn't draw a staircase. Michelangelo had the same trouble with the Sistine Chapel, and had to lie on his back to manage it. Thurber solved his problem by turning the staircase into a bookcase.

When Harold Ross, editor of *The New Yorker*, wanted to know if the woman atop the bookcase was alive or stuffed, Thurber replied she had to be alive, since his taxidermist had assured him you could not stuff a woman, and, furthermore, Thurber declared, he wasn't responsible for the behavior of the people he drew.

Ross was certain Thurber was crazy.

The jury is still out.

Jim had lost the sight of his right eye when he was seven, when a childhood friend tried to play William Tell and mistook him for an apple. In 1941, Thurber's left eye began deteriorating and had to be operated on; his mother insisted on consulting an Astrologer, who set the most propitious time for the surgery. It wasn't.

The surgeon told Jim his mother was, "As nutty as a fruit cake." But he operated on the given date.

It is rumored the Astrologer left town, perhaps having had a premonition. The operation was far from successful.

Thurber's good eye deteriorated until he could barely see, the ultimate calamity for an artist, even one who drew badly. That didn't prevent the nearly-blind Thurber from writing and drawing some of his best works, using special lenses and huge drawing tools, for almost twenty years. Helen nursed him through this black period, at times acting as both secretary and a seeing-eye dog.

When Jim was totally blind, he was visited by a *Life* magazine photographer, who handed him a lighted flashlight and asked him to draw something in the air with it, while the camera lens was kept open. Thurber produced a memorable drawing, in light, of a Thurber dog. It appeared in the pages of *Life*.

His last sketch.

James Thurber died November 2, 1961, after a long illness.

Helen was at her hairdressers at the time.

As Jim had long predicted.

You now know much more about James Thurber than I did when I first met America's greatest humorist—only Mark Twain might challenge that, but not after he saw Thurber's cartoons—when my then-agent (some men change wives; I change agents) Jules Goldstone asked if I would like to do a television series based on Jim Thurber's writings and drawings, to which he had just secured rights. It's a sign of our teenage times that his name and his work have been forgotten so quickly, but this was a couple of decades ago, when Thurber himself was very much alive and, as usual, kicking.

Today's television sitcoms are so far from Thurber's world that it is difficult to remember how relatively new television series were in the '50s, and how it was hoped the situation comedy might develop into some sort of American art form, as did the best of Hollywood's musicals. Also, Thurber was then in need of money, which may have influenced his aesthetic standards when he made the decision to enter the crass but sometimes lucrative electronic medium. Shakespeare, down on his luck after a poor opening night of *King Lear*, might well have succumbed himself. I know I did.

I quickly agreed to Goldstone's proposal—even though no money was involved. Just the opportunity to meet with Thurber, and to find a way to transform his gold into the dross of weekly television was more than enough.

I flew to London with Lucy—my Lucy—and with Rich and Lynne, on the start of a European vacation. We met with Jim and his wife, Helen, in a shabby residential hotel near Piccadilly, his home away from home. It was the kind of small, sagging British hostelry that might have been created from a Thurber drawing which had started out to be the Houses of Parliament and grew weary on the way. I remember he was leaning on a cane and Helen's arm as they came down into the tiny lobby. We had never met, but he looked more than vaguely familiar. Of course. The Thurber Man. He was small, somewhat frail, with a scraggly moustache, unkempt hair, on the arm of a large Thurber Woman. Helen was obviously in control, of her husband and probably the rest of the universe.

We were greeted warmly—I doubt he had any idea who I was, but I represented the hope of financial gain—and we all sat down to have lunch. Thurber was as whimsical and amusing as his writings, and treated me as an equal, proving he really didn't know who I was. I explained to him exactly what a television pilot was—the name "pilot" seemed to amuse him—and that I intended to write one based on his "If Grant Had Been Drinking at Appomatox," and send it to him for his approval before going any further.

Our lunch had arrived, and as we discussed how to dramatize the story, he placed both of his hands on his steak to locate it. For the first time I realized he was now almost totally blind; he lived in darkness, which hadn't affected his drawing, his writing, or his sense of humor. It impressed me so strongly that the image remained with me for years, long after the Thurber

"All Right, Have It Your Way—You Heard a Seal Bark!"

sitcom we called *My World—And Welcome to It* had gone to its unjust reward, along with Thurber himself. It was to be the inspiration for the movie *The War Between Men and Women* years later.

But if anyone had told Jim Thurber that afternoon, when his career was stagnating and *The New Yorker* was rejecting some of his cartoons, that many of us would still remember his stories and drawings today, just past the hundredth anniversary of his birth, he would have said what the Thurber Wife told the Thurber Husband when he told her he had seen a golden Unicorn in the garden, eating the lilies: "You are a booby and I will have you put in the booby hatch."

Only after his passing was Jim's work taken as a serious look at the human condition, which is one indication of how serious the human condition is. In the obituaries, when they were absolutely certain that he was dead, the Great Minds of journalism finally admitted his unassuming work to its true place in world literature.

To Thurber, Death was a temporary annoyance, not to be compared with Marriage, which can be permanent, if we allow women to have their way.

On the tombstone of Muggs, The Dog That Bit People, he placed an inscription: "Cave Canem. Beware of the Dog."

Beware indeed. Thurber firmly believed Muggs would come back from the grave to bite people. So if Thurber hasn't, he probably doesn't care to. Among the final tributes—to Thurber, not Muggs—is this:

> "If there was any doubt about Thurber's powerful effect on literate mankind, it was dispelled. He was most often compared to Mark Twain, as a confirmed American original who had lent another dimension to the art of humor. As Red Smith wrote in the *New York Herald Tribune*, 'Jim Thurber was the greatest humorist of his time and probably America's greatest since Mark Twain…one of the few great humorists in literary history.'"

The Times of London not only likened him to Mark Twain but to Lewis Carroll:

> "What he did was manufacture a unique world with its own creatures, its own foibles, its own madness—all remarkably similar to the real world, similar enough so we can laugh and then feel vaguely uncomfortable. It is a creation not to be taken lightly.
> "As for the man, he passed through with brilliance, suffered and caused some suffering, and then passed on. But most of all, he left something elegant and important behind."

Final Curtain

Something "elegant and important" does not conjure up the image of a television sitcom, but that was what I was discussing with Jim Thurber that distant day in the Thurberesque London hotel. He is one of the few authors, outside of the Bible, whose books have never gone out of print; while all of my own have, shortly after publication. I was more than reverent in discussing his writings. Jim Thurber wasn't. "We don't want to be immortal," he reminded me, "just rich. Don't let literature get in the way of television."

He also advised me always to take a pessimistic view of life, because it was least likely to prove false.

I came away from that meeting feeling blessed to have had the opportunity to meet that warm and friendly misogynist. I believe it was W.C. Fields who said, "No man who hates dogs and children can be all bad."

Add to the mix the female sex, and you have a reasonable facsimile of Thurber's credo. His real genius lay in making people believe it was just a facade.

With great enthusiasm, I returned to Hollywood and, in the current vernacular, proceeded to knock out a script, happily in line with Thurber's loathings. It didn't take long, because I found a way to include portions of three Thurber stories, as well as a few of his best drawings.

I sent the "pilot script" off to him and waited anxiously for his verdict. It didn't take long. He wrote a detailed letter, chastising me for being "too faithful to Thurber to make money." But he approved of the style and the characterizations, and that was heartening enough to enable me to rewrite very quickly and secure his blessing for the series.

I was home free, I thought.

Not quite.

Jules Goldstone insisted that Thurber was not exactly a hot box office name in the TV world. We would have to shoot a pilot film at our own expense, and present it to the networks in finished form. Networks, apparently, couldn't read, which is why Thurber had to be introduced to them as a television show, which they could understand if we indicated where the commercials would fall.

This first incarnation was known as *The Secret Life of James Thurber*, and featured Arthur O'Connell playing Thurber and explaining to the camera, "My name is John Monroe. Some people say my name is James Thurber, but that couldn't be because I have it on good authority there is no such person as James Thurber. My authority is James Thurber himself, who disclaims any resemblance to any person, living or dead or in a state of suspended animation. This is the State of Connecticut, which is more or less the same thing…"

After sketching a typical Thurber Woman, he continues, "I don't know if you can tell it by this drawing, but I hate women. Of course, I married one, but there wasn't anything else around. There never is. That's how they get you."

To save money, I directed the pilot on 16mm film, in black and white, with only a rudimentary attempt to animate some of the Thurber cartoons. Still, I thought it retained the Thurber essence. The pilot made the usual rounds, ABC to CBS to NBC, and they each made their informed judgement: who the hell is Thurber? It sank without a trace, except for a brief one-shot as a special on the *Alcoa-Goodyear Theater* in January of 1959.

Regretfully, I informed Jim and Helen Thurber of the sad facts, and abandoned the whole notion I had started with—an intelligent situation comedy.

A few years later, Jules Goldstone put together another pilot, starring Orson Bean as the Thurber character, written and directed by others. Although it was shot in glorious color on glorious 35mm film, it, too, did not sell and disappeared quickly.

It was about this time that James Thurber left us to meet Muggs and others of his creations somewhere in a Thurbersque heaven.

Although I had returned to the bigger screen, but smaller subjects, Thurber remained an unshakable image in my mind. For awhile I toyed with the idea of a musical based on his blindness, but it never seemed to jell. Thurber himself had starred in *The Thurber Album*, a collection of his works presented on Broadway, but it had enjoyed only a mild success.

By that time, Sheldon Leonard, perhaps best-known to the masses as Harry the Horse in *Guys and Dolls*, was at the zenith of his career as a television producer. I had known Sheldon since the beginning of the Danny Thomas show, *Make Room for Daddy*, when the Morris office representing Leonard—and practically everyone else—came to me with the same old story: Sheldon needed a job, he had directed a couple of television shows, would I approve of him to direct the Danny Thomas opus, whose pilot had just been sold to ABC? Fortunately, I approved, and Sheldon helped make that show an Emmy winner many times over and a goldmine for all associated with it. I bought the home I live in, all 3 acres, with my income from it.

Sheldon, in partnership with Thomas, was now the biggest force in network television, with a fistful of successful shows including *I Spy, The Dick Van Dyke Show* and *Andy Griffith*. He also had a unique contract with NBC, which guaranteed him two television series a year on the air, the closest thing to a license to steal in the industry.

Here was my opportunity. Sheldon knew who James Thurber was. He also had a fair idea of who I was. I asked him, as a favor, to run the Thurber pilot I had shot. He did, and immediately we were in business. The reason was simple: with Sheldon, you didn't have to make a pilot. If he said it was on the air, it was on the air.

In May of 1969, having secured all the rights from Helen Thurber, who was now in charge of the Thurber estate, I directed the first episode of what we called *My World—And Welcome To It!* and based it largely on "If Grant Had been Drinking at Appomatox." Sheldon had induced Danny Arnold, who had produced the highly successful *That Girl* series starring Marlo Thomas—Danny Thomas's daughter, of course—and was a gifted and somewhat insane comedy writer as well, to produce the series. Danny Arnold was a certified character. Large, forceful, outspoken, rugged good looks, with a cigar usually clamped between his teeth, he was the opposite of the stereotype of a Hollywood writer. He dressed well whether he could afford it or not, and had a seemingly unending supply of story ideas, without which no weekly television series can survive. For the Thurber role, he suggested an actor he had worked with named William Windom. I had never heard of him.

But lightning had struck twice. Danny had the same acid view of humanity as Thurber, and Bill Windom was a comedian who didn't seem to be a comedian; his humor was internal and bubbled out through his whimsical persona.

In this first episode, Joan Hotchkis played the long-suffering Thurber wife, and Lisa Gerritsen, the ten-year-old daughter, who was ages-wiser than her absent-minded father, who pretended to hate them both.

The opening titles of this new version—with much-improved animation, but the same terrible Thurberesgue drawings—rolled up on the screen, bumping into a drawing of Muggs, the dog:

JAMES THURBER

My World—
And Welcome To It

HARCOURT, BRACE AND COMPANY, NEW YORK

My World—And Welcome To It
Based on stories, inspirational pieces, cartoons, and things
that go bump in the night
by
JAMES THURBER

Muggs had had it. With a loud growl, he lunged for the name "JAMES THURBER," which immediately developed legs and ran for its life off the screen, followed by the triumphant dog. Windom, as John Monroe, approached the camera. He looked like all Thurber men, vaguely unhappy, righteously unattractive, and frightened to death of Life, somewhere in the gloom and darkness stage left. In the revised opening monologue, he told the television audience, "It's obvious now that women will eventually destroy the male sex and replace it with something involving transistors. As for dogs, they have been getting the upper hand for centuries, and the only reason they haven't taken over the world is because they don't want it."

Helen Thurber took very seriously her mission of protecting Jim's work. We sent her, with some trepidation, the four scripts Danny Arnold and I had prepared before the series took the air. I have a letter from Helen Thurber, dated July 9, 1969. These were some of her comments:

Dear Mel:

Your script, "The Night the House Caught on Fire," is by far the best, although it does seem a bit crowded. I love the sneezing house (a lovely idea) and think a lot of the reminiscent sequence is funny. It seems a pity to bury The Unicorn in the Garden in a story so essentially about grandfather, but that's just my opinion...I also liked, "The Disenchanted," although it has absolutely nothing to do with Thurber except the title...About the other two...

...Oh, well, I guess two out of four is a good average. Unhappily, I read the two bad ones first, and was thoroughly disheartened. I hate to blast them like this, especially when you yourself are so surrounded by the problems and difficulties of a Broadway play (Frank Gorshin, for God's sake!) and are probably getting ready to leave for the pleasures of a New York August. I really enjoyed your script (although I would like to see

Unicorn not drowned out by Barbara Frietchie and Grandfather) and I think The Disenchanted is good, and should play well. The other two are strictly, "For God's sake, Sally, switch to another channel!" scripts.

Love,
Helen
(Mrs. James Thurber)

It was easy to see where Jim got his attitude against all women, but I must say Helen's judgements were often right on the mark—sometimes too much so.

NBC put the first show on the air on September 15, 1969, and Thurber immediately shook up the world of the sitcom.

Cecil Smith, in the *Los Angeles Times*:

"'My World and Welcome To It' is reminiscent of nothing in television, not even Mel Shavelson's earlier attempt to bring the wondrous humor of Thurber to the little screen...

"The show opens with William Windom against a great Thurber drawing of a house which, as he talks, turns into a devouring Thurber woman...

"He helps his daughter with her history lesson by telling (and acting out) Thurber's, 'If Grant Had Been Drinking at Appomatox.' The impending visit of her teacher brings forth a wild fantasy of a rapacious beauty attempting to seduce him, which ends up with the woman on top of the bookcase...

"Shavelson is fond of telling of the time Thurber went to see the movie Samuel Goldwyn made of 'The Secret Life of Walter Mitty,' another Thurber classic, with a group of his friends. On the way out, Thurber turned to them and asked, 'Anyone catch the name of that flick?' I don't think the late humorist would ask that question about 'My World—And Welcome To It.'"

After the first half-hour episode of *My World* was aired, the critics were almost unanimous in their relief at finding that intelligent life could exist on NBC. So was the public, which started to tune in—in large numbers. *My World* achieved a creditable Nielsen rating, began rising further, and was the winner of the Emmy Award for Best Comedy Series of the 1969-1970 season.

And was promptly cancelled to make room for a half-hour program starring Red Skelton.

In part, I have only myself to blame; after the opening show, I departed for Philadelphia for the tryout of *Jimmy*, and its disastrous Broadway opening. I kept in touch with Danny Arnold and Sheldon, helping to rewrite some of the shows by mail, and flew back to Hollywood to direct an episode I had written, "The Night the House Caught Fire," but I should have remained in Hollywood throughout; I doubt I could have prevented the inevitable, but at least I could have shouldered more of the blame. Danny Arnold did a yeoman's job, as did Sheldon, but all the king's horses and all the king's men couldn't change NBC's eye on the bottom line. Unfortunately, Red Skelton didn't help them much; his show was also cancelled before it could get off the ground.

In a way, this marked the end of a television era. When *Make Room for Daddy* went on ABC back in 1954, the network hopefully kept the struggling show on the air for three years, until it developed a following and got a decent rating. Of course, when it did, it immediately switched to CBS, which had more stations, where it became the number one show on the air for several seasons. But then, costs were minimal compared with today. Quality was affordable.

Today, the prevailing television philosophy is to throw a new show to the wolves if it doesn't gain an audience immediately, sometimes defined as three weeks. To make an impression in so short a time, it usually requires shock value: flagrant sex, four-letter words, violence, crime. A show with human values and true humor is supposed to appeal only to members of the AARP. *Seinfeld* was an oasis in the desert.

Thurber is a cultivated taste. One abbreviated season was all NBC allowed us for cultivation. Only the British, that civilized nation of civilized tastes, kept playing and replaying the series in its entirety three separate times over the BBC.

Of course, mad dogs and Englishmen go out in the midday sun.

But, again, Jim Thurber refused to die. Years later, both Danny Arnold and I were at Warner Brothers working on separate projects when I told him my notion for a Broadway musical based on Thurber's blindness. The notion was outrageous enough to interest him.

Together, we wrote a screenplay using another Thurber title, *The War Between Men and Women*. It was an offshoot of *My World* on a more serious level, and concerned the failing eyesight of a Thurber-like cartoonist who met a hated female who had both children and a dog, and found himself stumbling into matrimony against his will. It would, like the television series, incorporate cartoons and animation of Thurber's drawings, including his classic work on world peace, "The Last Flower." Helen Thurber promised cooperation.

We submitted the screenplay to Warner Brothers, at that brief moment headed by Dick Zanuck, Darryl's offspring, and Dick immediately rejected it. Who the hell remembered James Thurber? Or wanted to see a movie based on a failed television series?

Well, someone did. My agent (the William Morris Office now) called with a message. A client had read our screenplay and wondered if we would allow him to play the lead?

His name was Jack Lemmon. There was something Thurberesque about Jack himself, illustrated in his best-remembered roles, the confused Gendarme in *Irma La Douce*, the female-impersonating musician in *Some Like It Hot*, and the forlorn patsy locked out of his own flat in *The Apartment*.

When we told Dick Zanuck that Lemmon had agreed to be our star, and we were taking the picture elsewhere, he was disturbed. "I suppose now you guys will make me look like a snook," he said. I realized he meant "schnook," and thought he was one, until the picture was released and the New York critics leaped on us for desecrating their James Thurber.

The film was made by CBS, through CBS Films, its theatrical operation at the time. Making the movie was a joy; Lemmon was the least movie-star-like movie star I ever directed, and one of the most talented. He could lift a comic situation to heights Danny Arnold and I could only pray for; and remove both the acid and the saccharine from the moments of the artist's going blind, in much the same way as Thurber himself did.

The Thurber wife was played by Barbara Harris, too pretty to be the traditional image, but she made up for it by being a loveable kook, as irrational as any Thurber Woman. In our later film together, *Mixed Company*, Barbara stepped off the plane at our Phoenix location with a huge vegetable pulverizer strapped to her back, so she wouldn't miss her morning carrot juice. She restricted her diet to liquid vegetables throughout the production.

Lisa Gerritsen played one of her children in the *War*, and the incomparable Jason Robards played another child, Barbara's ex-husband, who returned to her in the middle of Barbara's wedding to Lemmon.

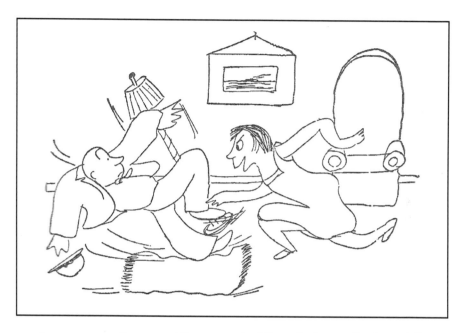

In one scene, Jason and Lemmon imbibe a little too freely and fantasize an animated war between the sexes, as in Thurber's famous sketch.

They then take their common hatred of the opposite sex out on Barbara, now Lemmon's bride and Jason's ex, who fights back fiercely.

BARBARA
I'm ashamed of you! You have no
regard for women! You're setting
a terrible example for our daughter
and you're talking about me as if
I were a-a-a motel room the two
of you shared for a night!

LEMMON
That's an unfortunate choice of
a simile.

BARBARA
If you're such a damned good
writer, how come Brentano's
can't give your book away?

LEMMON
That's beneath you.

BARBARA
You hardly know me! How do
you know how low I can stoop?

JASON
Barbara—

BARBARA
Shut up! Everybody just shut up!

She runs up the stairs.

That was supposed to end the scene, but Barbara, too far into the role to stop living it, turned at the top of the stairs, and shouted, "Come to bed—one of you!"

An ad-lib. The biggest laugh in the picture, Danny and I often took bows for it when Barbara wasn't around.

Although the New York critics savaged us when the film opened, those who were not self-appointed guardians of the Thurber legend were much more kind. The further west from New York City, the kinder.

> "The love affair Melville Shavelson and Danny Arnold originally had with the works of James Thurber in their Emmy-winning 'My World And Welcome To It' series continues in this amusing clambake of a Thurber-like character portrayed by Jack Lemmon...a first-rate comedy peopled with some delicious humans as well as a pregnant pooch...Film will need hard-sell, however, in certain situations"
>
> —*Daily Variety*, Hollywood.

As usual, *Variety* was prescient. Cinema Center Films, the CBS theatrical wing which produced it, shortly afterwards expired, like Muggs, and never returned. But there were other rewards that remain:

"... A delightfully warm comedy suggested by the writings and drawings of James Thurber. It is one of those rare movies capable of evoking an inner glow that continues long after you've left the theater.

"Jack Lemmon, Barbara Harris, and Jason Robards share top billing. Lemmon and Miss Harris are beautifully matched here and complement each other perfectly, with nicely restrained and deeply motivated performances that reveal both the humor and the humanness of the characters. Robards gives one of his best screen performances in some time...

"Throughout the film the Thurber drawings are used to good effect, and one especially delightful sequence features a war between men and women as enacted by these animated drawings, with Lemmon and Robards joining in. When Robards, a photographic journalist, is later suddenly killed during an assignment in Vietnam, animation is again used as Lemmon attempts to explain to Lisa Gerritsen the purpose of her father's life and work. For this Arnold and Shavelson have magnificently incorporated Thurber's tender and touching parable, 'The Last Flower.'"

—The Hollywood Reporter.

The *Reporter* critic also reminded us of our debt to Bob Dranko, who handled the difficult animation beautifully. Dranko could draw as terribly as Thurber himself when the occasion demanded it, and worked night and day in this era before computer animation to do all the design and action by hand, allowing us to use a system of front projection into which Lemmon and Lisa could walk and act and react to the animated drawings, before computerized special effects made it all too simple.

Arthur Knight, in *The Saturday Review*, headed his notice "The Men from Sitcom," and continued: "What makes a movie different from a television program? Some part of the answer may be found in the film, *The War Between Men and Women*, which has reversed the usual direction of going from screen to tube. Its origins lie in 'My World—And Welcome To It,' a series that provided more than a few sprinkles in television's sad wasteland and was prematurely axed...Shavelson and Arnold refused to let their 'World' die. Instead, they went to work on a movie script that moved their central character identifiably closer to Thurber. He became not merely a cartoonist with a good many hangups, but a cartoonist who was going blind. Best of all, they made room in their movie for extended passages of cartooning based not only on *The War Between Men and Women*, but on Thurber's seemingly naive, thought-provoking parable *The Last Flower*.

"In TV-land, one neither laughs uproariously nor weeps copiously. Watching *The War Between Men and Women*, one does both…The picture has a warmth, a humor and a sense of telling it like it is (or like it might be) that totally divorces it from the television medium."

One last note, in a critique of Jack Lemmon's career, written in 1978 by critic Will Holtzman:

> "Lemmon was becoming a superior actor for having been an adequate director on the film, *Kotch*. The proof was his next performance in Melville Shavelson's sleeper, *The War Between Men and Women*…
>
> The film is a unique melding of harsh wit and quirky slapstick, with an equally novel blend of film and animation. Like Thurber, Lemmon's Peter Wilson must contend with rapidly deteriorating eyesight in a world he views as barely sublimated warfare. His acid personality refuses to accept imminent blindness with even an iota of self-pity, and he walls himself off from others in whom he detects the least trace of sympathy."

Maybe that's a good thing, in the light of the demise of Cinema Center Films shortly after the picture's release. But I'll accept that last as a compliment.

Danny Arnold, of course, went on to considerable fame and fortune afterwards, as the creator—and owner—of the fantastically successful police sitcom *Barney Miller*. It enabled him to afford his true métier, that of owner of sick and lame race horses, which he pursued fanatically throughout the days I knew him. He asked me to join him on *Barney Miller*, but I refused, as I also refused to bet on his horses, with even more reason. Danny was warm and generous and extremely talented in every area, on his good days. On his lesser days, he hollered on people and fired anyone who displeased him, because he felt he could do their job better than they did. Which he insisted on proving. Becoming a multimillionaire didn't change him at all. Even when he was flat broke he had acted like one. He drove a white Rolls-Royce almost every day of his life, and on a few of those days he could afford it. He rented hotel suites as if they were motel rooms.

When the ubiquitous William Morris Office brought him the series idea by writer Ted Flicker that eventually became the highly-successful cop show *Barney Miller*, starring Hal Linden, Danny wrote his own version and made a pilot film, which did not sell. Somewhat disheartened, he invited me to view it at the CBS studios in the Valley. It was basically a portrait of the home life of a police captain and his wife, interspersed with a modicum of detective work. I was not impressed. I told Danny to run a film called *Detective Story*, from the play by Cornellian Sidney Kingsley, which won several Academy Awards with Kirk Douglas playing the lead. All the action in the original stage production took place in one set, the Headquarters of a New York City Detective Squad. Different characters were logically brought into the single set, where all the drama and comedy were acted out.

Danny ran the motion picture and saw my point. *Barney Miller* would take place in detective headquarters. That is when he offered me a piece of the show if I joined him, and I refused. That was also when he didn't offer a sizeable enough piece to Ted Flicker, who later sued Danny and collected a couple of million.

My refusal was validated by Danny himself after the show was on the air and a huge hit. He asked me if I would write an episode. I was making a film, but as a favor for an old friend, I wrote one.

He rewrote every line.

I think that was his purpose in asking me.

The problem with Danny was that he was not Walter Mitty; he was everybody Mitty imagined.

He's gone now, but every time I see a white Rolls-Royce, I wonder if it's paid for.

Chapter XII
End of an Era

How do you end an era? Simple, make the best motion picture of your career.

A generational change was taking place in the motion picture industry, which I was barely aware of. When *War* was finished, the President of Cinema Center Films, Gordon Stuhlberg, whom I had known very well when he was the lawyer for the Writers Guild, was so impressed with the movie that he sent me a newspaper clipping about a minister who had adopted a group of interracial children into his family. Gordon suggested I make a fictional movie about something similar, and Cinema Center would produce it. Was I willing?

This was a little like Cary Grant asking if he could tell Jack Rose and me a story. When the head of the studio suggests a project, you immediately go to work on it, with no questions asked. But, almost as I was reading the clipping, Cinema Center Films went belly up and Gordon Stuhlberg joined the army of the unemployed. Murphy's Law again.

However, the idea of an interracial family intrigued me; it was 1973, the first waves of boat people were arriving from Asia; blacks were still unacceptable in most of white society. Telling their story through children might be the best way to get a serious subject before the unpredictable moviegoing public. And comedy, good comedy, is never threatening. The fact that honest treatment of racial problems was years ahead of its time and public acceptance in the land of the free and the home of the brave, never deterred me.

I should have remembered *World in a Jug*. This novel, which I had bought for filming, concerned a little Negro girl (the unwieldy term,

161

"African-American," had not yet been coined) who was orphaned on a trip to Paris when her parents were killed in a traffic accident and she was left in the unwilling hands of an alcoholic, white American jazz vocalist in the twilight of his career. He immediately tried to get rid of her and send her back to the U.S.—and found all the planes grounded by a 24-hour airline strike, a French specialty. The entire story took place in those 24 hours that forced them together in an intimacy both resented. It was told as the improbable love affair between that small, 12-year-old black child, and the faded, 45-year-old alcoholic who had to fight both the bottle and his aversion to small children, regardless of their color.

By the end of the 24 hours, they both have recognized each other as human beings, just as the strike ends and she must return to what they both know is her segregated family in the United States—from a Paris that knows no color line. The end of an unstated love affair.

My first move was to change the singer to an American vaudeville comic, down on his luck and reduced to being a stage wait at Paris' Crazy Horse Saloon, to cover the time needed to undress the chorus girls for their next indecent exposure. The Comic's act was built around a nondescript dog which had been trained to do nothing at all but lay onstage and disobey him. As the story opens, the Comic has been fired, and is outraged to learn the dog has been rehired.

Obviously, the vaudevillian had to be Bob Hope. The dog did not have to be Rin Tin Tin.

Bob didn't care for the idea. Over the years, I kept sending the screenplay back to him, and getting a negative response or none at all; those close to him told me they tried many times to persuade him to take the role, but he always refused. I got the impression that neither he nor the American public was ready to accept a story in which a small black child was as intelligent and more responsible than a white, alcoholic comedian.

Some years later, when the invisible color bar was lifted, Bob was among the first who helped establish a 10-year-old black boy as one of the comedy stars of television. But by that time, the world had changed. Even the *World in a Jug*.

In the hope of securing some other leading man, I gave the screenplay to Jack Karp, then head of Paramount in Hollywood, He called me into his office and asked me if I could honestly pick a black child up in my arms and kiss it, her, or him? When I told him that might be up to the child, he dismissed the whole idea.

So I changed the hero back to the original—the has-been American jazz vocalist—and sent it to Frank Sinatra. The screenplay came back from Sinatra with no comment. Perhaps if the child had been not only black, but Jewish, and with only one eye, the story might have appealed to him. After all, Sammy Davis, Jr. was all of these. But if you had Sammy's tremendous talent, it didn't matter if you were black, white, or polka dot.

Some day, I hope to make *World in a Jug*. But it may seem an antique. As I may now be.

It was years later that I determined to make the film about an interracial family, even though Gordon Stuhlberg, who had suggested it, had been ousted from the studio, and Cinema Center itself had disappeared.

For assistance, I called on the talents of my collaborator on the biggest box office success I had ever enjoyed, *Yours, Mine, and Ours*. Mort Lachman was an ideal choice for this story. In addition to his genius for comedy, he had no prejudice against anyone or anything except a golf ball that refused to go into the little hole.

Mort worked in a rented apartment near Hope's home in Toluca Lake, which was Mort's somewhat office. I used to battle a typewriter in his Sears Roebuck-furnished living room while Mort battled a little white ball on a putting rug he had set up next to our desk. Every once in awhile he would look up in my direction and solve whatever story problem or punch line was holding us up, and then go back to trying to sink a hole-in-one on the carpet. Until he did, I didn't hear from him again.

We would have finished that screenplay in half the time if my collaborator had been Tiger Woods.

The story we came up with we called *Mixed Company*. It concerned a football coach suffering through a losing season. His warmhearted wife was determined to have more children to add to the three who were already making the coach's life miserable.

When a visit to the doctor convinces them that a childhood bout with the mumps has rendered her husband sterile, the wife suggests they adopt a child.

Pete, the coach, was played by Joe Bologna, and the always off-the-wall Barbara Harris played his wife. The key scene went like this;

JOE

Whoa! Who! Hold it down!
What are you and the doctor
doing? Am I here? Am I in the
room? Adoption! It's tough
enough loving your own kids!

BARBARA

You promised me a baby.

JOE

I promised you my baby!
I tried. Can you deny I
tried? You know anybody
could try harder?

BARBARA

You said you wanted me to
be happy. You said you...

JOE

Barbara, don't make jumps
on me! You always make
jumps on me! Whoa!
Whoa! You realize what it means
to adopt a baby? Somebody
else's kid they found in an
ash can some place? Maybe
the father was a murderer—a
sex fiend—

DOCTOR

...a football coach...

JOE

...a doctor! How would you
know? Ten years from now,
(more)

(cont.)
the kid might have a nose
over here! I wanna know
what my kid's gonna look
like. An adopted baby,
there could be something
terribly wrong with him,
you wouldn't find out for
years!

BARBARA
You take the same chance
with husbands.

Barbara, in a convenient twist of the story, works as a volunteer in a
home that specializes in the adoption of interracial children. Without
forewarning her husband, she has arranged to take one of them to a
basketball game on a trial basis. As they watch through the window of
their house, the child arrives in a car driven by the Supervisor of the
Children's Home, and steps out:

FREDDIE WILCOX is ten years old, unmistakably black, and
unmistakably appealing. He is frightened but by no means be-
wildered. He pauses to look at the house. Joe and Barbara are
staring at him from inside.

JOE
That's the baby you wanna
bring into this family?
You musta gone through a lotta
them before you found one that
would match! This isn't April
Fool, is it? This you really
mean? Kid's gotta be at least
eleven…

BARBARA
Twelve.

JOE
Probably from a broken home…
you know…got a lotta emo-
motional problems…

BARBARA
We can help him.

JOE
Did you happen to notice he's
also a spade?

MARY
Daddy, what's a "Spade"?

JOE
Lock your door and don't ask!

In 1973, when Mort and I were preparing *Mixed Company*, mixed families were almost verboten. Adding to the aggravation, we gave Bologna's exasperated basketball coach, yes, now basketball, a seven-foot African-American center who refused to play his best on a team that was losing almost every game, until he got a raise in his million-dollar salary. This gave the Coach an opportunity to vent his anger on the entire race, shouting, "We don't pay you five hundred dollars an inch to sit on your ass!"

A new prejudice was building in the United States against the sudden influx of refugees from the Vietnam war. So, naturally, the next child to enter the family was an eight-year-old Vietnamese girl, Quan Tran, along with her friend, a frightened little American Indian boy named Joe Rogers, aged five. Talk about the Rainbow Coalition.

With Gordon Stuhlberg in an important position at 20th Fox, I blithely met with him and handed him our treasured screenplay, the interracial family story he had suggested. I soon got the treasure back. No sale. Now that it was on paper, the studio didn't want to touch it. Too controversial.

But that was our purpose, to be controversial. I was determined to see this story on the screen. With Mort now unavailable, I kept rewriting alone until I felt I had improved the relationships and the characters enough to throw it onto the Hollywood crap table a second time. My major contribution, now that I recall, was to change the Coach's sport from football—with which we had started—to basketball, where the problem of a seven-foot spade who wanted more money was easily recognizable as reality. To my surprise, I immediately got favorable responses from both Paramount and United Artists. But Paramount wanted me to deliver Lucille Ball for the role of the wife, and that proved impossible. United Artists also presented a problem; they wanted approval of the leading roles, and my assurance that the budget would not exceed one million dollars. In the '70s, not many major films could be made for what even then was considered to be chicken feed, unless you could find a lot of cheap chickens. So I settled for United Artists.

I immediately enlisted Barbara, whose generous heart was as large as the character we had written; and, finally, Joe Bologna, a perfect fit for the outraged basketball coach who is prejudiced against the whole world to begin with, and regards Life as part of a cosmic basketball game.

The Phoenix Suns had just appeared on the scene and were such consistent losers that they were ideal for the team we needed. We used the name, and members of the Phoenix team played most of the athletes. In the opening sequence the Coach is lynched by the crowd when the team loses, in what we assured everyone was merely a dream sequence. In Phoenix, it was no dream.

Shooting in Phoenix in the summer was not conducive to harmony, but oddly the cast and especially the children we chose for the major roles seemed to enjoy it.

When the picture was finished, it had a major flaw. I had insisted on unusual reality in the color photography, to avoid the Disney candy-cane look I felt would interfere with the sense of reality. My cameraman decided on an effect that in essence involved fogging the negative after exposure, and, while certainly different, compromised the look of the film and, in some instances, made it look fuzzy and unfocussed. Viewing dailies when in production, fuzziness was not unusual, and we let it continue. When the final prints were struck, fuzzy was still fuzzy, and then it was too late to correct the problem, which was in the original negative.

The much bigger problem was United Artists itself. I didn't realize it, but *Mixed Company* would be the last theatrical feature I would direct. Because the stars were not of the stature of a Lucille Ball and a Cary Grant, and because the budget had been minuscule, someone in the organization decided United Artists could save money by throwing the picture away. This meant reducing the advertising budget and not pushing the distribution. Let it fail of its own lack of momentum. Who wanted to see a comedy about prejudice in America, anyway?

Lots of people, I felt, if they had known it was Playing At A Theater Near You. Often it wasn't. It has always been a mystery to me why the advertising department of a movie studio always wants something other than the pictures the studio makes. Don't they talk to each other before the studio buys a story? What usually happens is that the advertising department decides not to let the public know what the story those nudnicks in the front office bought, is about. *Cast a Giant Shadow*, for instance, was ballyhooed as, "WAR IN THE DESERT...THE YEAR'S GIANT ADVENTURE!" Nowhere did the dreaded word, "Israel," appear; maybe they wanted the public to think it was really *Lawrence of Arabia*. Not a bad idea, if it had worked.

Henry Blanke told me that Paul Muni's *The Story of Dr. Louis Pasteur* originally was called "The Death Fighter," but the advertising department, not having run the picture, produced a huge billboard showing Muni in boxing trunks, wearing boxing gloves and a fierce expression. The title was immediately changed and Dr. Pasteur's boxing gloves removed.

Mixed Company had billboards reading, "Congratulations, Dear! We're going to have a baby—three of them!"

Obviously, this movie was about fertility drugs.

Still, the critics had to be allowed to see it. And having seen it, most of them decided it was destined to be a hit.

Arthur Knight, again, in *The Saturday Review*: "Producer-writer-director Mel Shavelson is one of the few wearing triple hats who has been able to carve a very special niche for himself. With comedies like *Yours, Mine and Ours* and *The War Between Men and Women*, he has managed the tricky job of devising light entertainment out of fairly weighty and meaningful material. In *Mixed Company*, Shavelson has not only done it again, but done it better...To his credit, Shavelson offers no easy nostrums as he switches from the arena of the home to the equally harassing basketball court. Indeed, the answer that he provides for both is probably the most difficult of all—love, understanding, and respect. The kids are fine, Miss Harris is endearing, but ultimately it is Bologna's brash, brightly accented and altogether human portrait of a reluctant paterfamilias that carries the film, and makes it a modest but unmitigated delight."

There were many others in the same vein, but *Mixed Company* soon disappeared from the few screens it played. Some time later, critic Frank Wiswell wrote: "One of the delights of moviegoing is stumbling across an unheard-of, unballyhooed movie on the bottom half of a double feature or playing somewhere in a second-or third-run house that you find to do something unusual or special.

"'Mixed Company' is such a film.

"It had come out and died so quickly that I had to call United Artists to find out when it was released. The film was a year ahead of world events. Audiences who see it this summer are much more likely to find it a relevant, moving experience. Certainly the audience with which I saw it did. There was laughing, clapping, eye-wiping and nose blowing throughout…

"The kids are never used as cute human dolls to be hugged on screen and then to disappear. They are shown as complex human beings, sometimes lovable, sometimes not. The level of credibility Shavelson obtains from his three unknown children actors is devastating. Even W.C. Fields would be moved.

"Bologna especially gives a marvelous, touching performance. He drops the script's witty one-liners with the aplomb most of us just dream of. He always seems to be on a tight wire between a heart attack and ulcers as he meets each new crisis in job and family. But every time he goes into a one-to-one scene with one of the kids on the screen, something beautiful happens…

You would think, after notices like that, all I would have to do is relax and enjoy the million-dollar offers that would come rolling in. But, apparently, I was the only one who read the critics. The rest of the industry read the box-office returns.

In a town which is the only place where they would ask Shakespeare, "What have you done lately?," you are judged by your last movie. And mine made money for no one, including United Artists, the writer, the producer, and the director, all three of the last, unfortunately, being me.

A sea change was occurring in the business I loved; agents and lawyers were taking over the studios and the task of selecting what pictures would be made. I hold no brief against agents or lawyers; some of them, as the saying goes, are my best friends. But, just as I was becoming wiser and a better picture-maker, those in power became younger, which is really all that matters in this life. No longer were they experienced in the making of film; they hadn't grown up in the world of make-believe, amid the stages and cameras and prop departments and actors and writers and directors who were my whole universe. They hadn't grown up anywhere.

Jack Rose once said that whenever he met one of the new studio executives, he was afraid to shake his hand for fear of being arrested for child molestation.

A probably apocryphal story will be repeated here. The late Fred Zinnemann, director of such award-winning classics as *High Noon, From Here to Eternity, A Man for All Seasons* and *The Day of the Jackal*, had found himself in a dry period. His agent arranged for him to meet with one of the new generation of young, hard-driving producers who had a film ready to go. When Fred appeared in his office, the producer greeted him with, "Mr. Zinnemann, this is a great honor I've heard so much about you. Can you tell me exactly what it is you've done?"

Quietly, Zinnemann said, "You first."

And walked out.

I'm no Fred Zinnemann, but something similar was happening to my career. I grew impatient, waiting to start another theatrical film. A door had been closed, and I knew it.

My agent suggested I make a MOW. Movies for television were usually described as "Disease of the Week" films. I didn't want any part of them.

Again, you must remember this was a different age; no actor in theatrical film would risk his career by exposing himself to free television. It was beneath a true artist, until television money grew to match movie money, and it was no longer beneath any of them.

Also, television was willing to tackle subjects theatrical films wouldn't handle; the gamble was not as great, because costs were so much lower. Of course, costs were lower because schedules were much shorter; television pictures were made in days, instead of months. My agent (I believe, still the William Morris Office) encouraged me to take the plunge.

Once, in Naples, Pilade Levi had brought us to a seafood restaurant that had a huge table with an array of shellfish. The friendly Neapolitan waiter talked me into a large plate of them until Pilade stopped him. "Everyone knows the bay is polluted this month – he could die!" Pilade shouted, angrily. "How can you let my friend eat poisoned mussels and oysters?"

And the waiter shouted back, just as angrily, "I have a wife and six children!"

I presume my agent also had a wife and children, and urged me to take the plunge. Try a TV movie. I could always go back to making theatrical films when opportunity knocked.

I'm still waiting for that knock.

I accompanied him for an interview with Brandon Stoddard and Louis Rudolph at ABC. The network's offices at that time were in some nondescript type of warehouse in Hollywood

I have no Zinnemann story about that meeting. It was friendly, businesslike, and they both knew who I was, although I began to doubt it when they told me the subject of the movie they had in mind for me.

The life of Rudolph Valentino. And not for Bob Hope.

Why they should associate me with the screen's greatest lover, I have no idea. But it sounded like a welcome change, although I mentioned that Anthony Dexter had played Valentino in a highly unsuccessful theatrical film.

Forget it, I was informed. Nobody who watches television ever goes to a theater. Or vice versa. I hesitated, until I did a little research. I learned that the real force behind the Valentino legend was a woman. Her name was June Mathis, and all those years ago, she was a member of the select group of female screenwriters who included Anita Loos and Frances Marion and were at the top of their craft. June Mathis invented the character of The Sheik for a poor Italian immigrant who could barely speak the language and was embarking on a career of petty crime. She wrote most of his films, and made him an international idol who is still mourned on the anniversary of his death by women showering flowers on his grave. June was also for many years his lover; and so were many other willing females of his time. But Valentino well knew June was the major factor in his success. I felt this was a chance to do a film about a strong, intelligent, and beautiful woman, in the age before Women's Lib became just another Disease of the Week.

Rodolfo Guglielmi met June in Hollywood in 1920. She had just written the screenplay of *The Four Horsemen of the Apocalypse*. One of the first things she did for Guglielmi was to change his name to Valentino.

In the film's opening she tells the audience, "I was a screenwriter at Metro in those wonderful days before the screen learned to talk and say nothing."

She helped Rudy become the romantic idol of the silent era.

Valentino was all of thirty-one years old and a half million dollars in debt when he died. The American dream. Ninety thousand people a day fought in the rain to see him in his unpaid-for coffin in New York City. Rudy Vallee sang his epitaph: "The Sheik of Araby."

But I didn't really want to tell Valentino's story. I wanted to tell June's, and show how she created a legend. And have him admit to an audience that she was really Rudolph Valentino.

I labeled the film, *The Legend of Valentino...A Romantic Fiction.*

Aaron Spelling, the most prolific producer in the checkered history of television, was given the mission of producing the movie. Aaron was providing a large part of the ABC schedule in those days, and was practically autonomous. He was knowledgeable and very easy to work with, except that the shooting schedule he allotted the production was all of nine days. I protested that I had never shot a film in less than forty-seven, and he just laughed, and explained to me about television schedules. Studio space was rented by the day, therefore he had to use all twenty-four hours, or the owners would get spoiled. Nine shooting days were almost nine 24-hour days. There was little time for such unnecessary nonsense as sleeping or eating; there was little time to shoot more than one or two takes; there was little time for the actors to do anything but act.

For the role of Valentino, we chose Franco Nero, the handsome Italian star who had just played the role of Lancelot opposite Richard Burton in the movie version of *Camelot*. Franco had a little trouble with the English language, and a lot with Vanessa Redgrave, his longtime love, who had a long history of Communist sympathies. Franco told me Vanessa had once suggested they both give away all their money, so they could find out what it was like to be poor, and Franco had told her, "You give away your money. I already know."

Franco and I became friends during the hectic shooting, and he was a pleasure to work with. So was Suzanne Pleshette, who played June Mathis beautifully. When Suzanne found out I was allergic to penicillin, she gave me a gold locket to wear, listing the allergy, so if I was ever unconscious after an auto accident, the paramedics would see it and know the medication to avoid. Franco told me not to wear it. In Italy, he advised me, the paramedics would melt down the locket and give me penicillin anyway.

He educated me in what it was like to be a sex symbol in Hollywood. When Franco would visit me at my home, the phone would keep ringing with frantic calls from beautiful starlets who were imploring him to make a house call immediately. The fact that he must have left my phone number with them for just such an emergency told me a lot about him, as well as about the ladies.

The rest of the Valentino cast included my old friend Uncle Milty—Milton Berle, playing the role of producer Jesse Lasky—and Lesley Ann Warren, as Natasha Rambova, who became Valentino's wife…for awhile.

Shooting the film was an adventure and a lesson in how television films were made, racing from one location to another, sacrificing quality for speed, relying on the actors to know their lines and to give good performances the first time a scene was shot, because there never was enough time or money for a second chance.

I regarded it as a Tuesday film, following the Hollywood saying, "Do you want it good or Tuesday?"

In spite of all the problems, the picture received some respectable notices when it debuted on televison. The screenplay was nominated for a Writers Guild Award.

And ABC was immediately sued by Rudolph Valentino's nephew, who still worked in the sound department of Universal. He accused the network of using the Valentino name and image without the family's consent.

The case became a landmark in television history, because the Judge in the lawsuit ruled that you could not copyright a public personality, and that the film was prominently labeled, "A Romantic Fiction," so truth was not an issue. This opened the way for the wave of television biographies that have appeared on the tube ever since.

I never know whether to be proud or apologetic. Lou Rudolph and I had established a friendship and a business association that lasted for several years. Lou was ambitious, energetic, and made for the world of television. He chafed under the ABC jurisdiction – as their employee, he was not allowed to take a top producing credit on any of the films—and wanted very much to be his own man. And, some day, to write and direct. He was attuned to the television public's taste, and kept searching for projects that not only would interest them, but also, after *Valentino*, concerned a public figure whose family couldn't sue us.

What he came up with next was Harry Houdini.

I don't know how many pictures had already been made about the world's most famous magician, but neither Lou nor ABC cared.

All they wanted was for me to perform a little magic and pull a large Neilsen rating out of a hat.

Of course, I had known and was fascinated by the Houdini legend. Any man who could escape after being handcuffed, nailed into a wooden box and dropped into New York Harbor, was my kind of guy. However, would that make a movie for the ages?

What decided me to try was research that revealed what Houdini was really escaping from: his Jewish mother. Because Houdini had married a shicksa. I could empathize with that. It would be like writing about one of the family.

That, plus the doubt that still existed as to whether Houdini had actually managed to communicate with his wife from the grave, as newspapers of the time emblazoned on their front pages, intrigued me.

For the Houdini role, Lou suggested the hottest actor in television at the time—Paul Michael Glaser, the "Starsky" of *Starsky & Hutch*, then one of ABC's top series. I was startled when Paul phoned me from Florida, where he was on location, to tell me he had read the script and would be thrilled to play the Houdini role. He claimed his prime qualification was that he was very Jewish. I couldn't resist that kind of talent.

Next, the shicksa role, Houdini's wife. Again, to my surprise, Sally Struthers of *All in the Family* wanted the role so badly she offered to audition. Considering that she had played a key role in the top sitcom of all time for several years, why would she audition? Because, it turned out, she was sensible enough to realize her image was that of a daughter in *All in the Family*; she thought I might not have the imagination to see her as a wife. So she auditioned. The rest, as they say, is history.

The Jewish mother, I knew, would be no trouble at all. My top and only choice was Ruth Gordon, one of the leading actresses of the American theatre. She was married to Garson Kanin, the playwright and brother of Michael Kanin, a good friend of mine and brother member of the Writers Guild, along with his talented wife, Fay. The Kanins were one of the most prominent, gifted Jewish families in show business.

What I didn't stop to realize was that Ruth Gordon was not a Kanin. Except by marriage. Her family was all Episcopalian, or some similar strange cult. When she spoke, her accent was solid Gentile. Garson Kanin had married her anyway but he didn't have my problem. I had written a screenplay about a Jewish mother who opposed her magician son's marriage to a shicksa, and carried her enmity beyond the grave. She spoke with the accent that came with her from Europe, from a language she learned to speak as a child that had lived for centuries and doomed many millions of her people to the gas chamber. She had to be believed beyond question when she told the shicksa who wanted to marry her son how she felt about their diluting the race that had endured so long. The key was in one speech:

> MRS. WEISS
> Look at me. Look good at me.
> I'm five thousand years old.
> From the time of Abraham. You
> think that's nothing, five
> thousand years, the same people?
> Who else can say it? Do I have
> to tell you what it cost us?
> With fire they tried to finish
> us, with swords, with guns,
> with hate, you think I want
> to see them do it with love?

Could an Episcopalian deliver that speech and not be laughed at? Would Ruth Gordon's diction destroy one of the main points of the story? Her opposition to diluting the race?

Gar Kanin solved it for all of us. He taught his wife to speak with the Jewish accent he had been avoiding all his life.

The result? I give you the critics:

"Ruth Gordon, as the quintessential mother-in-law, steals all her scenes..."
– *The Hollywood Reporter*

"It would not seem possible by now to wring another variation on the classic Jewish mother, but Miss Gordon does, making her strength and piety the source of her destructiveness."
– Kevin Thomas, *The Los Angeles Times*

"Ruth Gordon, marvelously restrained, is outstanding as his doting mother who promoted the religious conflicts and jealousies..."
– Judith Crist, *TV Guide*

Judith Crist, the tough, uncompromising critic many call "Jesus" Crist, had panned *Valentino* unmercifully. I found it doubly comforting to read the rest of her critique of *The Great Houdinis*: "The tale itself—fact 'improved' with delightful dollops of fiction—has everything—magic, escapes, spiritualism, a love story, a mother-complex story, comedy, drama, mystery, dandy period atmosphere, and a topnotch cast...all join with Shavelson's literate script and brilliant direction to provide viewers with absorbing entertainment."

At the end of the film, when Houdini's secret message to his wife is revealed in a seance after his death, Vivian Vance, the narrator, concludes the story with:

> VIVIAN VANCE
> Until her death, Houdini's wife
> never denied that this was the
> exact message she and Harry
> had agreed on, that Hallowe'en
> night when he lay dying. The
> newspapers decided it was all a
> hoax, that Houdini hadn't come
> back. Me?... I believe...I believe
> the son of a bitch loved her.

The controversy raged in the press for some time after Houdini's "message" was received from the grave. Sadly, it was finally hinted that the Reverend Arthur Ford of the Spiritualist Church, who conducted the seance and relayed the message from the Beyond, had shared the same mistress with Houdini; it was presumed Harry had confided the message to her in an unguarded moment, and she had passed it on to the Reverend Dr. Ford, on a similar tender horizontal occasion.

"Oy, Gottenyu!" as Ruth Gordon would say.

There is a sad corollary to the film. Paul Glaser became a friend whose friendship lasted long after the movie was completed. He and his wife, Elisabeth, used to visit Lucy and me with their two playful children, to swim in our pool and lie in the sunshine.

Elisabeth Glaser contracted AIDS, apparently from a blood transfusion. Unknowingly, she passed it on to her children. Only Paul escaped the dreaded infection; no one knows why.

But Elisabeth was made of strong stuff; she became a leader in the crusade to combat the disease, and carried her fight to the White House and to Congress, where she became a symbol of the battle for its recognition and treatment. She publicly battled HIV all the way to her untimely end, losing one of her children on the way.

I don't know if Harry Houdini ever came back, but Elisabeth Glaser comes back every day in the treatment of HIV which she helped teach a whole nation to recognize, and take action against. As of this moment, years after her passing, newspapers are publishing the statistics that show, for the first time, deaths from AIDS in this country are decreasing rather than increasing.

Disease of the Week? Not this one. Disease of the Century and not *The Great Houdinis*. The Great Elisabeth.

Chapter XIII
Ike: The War Years
1977–1978

The Houdini film had hardly been laid to rest when I got another call from the indefatigable Lou Rudolph. ABC was considering purchasing a new book whose manuscript was just now going the rounds; the price was very high, and the bidding was going to be spirited. Would I read the book overnight and let ABC know what I thought of it?

The book was *Past Forgetting*, Kay Summersby's story of her wartime romance with General Dwight Eisenhower.

I called Lou the first thing the next morning and recommended that ABC buy the book at once and at any price; not for a quick two-hour MOW about a scandalous liaison that tarnished the Eisenhower image, but for the opportunity it offered for an in-depth account of America's role in World War II. That war had passed into the history books and been almost forgotten by a new generation, whose idea of their country's nobility had been soured in the rice paddies of Vietnam. Only Bob Hope and his Christmas shows had emerged successfully from that disastrous conflict, although he, too, was almost destroyed by it, as was President Lyndon Johnson.

At one point during the bloody Vietnam war, I had the demented idea there might be a comedy in its tragedy. I wrote a story about a comedian entertaining the troops in Vietnam and titled it *Love Thine Enemies*. The comedian's routines were pure Bob Hope: "I'm happy to be here at Da Nang…This place has changed hands more often than Liz Taylor…When I played here last time, the Cong had the best seats…I held out my hand to see if it was steady. And Ho Chi Minh shook it…" and so on. Bob, in some ways, had transcended the bad taste of that war, as he had WWII. In this story, his character proceeded blithely telling jokes that insulted the commanding General, who had a sense of humor like a Sherman tank. The

179

General turned to his Aide and was a little disappointed to learn he did not have authority to execute civilians.

He did the next best thing. The General informed the comedian he was honoring him by sending him to the U.S. outpost at Tran Khon. It stood, or rather, slouched, in the mud and jungle along the banks of the Mekong River. Six years of warfare made it so unattractive even the Viet Cong didn't want to live there. At least, not enough to want to recapture it. U.S. Army Headquarters knew vaguely that Tran Khon still existed, because occasionally helicopters were fired on when called to airlift another case of VD out of there. But for the most part, they chose to ignore it, in the hope that it would soon be retaken.

But in the middle of the forlorn outpost on the banks of the Mekong was a children's hospital; on the other side of the river, of course, was Charlie—Victor Charlie, acronym for the VC. Sometimes, at night, the VC would ferry some of their sick children across the river to the hospital, because it was the only one for hundreds of miles, even though it was in enemy territory. There is no enemy for a sick child.

One explosive night, the Tet offensive was launched. The VC crossed the river in force and overran the American base at Tran Khon. Our hero found himself fleeing for his life—in a leaky hospital launch containing both VC and South Vietnamese children who had been saved by a U.S. nurse, Lucille Ball, of course. The trip down the Mekong through enemy fire resulted in growing understanding between the children of both sides, including the two Americans, who also, at first, were sworn enemies.

It was, I hoped, an indication of how sanity might eventually prevail in that bloody conflict. I was so wrong. But so were American Presidents like Jack Kennedy, Lyndon Johnson and Richard Nixon. Only Dwight Eisenhower, who knew war better than any of them, saw the end of the conflict and had to admit America's first military defeat.

Bob Hope was then near the peak of his popularity from his Christmas visits to the Vietnam troops, and he, too, felt the movie might have something worthwhile to say. Bob agreed to star, and I brought in Marion Hargrove to collaborate with me on the screenplay, Marion had written the comedy classic of WWII, *See Here, Private Hargrove*, and had the military experience I lacked.

Private Hargrove was a joy to work with. We were getting along very well with the screenplay when I got an angry call from my secretary. She was quitting the project. She refused to continue working on a movie for

Bob Hope, who was by this time considered to be a leading Hawk, a defender of the military, and friend of the Administration in Washington which was prolonging an unpopular war. When I started to protest, she asked me, "Did you hear the news this morning? President Nixon has ordered the U.S. Air Force to bomb Cambodia."

Now, my secretary was a level-headed, hard-working girl. She endeared herself to me when she told me that she and her new husband were trying to rent an apartment, and were outraged by the intimate questionnaire the landlords asked them to fill out.

"Can you imagine?" she asked me. "They even wanted to know what kind of condominiums we used!"

You have to respect a girl like that, and I did. I knew she represented the change that was taking place in the nation's thinking about Vietnam,

I called Hope on the phone and told him Hargrove and I had decided to abandon the project. It was too soon to find humor in a conflict that was tearing our country apart, and Bob was becoming the focal point of much of the anger.

I was surprised when he quickly agreed.

"I was in Washington last weekend," he told me, "and I was outside my hotel putting my golf clubs in the back of my car when a convertible loaded with young guys drove by. One of them leaned out and shouted, 'Hey, Bob, we're bringing them home to you this Christmas!'"

There were no more Bob Hope Christmas Shows in 'Nam after that. There was no movie. It took years before Robin Williams could make *Good Morning, Vietnam!* and get laughs, by taking the attitude that the war was completely and absolutely wrong and had been from its beginning.

Again, I was ahead of my time. Or, rather, behind it.

Now Kay Summersby had given ABC the opportunity to portray a different kind of war, the last one where you could tell the good guys from the bad guys. The controversy that was sure to explode, even at this late date, when the book hit the stands with her story of her affair with Ike, would create a popular television audience. And once having their attention, I hoped to be able to tell the whole story of WWII through Ike Eisenhower, the five-star General who commanded the D-Day invasion of Europe and the conquest of Hitler's Third Reich, yet remained a recognizable human being with recognizable human frailties.

Lou Rudolph had been highly instrumental in getting Al Hailey's *Roots* to the ABC screen. That epic story had played out for an unheard-of eight hours in Prime Time, knocking off all the other network competition on the way. This story, Ike Eisenhower, World War II, and Kay Summersby, would need at least six hours to tell properly, but *Roots* had set the precedent.

ABC bought *Past Forgetting* for $250,000, almost a record price in television for an unpublished manuscript. And I was handed the job to write, produce and direct it, as the source material for a six-hour miniseries.

I didn't know it would take three years of my life. And not a little of my sanity.

I planned to call the film *Ike: The War Years*, and follow it with a sequel, *Ike: The Presidential Years.*

The best laid plans o' mice and men…

I had lived through all of WWII and had personally seen America's role from Bob Hope's first Army show at March Field to the stunning conclusion I heard in my car on Highland Avenue in Hollywood in August of 1945, while driving to my office at Paramount Studios. Over the car radio came the startling announcement of the dropping of the first atomic bomb on Hiroshima. Until that moment I had no idea there was an atomic bomb. Neither had the entire country, except those directly involved in what was called "The Manhattan Project." I don't remember the rest of that drive; World War II, I knew, was suddenly over.

At home, days later, I heard and recorded from my shortwave receiver the announcement directly from Tokyo Radio that the Emperor had accepted the Allies' terms for unconditional surrender—unconditional, except for Hirohito's job, for which there was no unemployment insurance in Japan. I learned the end of the story before the networks got the word. I still treasure that recording, made with a record-cutting machine, in the days before audio tape. Elmer Davis, the outstanding war commentator, once visited me at my home, and I played the recordings for him. Davis was then with the Library of Congress, and he took my recordings with him for the Library. They in turn gave me a tape cassette made from them, which I treasure.

The world would never be the same. War itself, on any truly major scale, would disappear. At least for my generation, and hopefully, my childen's, and their children. The Bomb itself made it easy to forget what a World War was really like. And that could be wrong. "Those who don't recall history's mistakes are destined to repeat them.

Kay Summersby's hopeless romance would make it possible to get the important story of WWII to television and the American public, and, hopefully, other audiences around the word. The film had to entertain for six solid hours, and in entertaining bring the past to life in a way designed to help prevent it from ever happening again.

I realized I didn't know enough about Ike Eisenhower to do the job. I didn't know enough about war. I didn't know enough about life itself. I was soon to learn. It took over a year of research and a great deal of help from others.

The first reactions to the news that ABC was going to make a miniseries called *Ike* were outraged screams from the Republican press, including the *New York Times*. Kay Summersby's book was anathema to all of them; it could destroy the good name of a heroic President. If we were using Kay's book as a source, they were determined not to allow the film to be made.

That made me angry. It didn't make Eisenhower less of a man, a general, or a human being, to have had an affair with a beautiful woman when he was separated from his wife for years, while carrying the burden of a terrible war on his shoulders. In fact, it made him more of a human being in my eyes. I felt that even the Eisenhower family would understand the importance of humanizing him.

Was Kay Summersby telling the truth? Was there actually a sexual affair? Did they or didn't they? The evidence on that crucial point was inconclusive. Kay herself had died before her book was published. Her story stated that there indeed was, and that when the war in Europe was ended, Ike had promised to bring her to the United States at his side, and the public be damned.

Kay never heard from Ike again after the German surrender. But in Harry Truman's posthumous papers there was evidence that General Marshall had told Truman that Ike had written to Marshall of his intention to divorce his wife, Mamie, and marry his wartime love. Truman supposedly hit the ceiling. Ike was recalled to Washington to face Marshall and was told it was tantamount to an act of treason. It could prevent a grateful country from someday rewarding him with the Presidency.

Eisenhower backed down, as he never had to the Nazi army whose officers he refused to meet with until they had signed their unconditional surrender.

In my innocence, I intended to open the film with that scene between Ike and Marshall. I never got the chance. A firestorm of protest appeared in the press, denying any of this had ever occurred, Kay Summersby's book was complete fabrication, her purpose, to make money. The only evidence, the editorial writers insisted, was hearsay. Nothing appeared on the record. The whole idea of Ike having an affair with any woman was nonsense, as long as Mamie existed.

I don't believe in angels or saints, even if they wear five stars for a halo. So I instituted my own investigation. A retired Army General, former member of Ike's wartime staff in North Africa during the first days of U.S. involvement in the fighting, was in Hollywood attempting to produce movies, a little tougher than battling Rommel. I made a point of meeting him at a party, and put to him the question of Kay Summersby's veracity. Yes, he told me, Kay was very beautiful, and very much Ike's constant companion, as his driver and later as his aide. Eisenhower made Kay the first Five Star Aide in history, and presented her with five stars. He also persuaded FDR to allow her to retain her British citizenship even after Ike made her a member of the American Army.

But what about Topic A? Did they, or didn't they?

The General merely said, "I once used Ike's bathroom at his headquarters above Algiers. When I opened the medicine cabinet, I was face to face with Kay's Kotex."

I went ahead with the screenplay, determined to tell their story just the way it happened. Of course, I wasn't allowed to. Some of the scenes that were changed or excised completely by the network will be included here later. Be of stout heart and continue.

My next move was to attempt to convince the Eisenhower family to cooperate in telling the truth. I wanted to emphasize that we did not mean to demean Ike in any way, merely to present him as the man he really was, for the purpose of history. We would ask their cooperation to make sure we didn't hurt his image, and that Mamie would be treated sympathetically. They would be given the screenplay and the opportunity to ask for changes.

Lou Rudolph and I made a pilgrimage to Gettysburg, Pa., where Gen. John Eisenhower, Ike's son, lived and worked. We were received with skepticism when we asked his help. He was, it seemed, writing his own book on his father; so was Ike's grandson, David. Lou proposed that ABC purchase both books in advance, at a considerable price, and use whatever material they included that would be helpful to make the record complete. We never got a conclusive answer, but the General promised to keep the door open.

Then he opened his door for us to leave.

We walked out onto the fields of Gettysburg, feeling a little like the Confederate Army. Still hopeful, I made an arrangement for a meeting with David Eisenhower in New York. I realized all of this might have some future historical value, so I made careful notes at the time. And here they are in their entirety:

NOTES ON MEETING WITH DAVID EISENHOWER
NEW YORK CITY, JANUARY 25, 1977

Present at the meeting: David Eisenhower, David Obst (acting as his Agent), Bridget Potter of ABC, Kathryn Seitz, her assistant, Shavelson. Meeting held in the private dining room in the ABC Building, NYC.

Among matters discussed was the timing of the release of the television motion picture to be produced about Dwight Eisenhower, in connection with the completion of the book David is writing about his grandfather. It became clear that David was still collecting material, the writing of the book had not started, and it would not be in print for some 18 months. [NOTE: "David" refers to David Eisenhower; "Obst" to David Obst.] Obst was not too happy about the network's plans to have the first half of the story on the air early in 1978.

In discussing Ike with David, I asked him specifically about Kay Summersby. He said he had read her book and did not know how much of it was factual. However, he felt it was all quite possible, and that the portrait of Ike that emerged jibed with his own knowledge and concept of Ike's character. Under direct question, he said that Mamie Eisenhower was well aware of Kay Summersby's existence. He did not think there would be any problem in treating the Summersby incident in the television film.

He also said that while his book was unwritten, he had completed its organization and wrote down some twenty or more chapter headings, which he handed to Bridget Potter. She later told me she felt it would be unfair for me to see them until the network negotiations to purchase David's book were completed. I have not seen them to this day.

David then gave us some insight into Ike's character, that he could explode quickly into anger, even at his grandson. David received a weekly allowance when he was young—25 cents a week, which was not increased. Once, visiting Ike when he was President of Columbia University, Ike was wearing a motorman's change device and gave David his allowance from that. Also, there was some incident earlier that caused Ike to explode at his grandson, and David said he was affected by the force of the anger, although later that day, when he caddied for Ike on the golf course, Ike never mentioned the matter and proceeded to treat David as if the incident had not occurred. David also said that Mamie ran the White House and, in a way, Ike, usually from her bed in the White House.

The meeting broke up on very amicable terms, the feeling being that there would be further negotiations about the details of money to be paid for David's book, and perhaps other contractual problems, but that both sides wanted to make the deal.

After that meeting, I was convinced we had all acted as adults, and that there would be no difficulty with the family in portraying Eisenhower as history, and Kay Summersby, remembered him.

By May I was well along with the six-hour screenplay, and there was no sign of the appearance of David Eisenhower's book. Another meeting was arranged, this time in California, and, again, I felt history might be interested—I know I was—so I kept careful notes.

And here they are:

NOTES ON SECOND MEETING WITH DAVID EISENHOWER CENTURY CITY, CA MAY 13, 1977

Present at the meeting: David Eisenhower, David Obst, Donald March of ABC, Shavelson.

Before we started the meeting, I was informed by Donald March that the negotiations for the purchase of David Eisenhower's book had been concluded, except for some small formality. I had made it clear I didn't want to have another meeting with David until the purchase was complete. I wanted to be certain I had the right to ask for any information I needed to complete the screenplay, without going through the frustration of the previous meeting, when I was not allowed to see his outline. I was assured by March that this time there was no longer a problem.

Since the first half of my screenplay was now completed, I had some specific inquiries to make. Most of them concerned the reality of the romance between Ike and Kay Summersby, and the reality of hte romance between Ike and Kay Summersby, as well as insights into the marital relationship between Ike and Mamie, which perhaps would contain the information I needed.

I inquired if he had seen the letters (between Ike and Kay) and he replied he had not been allowed to see all of them. I asked how this was possible, since he was supposedly given access to the Eisenhower papers by the family. He told me that some of the papers were marked, "C," and that "C" stood for a family committee that was to determine whether the papers should remain secret.

When I asked him who constituted the family committee, he said that for practical purposes it was solely made up of his father, John Eisenhower. He suggested ABC might want to buy his father's book to get access to the letters. I asked him if all the letters were to be published, and he said he didn't know. Perhaps some would be kept secret. But in his opinion, they did not reveal too much, because both Ike and Mamie were careful not to expose much of their real selves in correspondence.

There was further conversation as to when David's book would be ready for me to see. Apparently, he had not yet started writing it. I believe Don March informed David and Obst that ABC intended to put IKE: THE WAR YEARS on the air early in 1978, and that THE WHITE HOUSE YEARS would air in the Fall of 1978, supposedly synchronized with the release of David's book.

After the meeting broke up, I went down to the garage to get my car and ran across David and Obst deep in conversation near Obst's—or David's—car. The conversation ceased when they saw me. Later that day, I received a telephone call at my home from Obst, who said David was deeply disturbed by the fact that I apparently would be using a great deal of material from the Kay Summersby book in the screenplay, and wanted to know how I had become involved in the project. I told him that Lou Rudolph of ABC had sent me the galleys of Kay Summersby's Past Forgetting and asked what I thought of it. I called Lou the following morning and told him that while the book was far from a great one, it contained the essence of a wonderful romance, and that it was my opinion that ABC should purchase it at any cost.

Later, when the bidding on the book had raised the price, I reiterated this belief to Lou, adding that I saw not just the romance, but the entire story of World War II and Eisenhower's contribution to it, with the romance tying it together. It was a chance to do history with one of history's few gentle love stories counter pointing the war. I saw not a two-hour movie, as first envisioned, but four or perhaps six.

Lou agreed, and the purchase of the book was later made. Obst told me that he had been given to believe by Lou Rudolph that ABC had purchased the book merely to take it off the market; that there was no real intention to do the story of the Summersby-Eisenhower romance except in passing. He also said that if the Summersby story was as much as 20% of the final screenplay, the Eisenhower family would not approve. I said that was not my concern at that moment; my concern was to write the best possible screenplay.

Obst said that David had to get his father's approval before he could make a sale of his book to ABC, and that he probably would not get it under these circumstances, and that was the end of our conversation.

That was the end of the attempt to get the Eisenhower family's cooperation. David's book, an excellent one on his grandfather, was not completed until years after *Ike: The War Years* was aired. The actual Eisenhower-Summersby letters were finally released and were put up for auction by Sotheby's, in 1991, also long after the great success of the miniseries. Neither David's book, nor John Eisenhower's, was ever purchased by ABC.

Obviously, with an airdate, I had to proceed on my own. Kay Summersby was emerging as an interesting character in the screenplay I was writing, a perfect British foil for Ike's American General, and his equal in spirit and courage. I refused to consign her to the oblivion the family demanded. I was relying on her own words, and I felt they deserved to be heard. Today, after the publication of Ike's letters to Kay, there is now longer any doubt.

One scene to illustrate this is after Ike has returned from a visit to FDR in Washington and arrives in London, in the middle of the war, and is met by Kay and by Col. Tex Lee. At his quarters in Hays Lodge that night, this scene:

INT. ENTRANCE HALL – (NIGHT)

As Kay prepares to leave,

> IKE
> Kay—I've been ordered to present
> you with a gift by the President
> of the United States. Won't you
> stay a minute and have a
> nightcap with me?

Almost at the front door, Kay turns.

> KAY
> I thought you'd never ask.

She starts back, removing her uniform cap.

> IKE
> Gin and tonic?

> KAY
> Always. It's the only British
> drink you know how to make.

Ike exits to the living room.

> TEX
> (sotto)
> Summersby.
> (she -turns)
> It's no good. You'll be swept under
> the rug of American history.

> KAY
> I understand I'll have a lot of
> distinguished company under that rug.

She turns, proudly, and starts into the living room.

INT. LIVING ROOM – MED. SHOT (NIGHT)

Ike stands at a sideboard, mixing the drinks. He reaches into his
briefcase as she approaches.

> IKE
> Here it is.

He hands her a framed photograph of FDR.

> KAY
> (taking it)
> How kind of the President
> to remember, and not hold the
> Revolutionary War against me.

> IKE
> (a grin)
> That's because America won that one.

He hands her a drink. Kay sets the picture down.

> KAY
> (raising her glass)
> Cheers. To winning this
> one together.

They drink, silently. Ike turns, slowly, crosses to the sofa.

> IKE
> You might as well know that
> I'd made up my mind to order
> you back to General Spaatz…
> and then, there you stood on
> the train platform…waiting
> for me…like a lighthouse
> in the fog.

> KAY
> How flattering. Two hundred
> feet tall, solid concrete,
> and a beacon spinning about
> my head.

> IKE
> Shut up. In Abilene, that
> would be considered poetry.

> KAY
> (gently)
> I know, General. I do know.

She crosses and sits beside him, drink in hand. Ike lights up a cigarette, propping his legs up on the coffee table. For the first time, Ike looks completely relaxed.

IKE
Well, did you know that
the President has heard
talk about us?

KAY
Goodness. Is there nothing
better for American intelligence
to do? I'm actually flattered.

She pats his hand, lightly.

KAY
(continuing)
How long will it take for him to
find out about that, do you suppose?

IKE
What I'm trying to say is, I
don't want to see you hurt.

KAY
It's too late. You know
I'm one of the walking wounded.

She turns away and lights a cigarette.

IKE
The fact that you're on my staff
...that you're attractive...will
be enough for most people. You're
going to be scorned and you're
going to be ridiculed.

Kay gets to her feet, her back to Ike.

          KAY
I can take all that if I'm
also needed. At least, please,
let me have that.

          IKE
You're needed.

          KAY
My God. The Great Stone Face
can speak.

Ike rises.

          IKE
I knew that the moment I left
North Africa. I couldn't face
coming back to London and not
seeing you. It wouldn't really
be London.

Ike puts his hands on her shoulders.

          IKE (contd.)
But you must know I'm a soldier
and a husband. I love my country
and I love my wife. Whatever
small happiness we may have together
will only last as long as the
horrors of this war. Will you
promise to stay around on those
unfair terms?

          KAY
My God, Ike! They raise a lot of
corn in Abilene, don't they?

She turns away from him and picks up FDR's photograph.

IKE
It's honest corn.

Kay turns back.

KAY
My dear General Dwight David
Eisenhower, I don't know what
kind of women have been in love
with you before, but this woman
loves with all her heart and
that is why she is always hurt,
but, oh, the lovely, lovely
days between. I can make you
any kind of promise you wish,
because I am quite certain
there is no tomorrow. I don't
believe in heaven and I don't
believe in hell. What this
war has taught me to believe
in is Now.

She crosses and picks up her uniform hat, placing it firmly on her head.

KAY
(continuing)
So get yourself a good night's
rest because what you have to
do from now on is nothing short
of saving decency and honor
and the England I love, and you
go ahead and do your job, and I
will do mine, which is infinitely
less. It only involves loving you
so much that I don't give a damn
what happens to myself.

She turns and starts for the front door.

        IKE
Kay—

She stops but doesn't turn.

        IKE
        (continuing)
Dammit, Kay.

        KAY
Thank you. Shakespeare couldn't
have put it better.

And she is gone.

When the screenplay was finished, I sent it to Lou Rudolph. I got a call from him the next morning I hope I never forget, even though we went our separate ways long ago.

"I read it," Lou said. "I think it will be remembered a hundred years from now."

Of course, that's a little too long for a Neilsen rating, and in television terms he probably meant six months but I was heartened. Plans went forward quickly to put the screenplay into production.

By this time, the enormity of what we were attempting had finally dawned on us. Bill McCutchen, young, forceful and talented, was assigned as producer, and I was given the title of "Executive Producer" and freed from a lot of the daily harassment. Bill was also knowledgeable about stories, and was a great help—and sometimes a hindrance—in completing the script. We had many heated arguments, but we wound up in general agreement—and friendship—by the final Fadeout.

Screenplay completed, my first choice to play Eisenhower was my old friend from *War Between Men and Women*, Jason Robards. Jason was not only a great actor, but had the lightness and humor I felt Ike himself deserved. After *War*, Jason had a few two many martinis one night and rammed his car into a telephone pole, which rammed back. Robards was seriously injured, and part of his upper lip was torn away. It seemed as though his acting career was finished, but somehow in the wreckage they found his lip, and doctors sewed it back on. If they had put a zipper in, the old wartime warning to "zip your lip" would have been very appropriate. Robards grew a moustache to cover the damage and went on with his career as if nothing had happened. Eventually, he shaved the moustache off, and only the talent remained.

Jason told me he would like very much to play Ike, but he had just signed for another picture and would be unavailable when we were scheduled to shoot. Sadly, I had to give up.

The next actor suggested by ABC was universally recognized as a world-class performer. Robert Duvall had made a name for himself in *The Godfather*, and would later win an Academy Award for *Tender Mercies*. And also, he was bald, so he wouldn't need much time in makeup to play Ike.

McCutchen and I made a flying trip to New York to see Duvall, and got trapped in our hotel by the biggest blizzard I had been caught in since Jack Kennedy's Inauguration. All traffic was stopped by drifts of snow; New Yorkers were joyfully skiing down the center of Fifth Avenue, joined by several taxi drivers, since there was nowhere you could drive a taxi in the city.

Bill and I trudged across Manhattan ankle-deep in the white stuff, and finally reached the bar designated by Duvall as a meeting place. He seemed to be in a receptive mood; he had read the screenplay, and said he had given it to some cronies and they told him he should do it, if only to counteract the Godfather image. Of course, he felt television, after the Academy Award, was a step backward, but he thought *Ike* might be important enough to be worth taking that step. The conversation was straightforward and professional.

Bill and I reported to ABC that Duvall was available, and our choice. Even though he bore little resemblance to Ike, we felt makeup and caps on his teeth would help greatly, and he was naturally bald.

While Duvall's deal was being negotiated, I returned to the screenplay, and finally completed it, encouraged by several meetings in Washington with Maj. Gen. Robert Simon, Chief of Public Affairs for the United States Army. He and his department read the screenplay and felt its depiction of Ike and the U.S. armed forces was fair and favorable, and that Eisenhower as a human being was a better image for the Army than that of a saint or a military genius.

I was offered whatever cooperation I would need with the armed forces, and also complete access to all the combat footage shot in the European Theater during World War II, much of it never before seen, all of it stored carefully away in a vault. Further, I was given a complete catalogue of the shots available, each one numbered; I had only to order whatever I would like to view, and the Army would have it transferred to videotape and shipped to Hollywood. If I wanted to use it in the film, I was then given an internegative from the Army's original footage.

Not only was the combat footage dramatic, but it would allow me to portray the war on a larger scale than our budget would ever have permitted. However, it was all in black and white. All the color film available during WWII had been assigned to the war in the Pacific—because the light was better, I was told.

It was then I saw some early experiments in colorizing black-and-white film. The technique was rudimentary then, using relatively new computer technique, but it was effective and expensive. If we used the process, we would be the first to do so on a large scale. And it had to be a large scale, because I wanted it not only to show the war itself, but to be capable of integrating it with the new color film we would be shooting, thus allowing our actors to participate in history.

ABC also made a deal with Warner Brothers and Fox, allowing us to use outtakes from *Patton* and *Tora! Tora! Tora!* for *Ike*. This allowed me to open the movie with color footage of the Japanese attack on Pearl Harbor (restaged for *Tora! Tora! Tora!*), followed by the actual newsreel footage of the sinking of the *U.S.S. Arizona* and fire raging through the battleships crowded into Pearl Harbor, colorized for the first time so that the impact was much greater than the original black-and-white newsreel film that had helped send the United States to war.

We had now proceeded to the point where it was necessary for Bill McCutchen and me to go to London, to set up the locations, the personnel, and the studio space for the shooting of the scenes in England.

After we arrived, I got a phone call from Vanessa Redgrave, whom I didn't know except through Franco Nero's description of their tangled relationship. She was in London and somehow had secured a copy of the script, and insisted that she was the only actress who could play Kay Summersby, whom she had much admired. So much so that Vanessa invited me to have dinner with her. At her home. She would cook.

Vanessa, as no one has to be told, is one of our finest actresses, both onstage and onscreen. She is also outspoken on the subject of politics, but that hadn't prevented her from being awarded the Academy Award the year before for her leading role in *Julia*. I was delighted she wanted to play Kay, and was equally delighted with the steak she barbecued for me—barbecued, in Britain!—in her front yard. It was charred and tender. She was dressed in Levi's for this occasion, and we had a pleasant conversation about the story of *Ike* until the phone rang.

It was Franco Nero, who had no idea I was in Britain. I signaled to Vanessa to hand me the phone, and I started a heated conversation with him, asking Franco to leave my girl alone, until he finally recognized my voice and warned me against Vanessa's cooking, and not to allow her to convince me to give away all my money.

It was a great steak and a great evening, and I left firmly convinced that Vanessa Redgrave was the only possible choice to play the unconquered and unconquerable Kay Summersby.

My choice was immediately vetoed by ABC. Vanessa had not exactly endeared herself in Hollywood when, in her acceptance speech at the Academy Award ceremony, she had promoted the cause of the Palestinian terrorists. After *Cast a Giant Shadow*, I was doubly sensitive about the little nation of Israel, but I felt it was vital to show that free speech was important in America, and her political beliefs should not be held against her talent.

ABC was not in a forgiving mood. Lee Remick, whose TVQ—meaning, audience rating—was one of the highest of all women in American television, lived in London with her English husband. She, too, had read my script of *Ike*, and was actively seeking the Summersby role. I resisted, because Lee was an American, and I felt the conflict in the script between Kay's loyalty to the British Empire and Ike's Americanism would be weakened if a British actress did not play Kay's role.

Bill and I had lunch with Lee at Claridge's in London, and she was charming and intelligent, and demonstrated for us the British accent that came naturally to her, after her marriage and her home in London. I left unconvinced, but ABC insisted, and Lee Remick was to be Kay Summersby.

But not for awhile. Suddenly, the Eisenhower family sued the network to prevent the film from being made. They swung powerful forces to their support, including editorials against depicting an Eisenhower extramarital romance, in *The New York Times* and other papers. By the time I had returned to Hollywood, ABC had put the project on hold while the lawsuit was pending.

Time passed. I kept busy revising sections of the screenplay that might possibly offend Mamie, while retaining the basic facts. Also, the logistics of the shooting, the locations representing North Africa and other locales that could be found in Southern California, were nailed down.

After about a year of marking time, there apparently was a change of heart by the family. The lawsuit was dropped in favor of a request to be certain Mamie was represented favorably, and to soft-pedal certain elements of the Ike-Kay romance—which they tried to convince us had never occurred. Finally, *Ike: The War Years* was ready to roll. Bob Duvall arrived in Hollywood, and Bill McCutchen and I went with him to a dentist who was going to build the caps for his teeth, to promote his facial resemblance to Eisenhower.

The next morning shooting began, the scene of Ike's departure from North Africa for Washington on New Year's morning, 1944. Lee Remick as Kay and Telek, the puppy she had presented to Ike on his birthday, were there to see him off; both of them were being left behind. Here is the scene:

SUPER IN:

NEW YEAR'S MORNING
1944

SUPER OUT.

Several Army cars are heading across the field for the runway, Ike's Cadillac among them.

INT. CADILLAC – MED. CLOSE

Kay is at the wheel, a very disturbed Kay. Ike is in the back holding Telek on his lap. For a long moment, no one speaks.

> KAY
> (she keeps her eyes
> on the road)
> You will take care of yourself and not
> smoke so many cigarettes and not let
> the Germans shoot your plane
> down?

> IKE
> There won't be any Germans. I'm
> Heading for Washington.

KAY
Washington...that means your
wife. The one you love.

IKE
Yes, Kay. Mamie. The one I love.

KAY
It's been a hell of an affair, this
one. The Virgin Mary at Armageddon.
You've never said anything to me you
couldn't have said while saluting.

IKE
I'm not good at that sort of thing.

KAY
I *am*.

IKE
(to Kay)
Goddamit, salute me.

KAY
You know how terrible I
am at saluting.

IKE
That's what I want to remember.

She salutes, terribly.

KAY
Good luck, General. With all
my heart, good luck.

Ike returns the salute, hands her the puppy, and turns away.

He turns back for a moment, then starts for the B-17, where
Gen. Bedell Smith (BEETLE) awaits him. Ike is lost in thought.

>   IKE
>   (to Beetle)
> In the two years I've been
> fighting for the Channel
> invasion, I never once
> considered what to do if
> it failed. But I'm considering
> now.

>   BEETLE
> I know, Ike. I know.

>   IKE
> My God…there could be half
> a million of our boys dead
> on the beaches of France.
> And I'm the one who insisted
> the responsibility for this
> entire enterprise must be
> given to one man…alone.

>   BEETLE
>   Ike…

But he can't find the words. Ike enters the plane without looking back.
Nearby, Telek is struggling in Kay's arms.

>   KAY
>   (to the dog)
> Oh, no. If I don't get to go,
> you don't get to go.

The plane takes off into the Moroccan dawn.

I thought the scene had played well. It was difficult to open the shooting with, actually the end of the first act of the film. Duvall's performance held it together.

With the picture rolling I invited Lee Remick to dinner one night.

"You know, Lee, I fought very hard to keep you out of this film."

And Lee said, "I know."

"And you are very good in it."

"I know that, too," she said, sounding very much like Kay Summersby.

The critics all agreed it was one of her finest performances. It was a sad blow a few years after *Ike* was aired when Lee Remick died. The good die young.

I was using the *Queen Mary* as my temporary home while we filmed a sequence nearby in a seaside fortress representing Gibraltar. I received a phone call in my stateroom from Brandon Storddard, who was now head of ABC Films.

I was being removed as director of *Ike* when the production moved to London, and replaced by Boris Sagal.

I remember I was shattered. Boris Sagal was a fine and experienced TV director. He directed much more of the film, by the time it was finished, than I did, and much of its success belongs to him.

But problems that had developed on the set persuaded the network to make the change. It was their dollar. I had no choice but to step down.

The shooting continued professionally in London without me. I followed the dailies when the film arrived in Hollywood by plane—no satellite transmission in those days—and found the screenplay was followed, expertly directed, until what I felt was the key scene. When victory in Europe had been won, the truth of Eisenhower's wartime romance, since then confirmed by Truman's oral biography and Ike's many letters to Kay, was that Eisenhower asked Kay to return to America with him. She gently told him she knew she should not.

But my favorite scene was eliminated before it was shot in London. I had written it to take place at the end of the war, in the London Guildhall, after Ike made his famous farewell address to Winston Churchill and the British nation he had helped preserve. It contained the essence of what I felt was the true romance between Ike and Kay, now proven through Ike's letters that have since been discovered.

INT. GUILD HALL – MED. CLOSE – (DAY)

Ike and Kay are finally alone.

> IKE
> Kay—

Kay turns away.

> KAY
> Ike, I want you to know I would
> never ask you to keep any promises
> made in the heat of battle. You
> are free of me. I went into
> this with my eyes wide open,
> knowing I was to be swept under the
> rug when this moment came. I shall
> mind, of course, but it's been oh,
> such a lovely rug.

> IKE
> Have you got a cigarette?

> KAY
> Of course.

She hands him one.

> IKE
> Kay, I'm no good at saying things
> like this, but I'm going to try.
> You helped me keep my sanity
> during the most terrible moments
> of this war. I need you to keep
> helping.

He lights the cigarette. Kay turns to look at him.

KAY

Poor, poor Ike. Don't you know
yet who you are? Hitler blew
his brains out and Rommel killed
himself—all because of a Kansas
farm boy.

IKE

With a little help from some friends.

KAY

You stood up to Franklin Roosevelt
and you stood up to Winston Churchill,
and Abilene, Kansas, came out on top.
You're the only one who's finished
this war with the respect of the
mothers and fathers who gave you
their sons to send into battle.
Respect, Ike. It's not yours to
be tampered with in any way.
It was given to you by the 80,000
boys who gave up their lives
for their country. You may
have to give up yours. I don't
know what the future holds
for you, but I'm certain it's
something marvelous…I'm a
big girl, Ike. I know when
I'm out of my class.

IKE

Kay…dammit, Kay.

KAY

Thank you, General. Now we'd
better go, there is so much
more cheering to come.

The scene that was actually shot was no more than a farewell, the two of them smoking a last cigarette together. There was no implication that Ike wanted Kay to come back with him, or that Kay was wise enough to know she had to give him up. This was merely the end of another summer romance. Thanks for the memory.

I felt it was beneath the characters, and beneath the real persons they represented, and destroyed the meaning of the relationship I had taken so much care with.

To remain true to history, I had written other scenes to cover Ike's return to Washington and his encounter with General Marshall. These scenes were eliminated during the jockeying with the Eisenhower family, although I felt someday they would be revealed to be accurate. The first scene is in Gen. Marshall's office after Marshall received the letter mentioned in President Truman's oral history.

INT. MARSHALL'S OFFICE – MED. CLOSE – DAY

Gen. Marshall is on his feet confronting Ike, who is also standing.

> MARSHALL
> That was the goddamdest letter
> I ever read in my life, Ike!
> You must be out of your mind!

> IKE
> (quietly)
> I meant every word.

> MARSHALL
> Idiotic! Foolish! You, of
> all people! The Supreme Commander
> acting like a schoolboy who's
> been in the bushes with his
> teacher! Have you told Mamie?

> IKE
> Not yet.

MARSHALL
Eisenhower, mention one word of
what you said to me in that letter
to that wonderful woman, so help
me God, I'll hound you out of the
United States Army if it's the last
act of my military career!

IKE
Well, goddam it, you go ahead and
try! I'm no schoolboy; I know
exactly what I'm doing. I've
given Kay my word, goddamit, and
my heart, not that I expect you
to understand.

MARSHALL
I don't understand one damn thing
you're saying. Except that you're
throwing away the most promising
career in American military history.

IKE
It's my life, I can throw it away
if I want to.

MARSHALL
The hell you can. The hell it's
your life. How many thousands of
men did you order to give up theirs
for their country? How many boys
in the 101st Airborne came back
after you shook their hands?

He takes Ike by the arm, hauls him toward the window, where
the Washington Monument is visible in the distance.

        MARSHALL
I want you to be the next
Chief of Staff. You divorce
Mamie and marry that English
girl, I won't have a prayer of
getting that appointment past
Congress. Look out of that
window. If you look real hard,
that's the White House. It may
look far away now, but it's getting
closer all the time.

        IKE
To hell with the White House.
I'm no politician and I never
want to be one.

        MARSHALL
What are you, Eisenhower?
Don't you understand your country
may need you? It needs you
right now. Because you stand
for something. You stand for
116,000 American dead; you're
the only one who has come out
of this war with the respect of the
mothers and fathers who gave you
their sons to kill. Respect. Remember
that word. It isn't yours. It was given to
you by your country. By the soldiers and
sailors and airmen who died for it.

He is pacing now.

        MARSHALL (cont'd)
And if you want to throw it away
so you can climb in the sack with
        (more)

(cont.)
some girl half your age, you go
and do it, because you're going
to live in history, right next
to Benedict Arnold.

                    IKE
That's hitting below the belt.

                    MARSHALL
Where do you want me to hit you?
How do I make you come to your
senses? Your life is not your own any
more. It belongs to the United States.
Now, I order you to go back to Mamie
and forget everything that's happened
in this office and so will I. Eisenhower,
you owe this nation something. I've given
you a direct command. Are you still a
soldier?

                                        DISSOLVE TO:

EXT. SHAEF HEADQUARTERS-BUSHEY PARK- (DAY)
    Kay, almost as we first saw her, running breathlessly along the sidewalk
    toward the still-sandbagged entrance of Supreme Headquarters outside
    of London, pulling Telek, the Scotch terrier, along by his leash.

INT. SHAEF HEADQUARTERS-MED. SHOT
    Tex is standing up on a desk, surrounded by members of the
    Headquarters staff, finishing the reading of a list of names.

                    TEX
All of you are to report to Hendon Airfield
at 0800 hours Friday for transport to
Washington and the office of the new
Chief of Staff of the United States
Army, General Dwight D. Eisenhower.

There are CHEERS and some WHISTLING as he gets down from the desk. Kay has just rushed in with Telek in her arms; she reaches his side.

          KAY
Sorry I was late—it was Telek's morning
at the Vet and he was impossible —
should I ask?

          TEX
What do you think?

          KAY
I honestly don't know.

          TEX
Not on the list.

          KAY
Oh…Any message?

          TEX
Not a word.

          KAY
Strange. I thought there
might be a message.

          TEX
Dammit, Kay, it's not like
him. It's not fair. Even
though I warned you long ago.

          KAY
I didn't think it would hurt,
really. It does, dreadfully.
What am I to do with Telek?

TEX
What do you mean?

KAY
He's the General's dog.
I gave them to each other.

TEX
Not on the list.

KAY
You looked under the "T's"?

TEX
Sure.

KAY
Strange…I don't know how being
kind to a poor little dog could
damage the United States of America…
but then, I'm not a bloody Yank.

TEX
Kay—I'm so goddam sorry.

She is at the door. She turns.

KAY
Sorry? Sorry for Kay Summersby?
Why, I fought this whole bloody war,
 didn't I? We British gave everything
we had…everything we had. And
we're still here. We'll muddle through,
thank you.

She sets Telek down.

KAY
Come on, you little Scotch bastard
Hold your head up high.

And she pulls the Scottie off with her.

EXT SHAEF HEADQUARTERS BUILDING—NEAR ENTRANCE

As Kay comes out with Telek, they walk away, oblivious to passersby, across the broad lawn toward the British countryside. The MUSIC IS "Rule Britannia."

The preceding scenes were never shot.

Six hours of *Ike: The War Years* were broadcast over the ABC Network, two hours each successive night, that May of 1979. We almost didn't make the airdate. I had been editing the final cut of the picture up to the last moment, and had been battling the network over the colorized sequences. Everything is put on the air from videotape; that meant that those scenes, which had been computerized onto video tape for the colorization process, then converted back to 35mm film, would then be converted back to tape again, with consequent loss of quality. I finally convinced ABC to transmit the colorized sequences directly from the original tape.

Ike has never looked that good in subsequent broadcasts.

I knew we had a good film, in spite of all the problems. I was disturbed that it wasn't as good as it might have been. But I was astounded by its reception, which was far beyond what either I or the network had hoped for. It knocked every other program on every other network off for every half hour it was broadcast. ABC took a huge ad in the trade papers to make certain no one missed the point: *Ike* averaged a 40-share, smashing its competition every show, every half hour, every night it was presented.

"Surprisingly absorbing drama…The canvas, covering all of Europe and parts of the military campaign in North Africa, is vast. The key historical details are remarkably comprehensible. Lee Remick contributes one more impressive performance."
– John J. O'Connor, *The New York Times*

"It's stirring stuff, beautifully edited and scored. Told in 1945, tears will flow and if you were over 10 years old your heart will break all over again."

— Harriet Van Horne, *New York Post*

"Duvall cuts a forceful figure. Remick could cause any man to swoon, regardless of age, rank, or marital status. Her feistiness meshes well with Duvall's homey gruffness. They're the Hepburn and Tracy of the European Theater."

— Frank Rich, *Time* magazine

"A remarkable achievement. Central to the action is the war itself. Never was it more graphically shown…the glow of Lee Remick remains after the six hours end."

— Cecil Smith, *Los Angeles Times*

"But the most credit for a crackerjack production is reserved for Mel Shavelson's screenplay. Altogether, Ike, is an engrossing drama coupled with a most peculiar yet moving love story. It's sure to be controversial among Eisenhower scholars, but I think America is going to say, 'I Like Ike' all over again."

— Ron Miller, *San Jose News*

And on, and on, and on. I have two large scrapbooks filled with similar critical acclaim from all over the United States. I knew that much of it was due to all those who, on two continents (is England a continent?) had labored for so long under such difficulties to make it happen. I also knew that Robert Duvall had brought off his own interpretation of Ike by disregarding much of my wise counsel. As for Lee Remick, she was the one I had leaned on to bring Kay to life exactly as I had envisioned her. I was saddened beyond belief by her untimely passing; and as another sad footnote, Boris Sagal was killed a few short years after *Ike* was completed, when he accidentally walked into the whirling blades of a helicopter while shooting a television film in Alaska. Boris actually directed a major portion of *Ike*, and brilliantly.

Mamie Eisenhower herself had passed away before the film was aired. I would have loved to have known her reaction to the finished product.

Vindication of my interpretation of Dwight Eisenhower did not come until long afterward. In 1991, an old adversary, *The New York Times*, the respected newspaper that had insisted we would Hollywoodize history, that there never had been anything between Kay Summersby and the Commander in Chief of Allied Forces, and urged that the film not be made, published an essay by William Safire, headed,

"Indeed a Very Dear Friend" – Ike's letters to Kay

"I thumb through auction catalogs, you can never tell what you may find.

"In a Sotheby's catalog for a sale in New York on June 13, I found a historical love story in a collection of letters. The romance, its evidence now for sale to the highest bidder, was between Gen. Dwight Eisenhower and his secretary-driver, Kay Summersby.

"Rumors of the wartime relationship were denied at first by Ike's loyal friends…But in 'Plain Speaking,' Merle Miller's 1974 oral biography of Harry Truman, the former President—who detested his successor, Eisenhower—told the whole truth and perhaps then some.

"According to Truman, 'right after the war was over, Eisenhower wrote a letter to General Marshall saying that he wanted to come back to the United States and divorce Mrs. Eisenhower so that he could marry this Englishwoman,' which Truman thought 'shocking.' Apparently, General Marshall denied the request in such coldly furious writing that 'one of the last things I did as President, I got those letters from his file in the Pentagon, and I destroyed them.'

"Curious; Truman could have elected his fellow Democrat Adlai Stevenson in 1952 by leaking, rather than destroying, those letters. 'Most biographers and other students of Eisenhower,' writes Selby Kiffer of Sotherby's in tasteful catalog narration, 'have dismissed Truman's account as a vindictive falsehood. One who did not was Kay Summersby.'

"She wrote a book after the Truman revelation, 'Past Forgetting,' asserting but not detailing her love affair with the General who became President. Lee Remick starred in the miniseries. Was Kay's story true? David Eisenhower, in his superb biography of his grandfather, noted that the truth 'was only known by them, and both are gone.'

"It turns out the evidence is not gone. Thirty-seven lots of letters, documents and signed photographs from the estate of Kay Summersby are up for auction next week, offered for sale by anonymous people to whom she left the precious papers.

"Although there is no smoking profession of love, nobody who reads these handwritten notes and letters from a caring, sensitive, sometimes gruff, sometimes distraught Eisenhower can easily say that Harry Truman was a liar...

"A scribbled note to Kay on what must have been a quiet day:

'Irish: (Summersby was not, as Truman thought, an English-woman)—How about lunch, tea & dinner today? If yes: Who else do you want, if any? At which time? How are you? D.' (Sotheby's estimates this will go for $3,000 to $5,000 to historians, that romantic ampersand—'lunch, tea & dinner'—makes it worth more...

"The mystery remains why she did not include all the correspondence in her final book, but this we now know:

"Dwight Eisenhower, separated by war from his wife, became intimately attached to a woman who served with him. Kay Summersby returned his love. He extricated himself because that was the path of loyalty and duty. She understood, steadfastly protected his secret until it could hurt nobody, then made it possible for their story—of four-star crossed lovers—to be appreciated by a later generation of admirers of a great man."

I rest my case, what's left of it, now that it's too late to be of help in getting that crucial moment reinstated when Ike intimated he wanted Kay to remain with him after the war. Except here, in a history of my own history, where neither the Eisenhower family, the *New York Times*, the ABC Network, or anyone else, can rewrite me.

One more pat on my own back before leaving *Ike*. To make the following letter more impressive, I reproduce it on its original taxpayer-paid-for stationery:

DEPARTMENT OF THE ARMY
OFFICE OF THE SECRETARY OF THE
ARMY WASHINGTON. D.C., 20310
14 MAY 1979
SAPA-CI

Mr. Mel Shavelson
Dear Mel,
    It was a pleasure viewing your feature motion picture "Ike." Both the Department of the Army and the Office of the Assistant Secretary of Defense for Public Affairs consider it positive and an excellent example of how the military working with a producer can turn out a film of mutual advantage
    May we enjoy continued good fortune and success with ABC in the years ahead.
Sincerely,
Robert B. Solomon
Major. General, GS
Chief of Public Affairs

I realized I was now an established authority on the American military, which had once declared me 4F as unfit for duty, when I received an official invitation from the War Department in Washington, asking me to join a select group from Hollywood to a secret underground base of the Strategic Air Command, somewhere in Nebraska, location classified, to be given an indoctrination in the Army's latest weapons in the Atomic Age.

I carefully zipped my lip and joined a flight of the top brass in the motion picture industry, including my old friend Jay Kanter, former agent, now a Vice President of MGM.

We had a long flight in a C-130, an army transport which had no windows, so we could not see where we were going. Fortunately, the pilot had a window, and we managed to land safely, in the cold and snow, at some hidden Army base in that frozen state. We were comfortably housed in barracks, fed far beyond GI standard, and then, for two days, extensively toured a facility built far underground so it would be impervious to the nuclear attack all its officers were certain was soon to come from the Soviet Union.

First we saw one of the two large planes, one of which was always in the air so it could not be targeted, which contained the radio controls for America's nuclear missiles. Each plane could receive a special signal from Washington if the President of the United States decided to launch a nuclear attack against an enemy, but that fatal signal could not be transmitted from the plane without an officer inserting a special key into the control mechanism. As a precaution against any spies who might have infiltrated the Air Force, a second officer had to insert a similar key at his end of the plane, and the two were separated by bulletproof glass so they couldn't threaten each other with a gun at the crucial moment. Thus, Fail Safe had been achieved, unless they were both spies. I put this as a question to the officer who was showing us the plane, and got a cold stare in reply. Don't worry; the Army had thought of everything.

Next, we went far down into the bowels of the earth and were shown the huge computers—this was in the age when all computers were huge, but these were much huger than any others—and we were told they controlled all the nuclear weapons and communications the United States possessed throughout the globe. To demonstrate, another officer called in, via satellite, 120 different SAC bases in both hemispheres; all the replies were received within 120 seconds.

Tremendously impressed, we were assembled the next day in a large auditorium, where we were told we were to be given our diplomas as Bachelors of Sacology for completing the course. The event began with the showing of a secret film on the Cruise Missile, so new it was barely whispered about. The film informed us that the Cruise was self-powered, and when launched traveled at incredible speed at an attitude of only 600 feet, so it could fly under any radar detectors the Enemy might have. The Enemy was not identified, but we were told the Cruise had been targeted on certain key buildings in Moscow, some 6,000 miles away, so we could hazard a guess. Each Cruise was controlled from the Pentagon in Washington; it contained a video camera in its nose which transmitted its pictures back via orbiting satellites, and it was interactive, like a video game. The Generals in Washington could see and direct its course so accurately, it could not only hit a Moscow building, but go through whichever window they chose. All of this was possible, we were told, because the computers in the Cruise had been programmed with a topographical map of the entire world, including not only mountains, but any building higher than 600 feet, so it could automatically avoid them. And each Cruise missile contained a nuclear bomb, which would detonate on impact. There were now 200 nuclear armed Cruise Missiles.

I inquired—reasonably, I thought—what would happen if the system failed and the Cruise hit a Hilton Hotel in Istanbul that was 601 feet high?

I was stared down by the officer giving the lecture, who asked if I had paid attention when being shown the huge computers which controlled the entire United States' military capability? Each one cost a hundred million dollars.

I nodded, meekly, and sat down. Another officer called us each up by name, and issued us each a diploma announcing that we were now Bachelors of Sacology. And then the Commanding Officer called up Jay Kanter. He announced that since Jay had been through the course once before, he was entitled to a Ph.D, a Doctorate, and that he would henceforth be known as Dr. Kanter. Jay went up and accepted his doctorate with great enthusiasm, and then we were all piled into a bus for the trip to the airport and the C-130 for our flight back to our secret destination, Hollywood.

Except for Jay. He was given a military limousine, and a red carpet was spread out on the tarmac for him to tread while getting into the plane with the rest of us simple peasants.

Once we had taken off—at least we were told we had taken off, the plane still had no windows, showing how much the Army trusted us—I turned to my old friend and said, "Jay, I didn't know you'd taken this course before."

And Jay said, "You think I'm crazy? This is the first time I've ever been in Nebraska."

"Then how come you were given a Doctorate, while all the rest of us only got our Bachelors?"

Jay shrugged and said, "The computer fucked up."

There is a temptation in any recounting of one's life and adventures, to turn it into a complete ego trip, since there is no front office to complain about the cost, no historian to check the facts inside your own mind, and no collaborator to turn thumbs down on the jokes.

I'll try to be brutally frank about the years that have followed *Ike*. I had reached the top of the mountain, both artistically and financially, and there was no place to go but downhill. At least, that seems to be the way it turned out.

I never thought that my chief benefactor would be the United States Internal Revenue Service. ABC had established a subsidiary called "ABC Circle Films," which was to produce motion pictures for the TV network outside of the network's regular programming. The IRS declared this was a tax dodge, since ABC Circle had produced exactly zero product, while charging off various operating expenses. So ABC decided that *Ike* would be the first production of ABC Circle Films. And because the U.S. government was watching, ABC could not try the usual Hollywood bookkeeping. *Ike* was given no budget limitations. ABC could not charge off losses from previous productions, because there had been no previous productions. And, after paying me my salaries as writer, director, and Executive Producer, my Llenroc Productions (whose name confuses a lot of people until they realize it is "Cornell" spelled backwards) was given 100% of the profits of *Ike* after three network runs on ABC, and 50% of the profits, from the first dollar, on foreign showings. ABC was afraid of keeping too much of the profits from *Ike* and risking an IRS audit.

Nirvana!

Hindsight, in my case, is much easier than foresight. Llenroc sold off my U.S. rights to Viacom for what I thought was a very tidy sum, considering that ABC could run *Ike* three times before turning it over. But the network only ran it twice. So Viacom got a windfall, a run they hadn't paid for. They showed their gratitude by making me pay a considerable sum owed as residuals to the actors for the third run, since Viacom hadn't expected to own *Ike* for that one. I never figured that one out.

But I didn't complain. Llenroc still owned 50% of the foreign revenues, and *Ike* turned out to be the largest foreign grosser of any U.S. television film to that date. Almost every civilized and non-civilized country in the world bought it, except for Germany, whose hesitation was understandable. They didn't like the ending. But, eventually, *Ike* did play German television, and for a substantial payment.

Freed of financial problems for a lifetime, and with an international boxoffice hit to my credit, you would think I could now make any film I cared to. But this was Hollywood.

I decided to find another biography with the size and importance and controversy that had distinguished the Eisenhower story. It was already obvious to the network and to me that *Ike: The Presidential Years* would never be made.

I presented ABC with the story of another American hero, who fought a different sort of battle; the difference was that this hero was black, and a Communist, and his battle was against the government of the United States of America, and he won, for himself and for his race.

In researching his life, I came to the conclusion that, as with Eisenhower, his story was really the story of the woman he loved, and betrayed, and loved again.

This is the storyline I presented to ABC:

BALLAD FOR AMERICANS
The Life of Paul and Eslanda Robeson

She was born into trouble, the illegitimate niece of Supreme Court Justice Benjamin Cardozo, the appointee of Herbert Hoover who shocked the nation by writing the majority opinions that upheld the Roosevelt New Deal's social legislation.

That family relationship meant Eslanda was half Jewish...She called herself, openly and defiantly, Eslanda Cardozo Goode. Defiantly, because her other half was black. Although you couldn't tell it. Eslanda—Essie, as she preferred to be known—could and did, when necessity demanded, pass for a white woman. Her beauty and intelligence would have taken her anywhere she wanted to go beyond the color line. But she chose to fall in love with a man who couldn't, a man who was also born into trouble, a man as black as the back door to Hell, through which they traveled together. He was a giant of a man, with a giant voice and a giant heart, who made giant mistakes, in life, in love, in politics. He was All-American and Phi Beta Kappa when he graduated near the top of his class at Rutgers, but the smartest thing he did in his entire life was to turn Eslanda Cardozo Goode into Mrs. Paul Robeson.

Or was it that smart?

Eslanda took his life and shaped it in strange ways; Paul was a lazy man, she gave him ambition; an untrained talent, she helped him become the greatest Othello of modern times, and its greatest balladeer; a non-political man, she forced him to become a symbol for his race, an outcast, an exile, a wanderer, disgraced and ashamed; and in the end, it was Eslanda Cardozo Goode Robeson who stood proudly at his side when finally they returned in triumph to the land that had borne and banished both of them. Her triumph was mixed with pain, because once before when Paul Robeson had returned to the United States at the height of his fame, it had been with a woman who was truly white, whom he introduced as his wife, while Eslanda remained in England, forsaken but determined; now she had won that battle, too.

I heard Paul Robeson sing "Ballad for Americans" one electrifying night during World War II. The audience in the Hollywood Bowl stood and cheered for fifteen minutes. Things weren't going too well for America and Americans at that time; Hitler's star was in the ascendancy, the Allies were being pushed back, and the specter of surrender to a Master Race which stood for the extinction of both Jew and Negro as well as the end of freedom, seemed more than a possibility. Until Paul Robeson's powerful voice sang us that song of the America he believed in.

In gratitude, his native land banished him from the stage, destroyed his career, and attempted to take away his passport and his birthright when Eslanda persuaded him to speak out and stand up for his brothers. He was stoned by the spectators when he attempted to give a concert for charity at Peekskill, New York. The police turned their backs. Defiantly, Paul came back and gave a second concert, and was stoned again.

He and Essie left their native land and went, of all places, to Russia. Sergei Eisenstein, the great Russian film director, had invited them to Moscow to discuss a movie. They traveled by train from Paris, and when they stepped out on the platform at Friedrichstrasse Station in Berlin for a few moments en route, Nazi Storm Troopers guarding the station took one look at the big Negro and the beautiful fair-skinned woman with him, and started closing in on them. Paul, who understood German, realized the Nazis thought Eslanda was a white German girl traveling with a black man. The SS men were working themselves into a frenzy against both of them. Paul faced them down, grabbed Essie and hustled her aboard the train, realizing that she was in far more danger than he was. He was only black. She was Jewish.

Frightened and angry after their escape, Paul was even more susceptible to the friendship and understanding he found at the Russian border, where the way had been prepared for him. The Customs officials played recordings of "The Volga Boatman" sung by "Pavel Robesona," crowds cheered him on the streets of Moscow, and the contrast with Fascism couldn't have been more pronounced

Then came World War II, and Paul and Eslanda returned "home," but the Russian experience had convinced Essie that only in the Soviet Union was there true freedom for minorities. Blacks were not persecuted in Russia because they weren't numerous enough to matter; Jews were persecuted because they were, but Essie did not permit herself or her husband to face that fact.

When America entered the war, Paul threw himself into patriotic endeavors for his native land. "Ballad for Americans" became his theme song.

But when the war was over and the tide of feeling created the McCarthy era, Paul and Eslanda found themselves in the minority who defended Russia. Paul Robeson was hauled before the House UnAmerican Activities Committee, where he refused to recant.

"My mother was a Quaker," he told the Congressmen. "My ancestors baked bread for George Washington's troops when they crossed the Delaware. My father was a slave. I stand here struggling for the rights of my people to be full citizens of this country. And they are not."

The force of public opinion banished Robeson from his own land. When "Show Boat" opened on Broadway, the role Robeson was born for was given to another; Paul played the part in London. Then he left Essie—or Essie had left him—for Uta Hagen, when Hagen played Desdemona to his Othello despite her marriage to Jose Ferrer. After her, it was Lady Peggy Ashcroft who saw herself as the next Mrs. Paul Robeson.

But Essie fought back. When the smoke had cleared, she was at Paul's side, in Russia once more, after the United States had finally revoked his passport, so he could never return to America. She made Paul hire the best lawyers he could afford, and they fought the United States government to a standstill until he got his passport back.

Paul returned to America to no hero's welcome but the one in his heart. He returned with his wife, who had never left him even when she might have and should have. And he knew the mistakes he had made and didn't know how he could have avoided them, because he was only a man.

He had thrown away a career and a large part of his life because Eslanda had taught him to believe in the kind of real freedom that wasn't popular then; it seldom is, even now.

On his sixtieth birthday, his friends arranged a concert for Paul Robeson at Carnegie Hall. Calling Essie out of the wings, he stepped proudly to the center of the stage and waved the passport that had been returned to him. For the last time in public, he sang, "Ballad for Americans." It had become a love song.

> Out of the cheating,
> Out of the shouting,
> Out of the murders and lynchings,
> Out of the windbags, the patriotic spouting
> Out of uncertainty and doubting
> It will come again.
> Our marching song will come again!
> For I have always believed it
> And I believe it still
> And you know who I am—

> CHORUS
> No! Who are you?

> PAUL ROBESON
> AMERICA!

In 1972, shortly before his death, they dedicated the Paul Robeson Campus Center at Rutgers to him. The President of the University had this to say: "He transcended his time, his race and his person to join that select group of souls who speak for all humanity." A black prisoner in the Marion, Ill. Penitentiary wrote this monosyllabic tribute:

> They knocked the leaves
> From his limbs
> The bark
> From his
> (more)

(cont.)
Tree
But his roots
Were
So deep
That they are
A part of me.

I got that story line back from ABC so quickly the breeze almost knocked me over. Was I out of my mind? A national network doing a film about a black Communist?

I tried to explain that I had obtained the first computer-reconstituted recording of Robeson's singing, his incomparable bass-baritone restored to its original glory, and I wanted to use Robeson's actual voice, as Al Jolson's singing was used in *The Jolson Story*, so audiences hearing it would understand how a black man, in those prejudiced times, could have gained so much success in the white man's world and then thrown it away. For this film was to be an Entertainment, and the focus would be on the greatest voice of its time, and the love story that was his romance with a beautiful girl who was both black and Jewish, and knew prejudice better than he did.

No dice. No one at ABC was listening. No one heard the voice I heard. So I took the project to CBS and "pitched" it.

Four hours later, to my amazement, I had a deal. A contract to write the screenplay. CBS was willing to stick its corporate neck out.

I began writing again. While I wrote, a whole platoon of CBS executives was kicked out of office. The annual housecleaning. When I turned in my screenplay I was asked, "You don't think CBS would really do the story of Paul Robeson, do you?"

Neither would anyone else, I discovered, although I tried determinedly for years. I don't give up easily. I'm still trying.

Along the road, or the detour, I submitted the script to Columbia Pictures, which had a new, liberal head of production, David Puttnam. He turned it over to his Senior Vice President of Production, Stanley Robertson, who was the highest-placed black man (by then, Afro-American) in the motion picture industry. I was particularly interested in how it would be received by an outstanding, intelligent black executive. Here again, the actual letter:

Columbia Pictures

Stanley G, Robertson
Senior Vice President
Production
February 4, 1987

Dear Mel:

Thank you so much for giving me the pleasure and the opportunity to read BALLAD FOR AMERICANS. It is a dazzling and fascinating piece of work and I wish you all success in ultimately getting it made.

Sincerest regards,
Stan

SGR/tb
Encl

Nothing much happened after that, except that both Stanley Robertson and David Puttnam soon left Columbia Pictures.

But don't get me wrong. I love Hollywood.

The years that have followed continued the roller coaster ride that now includes some 35 produced screenplays, including a dozen directing credits. Some stars have remained friends, others are not mentioned on advice of counsel.

In an industry which has come to regard Youth as its main audience, I now find myself content to be Yesterday, the comfortable Yesterday when dialogue in cinema was more important than car crashes, and sexual encounters sometimes included that weird emotion, Love. Of course, that slowed things down quite a bit. Sometimes to *my* speed.

That now includes several years on the Faculty of the Master of Professional Writing Program at the University of Southern California, at the invitation of its head for over 25 years, Professor James Ragan, considered one of America's leading educators in spite of having employed me. However, he has now left that post. Jim Ragan has also managed to produce some of the best poetry of this or any other time, without falling into the error of allowing it to rhyme. Or to contain traces of his native tongue, which he claims is Czechoslovakian.

My classes at USC always opened with a quotation from my favorite writer-director, Woody Allen: "Those who can, do. Those who can't, teach. Those who can't teach, teach Gym."

My finish: "Welcome to my Gym class."

As I said before, there are a lot of *good* things about growing older... and I wish I could remember what they were...

GOOFS

Confession, it is said, is good for the soul, so it is time to record some of the incidents I have carefully skipped over.

In no particular order, I remember first an incident with Judy Garland, whom I had known since she was 14 years old when she was appearing on the Bob Hope Pepsodent Show. She left, as I have recorded, to play Dorothy in a film you may have heard of, *The Wizard of Oz.* Some years later, after Judy had married Director Vincente Minnelli and Jack Rose and I were writing *The Five Pennies*, we needed a child for the role of Danny Kaye's daughter, small and young and able to deliver comedy and sing a song or two with him. Hearing about it, Judy invited us over to her house—as I recall, large and spacious and located expensively somewhere in Beverly Hills. Judy seated us and called one of her daughters to appear and sing for us. A little girl quickly entered, somewhat frightened but apparently well rehearsed by her mother. She stood in front of us and without hesitation, sang three songs for her audience, in a small voice, but on key. After she left, I turned to Judy and asked her why she would want her daughter to go into show business, where she herself had found so many difficulties? Besides, I informed her, her daughter was lovely, but obviously she had no talent.

Jack agreed with me, and jointly we became the first musical experts to turn down Liza Minnelli.

At another time during our careers at Paramount, the story department sent over a German film that had just been released, and asked if the studio should buy it for us to make into an American movie. Jack and I ran the picture, which was in black and white with German subtitles, and both agreed that *Die Trapp Family* was too Austrian to ever be made palatable to an American audience. Of course, after almost every other studio turned it down, Rogers and Hammerstein disagreed, and *Die Trapp*

Family became *The Sound of Music* on Broadway, and later was written as a film by my good friend Ernie Lehman. He and Director Bob Wise turned it into one of the most successful and profitable Hollywood musical films in history.

Some time later, Producer Martin Ransohoff sent me a screenplay that had been written by Paddy Chayefsky, which Ransohoff had given to William Wyler, one of Hollywood's greatest directors, who won an Academy Award for directing *Ben Hur*. Willy Wyler turned it down, and Ransohoff wanted to know if I would direct it. Unfortunately, he sent me the screenplay on which Wyler had written adverse comments. I was too foolish to recognize it as being far from anti-American, but strongly anti-war. And beautifully written. I was involved with preparing another film at Paramount, and finally decided to turn down *The Americanization of Emily*. It was promptly made into an outstanding motion picture, starring Julie Andrews and James Garner, well directed by Arthur Hiller in a memorable production. It is still remembered today, especially by me.

Somehow, Wyler and I had become friends, and guests in each other's homes. It was about the time that doctors told Willy he had to stop directing films and take life easy. For Willy, that was close to impossible. He told me he had decided to get away from Hollywood, so far away that he could forget about all its telephone calls and truly relax. He was going to take a trip with his wife Tally to Antarctica. He made the mistake of letting me know the name of his ship and its schedule.

When the liner was arriving at its port near the South Pole, he was startled by an announcement over the ship's speaker: "Mr. Wyler, there is a phone call for you!"

I have mentioned my dubious career as an Amateur Radio Operator. Over my amateur radio station, W6VLH, I had contacted an Army Amateur Radio station located at an American base near the South Pole, after I had arranged with Willy's daughter in San Francisco to have her speak with her father at the end of the earth, via telephone over my transmitter.

The amateur station in Antarctica had contacted the ship by radio, and everyone could hear everyone perfectly.

I'm not sure Willy was thrilled by that phone call. But I know *I* was.

* * * *

I recently taught in the Master of Professional Writing program at the University of Southern California. I tried to start my students out as I started, believing in themselves, and believing that this is the best of all possible worlds. And that truth and honesty and talent will always lead to success.

So you may understand why that class no longer exists; in fact, the entire department has been closed.

In today's world, everything changes. Not necessarily for the better.

I comfort myself by following Irving Berlin's advice: Count My Blessings.

Foremost among them, as I look back at my past, were the sixty-three years I spent in marriage to Lucille Theresa Myers, for whom I wrote, on her 75th birthday:

> The girl I met
> On the steps of Sage
> Refuses to learn
> To act her age
>
> I love her still
> As I did that day
> In the rumble seat
> Of a Chevrolet
>
> At Father Time,
> If he should pass
> We'll thumb our nose
> And kick his ass
>
> For its plain to see
> Love improves with age
> Like the girl I met
> On the steps of Sage.

Unfortunately, Father Time refused to pass Lucy. With unbounded courage and undimmed compassion for all of us in her life, she drifted away and lies, as she wished, in the garden of our home amid the roses she adored.

I never promised her a rose garden when she married me—all she got was a 35-cent wedding ring. But she treasured it as much as her roses. I found that very ring when I went through her possessions. The glass diamonds a little worn, the gold a little greener than when the Rabbi held it up to the light, but like our marriage, it had survived all the troubles and problems of our marriage. Much better than I did.

Lucy's obit summed it up:

> "Lucy Shavelson, as she was known to her many friends and admirers, was a legendary hostess. She and her husband entertained such Hollywood 'Golden Age' celebrities as: Cary Grant, Kirk Douglas, Lucille Ball, Groucho Marx, Edith Head, Sophia Loren, Paul Newman, Bob Hope, Charlton Heston, and William Wyler. A lover of art, music, and poetry, Lucy Shavelson kept clipped to her notebook this verse:
>
> > Do not stand on my grave and weep.
> > I am not there, I do not sleep.
> > I am a thousand winds that blow;
> > I am the diamond glints on the snow…
> > I am the swift uplifting rush
> > Of quiet birds in circled flight
> > I am the soft star that shines at night.
> > Do not stand on my grave and cry.
> > I am not there, I did not die."

Of course she didn't. Lucy lives on in the roses, and even more in the son and daughter she raised when I was too busy with what I laughingly called my career. For Richard and Lynne, I have love tinged with resentment at the way they have grown up so successfully without my help. Richard has been the Dean of the School of Education at Standford and has received honorary degrees from several prominent European universities I never attended and can't pronounce.

Lynne, at an early age, learned that the road to success lay in completely disregarding her father's advice. When I pointed out to her that news photography was one of the most difficult professions for a female, a month later she was on the photo staff of *Time* magazine. Soon tiring of that, she eventually decided to get married (to Marine Captain Joseph Joiner, then recently returned from combat in Vietnam) and told me she was going into television journalism in San Francisco. I told her that was the most overcrowded profession in an overcrowded city. A year later she was anchoring the news on camera at KCOP and soon managed to find time to mother a son as well.

In quick succession after that she filmed two documentaries in China and one in Russia, acquired the obligatory modern divorce, and later moved to Washington, D.C. Her son, Scott, grew up to become a successful lawyer and quit to enlist in the Judge Advocate Group of the United States Marine Corps where he is now Captain Scott Joiner. As this is written, he is headed for Iraq. His mother has now authored a soon-to-be-published book on—China? Of course.

*   *   *   *

The most beautiful woman of my acquaintance had also lost her love only a month or so before Lucy left me. Ruth Florea had seen her husband, the great *Life* magazine photographer, director, and human being, John Florea, gradually droop and pass away in a hospital while she was at his side, leaving her as alone as I felt. Almost in desperation, I invited her to watch a Monday Night Football game on the large television screen in my now-empty home, installed to make me attractive to anyone who only had a small television screen of their own.

She told me later she had given up all hope of ever committing herself to another man.

No matter what kind of television set he had.

Persistence conquers all. I took her to the movies, and found she liked the same films I did—including some of my own. That did it.

After a while, I learned more about her. Ruth had left college for a marriage, and found she couldn't bear it after having three children. She had the courage to get a divorce. And, in her early forties, had become a professional model and an actress. Her beauty was such that she became the first Mrs. America when that competition was begun, and on stage she appeared in many regional productions of *The Sound of Music*, several films, and became the wife of John Florea, whose camera had made beauty a part of daily life. They battled their way through the Hollywood I knew, occasionally meeting Lucy and me through friends. Ruth remained a mother to her children, and a grandmother to theirs, until John became ill, and she had to become a nurse who stayed with him to the end. It was not pretty, but her faith was strong enough to sustain her. Afterwards, her spirituality occasionally conflicted with my Jewish reality, but perhaps that added to our attraction for each other.

I proposed marriage. She hesitated, for all the reasons a woman hesitates. Perhaps, in my case, many more. Then, after more than a year together had passed, we had a Hollywood wedding in my living room, presided over by Arthur Hiller, the talented director of *Love Story*, among others, who had become a mail-order minister and had performed many marriages in "the business." I presume Ruth and I are legal, and our unlikely love story is a match for Arthur's film, unless he received his ministry in his mail by mistake.

However, I regret that, recently, Arthur's eyesight has become limited, but not his heart.

If we aren't legal, I'm happy to add, we don't give a damn. And we know, each of us, that Lucy and John would have approved.

Ruth adopted not only my family, but my two most loyal friends— Barbie, our regal Collie, and Annie, our half-breed Who Knows? Both shared our bedroom each night until they barked and were released to share the night with our neighbors. Consequently, the following:

> To Ruth
>
> My love is like a melody
> That came along so late
> I thought I'd never sing again
> And that would be my fate
>
> But you have given back my voice
> And turned to light the dark
> I'll sing my love the Barbie way
> And bark, and bark, and bark.
>
> Happy Birthday! Arf!

Unfortunately, Barbie is no longer with us, but I can still hear her bark.

And so, I will thank all my lucky stars, from Lucy and Ruth to Bob Hope through Sophia Loren and Kirk Douglas and John Wayne and Clark Gable and Cary Grant and Paul Newman and Joanne Woodward and so on and so on, all the stars who have brought me safely to wherever I am today. Did I forget Sinatra? Well, I can only turn to Ol' Blue Eyes again, and repeat the finale he sang for some thirty years. Overly dramatic, overly sentimental, like Life itself.

> And now, the end is near;
> And so I face
> The final curtain.
> My friend, I'll say it clear,
> I'll state my case,
>   (more)

(cont.)
Of which I'm certain.

I've lived a life that's full
I've traveled each and ev'ry highway;
And more, much more than this,
I did it my way.

* * *

And that was my biggest mistake.

* * *

THE END

AFTERPIECE

Recent events have taught me that no story is ever finished. Life reserves its surprises for when we least expect them.

My days in the Master of Professional Writing Program at USC were limited, enjoyable, and consisted often in presenting outstanding films and their writers and directors to the students in the film program and then getting out of the way. Sometimes I could inflict one of my own films, since the audience wasn't permitted to walk out.

All of this under the watchful leadership of the outstanding head of the program for over 25 years, Prof. James Ragan, whom I called the Poet Laureate of S. Figueroa Street, although his poetry never rhymed. It took me a while to realize it didn't rhyme because he didn't want it to. Shakespeare sometimes had the same failing.

It all came to a crashing halt in the Fall of 2006, when Ragan and the entire program were eliminated for reasons beyond me. Perhaps because it was an intelligent way to bring students into the reality and insanity known as the Motion Picture Industry, which William Goldman described as the place where nobody knows anything.

At any rate, it seems I won't have to pay for a USC parking pass any longer. And I will miss it.

Acknowledgement

Anyone who claims he doesn't have anyone to acknowledge in the telling of his life's story is merely acknowledging his own ignorance. Those who have helped me most in my lifetime include my parents, Joseph and Hilda Shavelson, my wife Lucille who endured me for more than six decades, offspring Richard and Lynne, my beautiful wife Ruth, Maureen Solomon who helped to edit and advise on all these pages, and, finally, those who helped in the world of show business, headed by Bob Hope and including, even a few who didn't...

Credits

WRITER:

Ike: The War Years (1978) TV
The Great Houdini (1976) TV
The Legend of Valentino (1975) TV
Mixed Company (1974)
The War Between Men and Women (1972)
Three Coins in the Fountain (1970) TV
"My World and Welcome to It!" (1969)
Yours, Mine and Ours (1968)
Cast a Giant Shadow (1966)
A New Kind of Love (1963)
The Pigeon That Took Rome (1962)
On the Double (1961)
It Started in Naples (1960)
The Five Pennies (1959)
Houseboat (1958)
Beau James (1957)
The Seven Little Foys (1955)
Living It Up (1954)
Trouble Along the Way (1953)
April in Paris (1952)
Room for One More (1952)
Double Dynamite (1951)
I'll See You in My Dreams (1951)
On Moonlight Bay (1951)
Riding High (1950) (additional dialogue)
The Great Lover (1949)
Always Leave Them Laughing (1949)
It's a Great Feeling (1949)

Sorrowful Jones (1949)
Where There's Life (1947)
KTLA Premiere (1947) TV
The Kid from Brooklyn (1946)
Wonder Man (1945)
The Princess and the Pirate (1944)

DIRECTOR:

The Other Woman (1983) TV
Ike: The War Years (1978) TV
The Great Houdini (1976) TV
The Legend of Valentino (1975) TV
Mixed Company (1974)
The War Between Men and Women (1972)
"My World and Welcome to It!" (1969)
Yours, Mine and Ours (1968)
Cast a Giant Shadow (1966)
A New Kind of Love (1963)
The Pigeon That Took Rome (1962)
On the Double (1961)
It Started in Naples (1960)
The Five Pennies (1959)
Houseboat (1958)
Beau James (1957)
The Seven Little Foys (1955)

PRODUCER:

"Ike: The War Years" (1979) TV
Mixed Company (1974)
Cast a Giant Shadow (1966)
A New Kind of Love (1963)
The Pigeon That Took Rome (1962)
Trouble Along the Way (1953)

Index

Printed in Great Britain
by Amazon

52034580R00145